Green
from the
Ground
Up

A BUILDER'S GUIDE

Green from the Ground Up

Sustainable, Healthy, and Energy-Efficient Home Construction

David Johnston & Scott Gibson

The Taunton Press

Text © 2008 by David Johnston and Scott Gibson
Illustrations © 2008 by The Taunton Press, Inc.

The Taunton Press
Inspiration for hands-on living®

The Taunton Press, Inc., 63 South Main Street, PO Box 5506, Newtown, CT 06470-5506
e-mail: tp@taunton.com

Editor: Peter Chapman
Copy editor: Anne Jones
Indexer: James Curtis
Cover design: Scott Santoro, Worksight
Cover illustration: Bob La Pointe
Interior design: Scott Santoro, Worksight
Layout: Scott Santoro, Worksight
Illustrator: Martha Garstang Hill

Library of Congress Cataloging-in-Publication Data

Johnston, David, 1950-

  Green from the ground up : sustainable, healthy, and energy-efficient home construction /
David Johnston and Scott Gibson.

     p. cm.

  Includes bibliographical references and index.

  ISBN 978-1-56158-973-9 (alk. paper)

  1. Sustainable buildings—Design and construction. 2. Buildings—Energy conservation. 3.
Sustainable architecture. I. Gibson, Scott, 1951- II. Title.

TH880.J638 2008

690'.837—dc22

                    2007028844

Printed in Singapore

10 9 8 7 6 5 4 3 2 1

The following manufacturers/names appearing in *Green from the Ground Up* are trademarks:
air-krete®, Andersen®, Cedar Breather®, Cor-A-Vent®, Corian®, Cracker Jack®, Duette®, Dumpster®,
Durisol Wall Forms®, EnergyStar®, Enerjoy®, FSC™, Gortex™, Grace Ice and Water Shield®, Gravely®,
GreenSure®, Heat Mirror®, Home Slicker®, Hunter Douglas®, Hylar®, IceStone®, InterfaceFlor™,
Kynar®, Lyptus®, Medite™, Metlund®, Micronal® PCM SmartBoard®, Milgard®, Mylar®, NuCrete®,
PaperStone™, Polyureseal BP®, Rainscreen®, Richlite®, Silestone®, SkyBlend®, SolaHart®,
Superglass®, Thermafiber®, Trex®, Typar®, Tyvek®, Tyvek Drainwrap®, Ultra Touch®, Wal-Mart℠, Zodiaq®

For Charlie Wing, who taught me how to build
from the ground up.
—DJ

ACKNOWLEDGMENTS

First, I want to thank Kelli Pousson and Kathryn Koberg for their dedication and tireless work to make this book as beautiful and illustrative as possible. I thank my wife, Elena, and my two dogs, Sundancer and Wind Dancer, for their patient understanding these last few months. Without their support, I don't know what I would have done.

It has been an absolute pleasure working with coauthor Scott Gibson and editor Peter Chapman. They have been positive and inspiring. Most of all, I want to thank all the builders, remodelers, and architects who have provided so much content and hundreds of photos to make the book rich and accurate. I especially want to thank the Boulder Green Building Guild, the California Build It Green program, Stopwaste.org, and the Master Builder's Association of Seattle for their input, suggestions, and contributions. They are leaders in the green building movement, changing the way we build homes in America.

As always, a book like this follows in the footsteps of the pioneers who have made green building such an amazing phenomenon. Many thanks to Bill Reed, Doug Parker, Marc Richmond, Brian Gitt, Carl Seville, Mark LaLiberte, Kristen Shewfelt, John Viner, Larry Kinney, Tom Hoyt, Jim Leach, Debora Wright at CMHC, and Johnny Weis at Solar Energy International.

—DJ

Contents

INTRODUCTION

My passion for green building is based on experience. I know that building green results in better houses and that it improves the lives of the people who live in them, not to mention the health of our planet.

For 10 years, I ran a construction company in Washington, D.C., called Lightworks Construction. We focused on solar construction. When the solar tax credit expired in 1985, everything changed. The momentum of the solar industry ground to a halt, and it didn't get going again for nearly 20 years. With the financial incentive gone, we began specializing in building and remodeling super energy-efficient and innovative houses, offices, and restaurants. Our job was to over-deliver and delight our clients by transforming their homes and offices into more comfortable, efficient spaces. Although the term had not yet been coined, we were pioneers in what is now known as "green building."

In 1992, I sold my construction company and set off to discover the new, big-business ideas that would make the world a more sustainable place. I interviewed CEOs from over 50 cutting-edge companies. I spoke with manufacturers, investment firms, inventive providers of services, and consultants and leaders in the construction industry. Over the course of those countless conversations, it became clear that many sectors of the economy were converging on a new business model, one with the potential to change the way our homes are built and how they work—and, I hoped, with the potential to lead us to a less challenging future for our children.

Jim Leach, a leading solar builder in Boulder, Col., was one of the visionaries who illuminated this fresh way of thinking for me. He was also the one who first told me about a new field called "green building." Finally,

there was a word that described how we built at Lightworks. For me, green building was the perfect way to marry my love of construction with my desire to improve the quality of life for America's homeowners. And I got to do something good for the planet.

Grand aspirations are fine, but the real difficulties always show up in the details. I moved to Boulder, where I'd gone to school, explicitly to start a green building program. I met with the Boulder Home Builders Association (HBA), and we started a green building committee to explore the issues and opportunities in green building. A few builders, inspired by Jim Leach's enthusiasm, joined forces with us, and the HBA board soon passed a resolution to develop a program.

At about the same time, the city of Boulder decided to update the local energy code, which had been adopted after the energy crisis in the 1970s. They wanted to incorporate resource conservation and indoor air quality into a green building program that would keep up with the growing number of local green builders. Within a year the second and third green building programs in the country were on the books; the Denver Home Builders Association adopted the Boulder program and the City of Boulder enacted a green building code. That's what launched this stage of my career.

My new company was called What's Working. As a recovering builder, I was actively involved as a consultant and trainer in green building programs around the country. With Kim Master, who joined the company in 2003, I wrote *Green Remodeling: Changing the World One Room at a Time* to fill the niche for homeowners and remodelers who wanted a how-to book to guide their green remodels.

Since then, the increased interest in green building has been nothing short of astonishing. Green is everywhere, and everything points to long-term changes in how home buyers and home builders will do business. Where this leaves builders is another story. It's fine for consumers to clamor for "green" houses, but what does that mean, exactly, to the person who is responsible for translating that into a real house? It's no less confusing for the prospective homeowner who wants a green house but isn't sure what that entails.

This book offers a way to get there, not by adopting wildly new building technologies and materials but mostly by using what's already on hand. One step at a time, builders can move from conventional construction to something far richer for themselves and the people who buy their homes. It works.

David Johnston
Boulder, Colorado

Green Building Basics

Our built environment is changing the world significantly and, it would seem, irrevocably. Global climate change and the steady depletion of essential natural resources are making the news. More devastating natural disasters, such as Hurricane Katrina in 2005, and painfully high energy costs may be an inevitable part of our future, and residential construction is partly to blame. More than a million single-family homes are built every year in the United States alone. All of those houses consume an inordinate amount of natural resources and energy. Maybe that's why green building seems to be taking root, not as a passing fancy but as a fundamental change in how and why we build the houses we live in.

What we alternately call green building or sustainable building is a way for people to make a positive difference in the world around them—if not reversing, then at least reducing the impact of humankind on the planet. Not coincidentally, it has its own practical rewards on a scale that all of us can immediately understand. If becoming model citizens of Planet Earth is too much to get our arms around, living in healthier, more comfortable houses that are less expensive to operate and last longer is certainly an attractive idea. Who wouldn't want to participate in something like that?

THE GREEN FACTOR

Green building encompasses every part of construction, not just the house itself but everything around it, and how the house and its occupants relate to the community around them. In theory, it can seem simple. In practice, it can get complicated. At its most basic, green building is a tripod of three interrelated goals:

- **Energy efficiency**, the cornerstone of any green building project. A well-designed and green-built home consumes as little energy as possible and uses renewable sources of energy whenever possible. Lower energy use not only saves homeowners money but also has broader societal benefits, including fewer disruptions in energy supplies, better air quality, and reduced global climate change.

- **Conservation of natural resources.** Conventional building needlessly consumes large quantities of wood, water, metal, and fossil fuels. There are great varieties of effective building strategies that conserve natural resources and provide other benefits, such as lower costs. Strategies include the use of durable products to reduce waste and specifying recycled-content products that reuse natural resources.

- **Indoor air quality.** Poor indoor air quality is often caused by mold and mildew that are the result of leaks or poorly designed and maintained heating and cooling systems. Another common source of indoor air pollution is the off-gassing of chemicals found in many building materials. Some are known carcinogens.

Green building is ultimately about the relationship of a house and its occupants to the world around them. It's a process of design and construction that fosters the conservation of energy and other natural resources and promotes a healthy environment.

In essence, that's what green building is about. It's not a scorecard where we rack up the number of recycled building materials we use, nor is it a requirement to buy a roof's worth of solar panels or put a wind generator up in the backyard. Green building might include some or all of these things, but it's a lot more than that. Green building is a systematic approach that covers every step of design and construction from land use and site planning to materials selection, energy efficiency, and indoor air quality. All of this will be covered, step by step, in the chapters that follow.

Green Is No Longer on the Fringe

Green is hot. According to a survey conducted by McGraw-Hill Construction, demand for green building had outpaced supply by early 2007 as home buyers looked for greater energy efficiency. The National Association of Home Builders (NAHB), a trade group not known for making wild predictions, now believes we've reached the tipping point when half or more of its members are incorporating green features into the homes they build. Even the modular housing industry is getting into the act with a growing list of designers coming up with houses that embrace the goals of sustainable building, not simply fast construction.

Green building shows every sign of becoming a self-fulfilling prophecy: The more people are exposed to the benefits of green homes, the more green homes will be built.

Interiors built to sustainable building standards don't have to look odd. These cabinets are made from panel products that don't off-gas toxins and are manufactured with materials that can be harvested sustainably. Water-based and natural finishes keep occupants healthier than those loaded with volatile organic compounds. The wallpaper is made from renewable cork.

Coast-to-coast, the home-buying public is asking for green features from their architects and builders.

So where did all this start?

It really began in Austin, Texas, in 1992 when the city's green building program won a sustainable development award from the United Nations' Earth Summit in Rio de Janeiro. That put green building on the map, and builders working on the fringes of conventional construction used the healthy-living, energy-saving objectives of green building as a unifying theme. Over the next several years, alternative building techniques such as straw-bale, rammed earth, and adobe construction received a lot of press.

By 1996, the Denver Home Builders Association was developing the first private sector green building program in the country. Although it met with great resistance, the board approved the plan by a single vote. At the same time, Boulder, Col., became the first city in the country to make sustainable building part of its city code. If you wanted a building permit, you had to have 50 "green points" on the permit application. Both the Denver and Boulder programs got the attention of the construction industry as well as city officials

Alternative designs of the 1970s may have been inexpensive to build and heat, but they lacked a diversity of design that turned off many potential converts. This house incorporates structural insulated panels, insulating concrete forms, and other green features yet looks entirely contemporary.

Smart planning can include the placement of windows for solar gain, thereby reducing energy bills, and using concrete as a finish material on floors. Minimizing carpeting reduces the threat of mold and allergens. A ceiling fan and operable windows aid ventilation.

across the country. Cities from Atlanta to Seattle launched green building programs, then home builder associations around the country picked up on Denver's example. By 1999, there were more than 50 local programs countrywide.

Lots of Green, Few Common Standards

There were plenty of green building programs, but not much common ground. Each of the country's local programs had its own definitions of what it meant to be green, and builders working under more than one of the programs could easily be confused. In the Aspen, Col., area alone, for example, builders in the late 1990s could choose from among four separate green programs.

The NAHB soon started thinking about what production homebuilders needed to know, and the association later published its own set of guidelines. They are just that—guidelines that may be adopted by builders as they see fit. Local or statewide programs scattered elsewhere across the country may follow the NAHB Green Building Guidelines' lead of suggesting without requiring, or they may set measurable performance standards. The Energy Star® program of the U.S. Environmental Protection Agency has included indoor air quality as part of its energy-saving initiative. MASCO, a large conglomerate of building product manufacturers, has its Environments For Living (EFL) program that certifies builders at progressive levels of home performance (see www.eflbuilder.com).

BUILDING WITH STRAW

Straw-bale construction will probably never be mainstream but it does satisfy at least three important goals for green building: straw is a renewable resource that can be harvested locally, it's relatively inexpensive, and straw-bale walls have high R-values for energy efficiency.

Straw can be used as infill—meaning a structural framework actually carries building loads—or the bales can be formed into structural walls without any additional framework. Once the bales have been stacked into walls and pinned together, they're covered with wire mesh and finished with stucco to make them weather tight and durable.

It can take several hundred bales of straw to make a house, but the raw material is an agricultural waste product that can come from any one of several crops—wheat, oat, barley, and rye among them. Some 200 million tons of straw are produced in the U.S. annually, so there's plenty of it available.

Straw bale is a low-tech construction method that can be managed without a lot of building background, which makes it appealing to owner-builders trying to save money. If low cost is appealing, so is performance. A bale of straw has an R-value of about 28, and the stucco finish protects against both pest infestations and fire.

On the downside, the availability of straw probably has something to do with where you live. It must be kept dry during construction, and code officials in some parts of the country aren't familiar with it so approval is not likely to be automatic. If you want to learn more, there is a variety of sources for information, including www.greenbuilder.com.

Early green building programs were a magnet for new ideas and practices aimed at making houses more energy efficient and less expensive to build. One result was a wider interest in straw-bale construction.

RAMMED EARTH AND ADOBE

Both rammed earth and adobe houses seem nearly ideal from a green point of view and, in many ways, they are. The appeal of both techniques is that the Earth itself is the basic raw material for the building envelope. It would be hard to top that on a scale of sustainability.

Traditional adobe houses are made from earthen bricks that have dried in the sun and are laid in courses to form walls. Modern versions can be stabilized with cement. The gently rounded contours and thick walls of these houses are an architectural trademark of the southwestern U.S. and Mexico. Because building materials can be taken directly from the site they're inexpensive, and adobe has high mass, although not necessarily a high R-value.

There's probably no reason that adobe houses couldn't be built outside their traditional geographic stronghold. But on a practical level, you'll also need hot, sunny weather and the right kind of soil to make the bricks, as well as experienced builders who know how to work with the material. You're not likely to find those conditions in Tacoma, Cincinnati, or Boston. If you have adobe bricks trucked in, it's going to get very expensive.

Rammed earth is another green-friendly building technology in which soil mixed with a small amount of cement is compacted with hydraulic tools in forms to create walls up to 2 ft. thick. Walls are extremely heavy—100 lb. or more per sq. ft.—so these houses call for sturdy concrete stem-wall foundations.

Building a rammed earth home is not a beginner's game. It takes specialized equipment as well as know-how, and the labor-intensive process isn't inexpensive. Rammed Earth Development, a Tucson, Arizona-based company specializing in this technique, estimates that a rammed earth house starts at nearly $200 per sq. ft. Ironically, even though walls are made from earth, not any kind of soil will do. Rammed Earth says site soil is used only rarely because most of it doesn't have the right mix of ingredients. It's actually cheaper to buy screened fill, according to the company.

Both building techniques are appealing for their use of natural materials, if not their inherent beauty. But a variety of factors is likely to keep them confined to a limited geographic region. Good sources to learn more about it include Rammed Earth's website (www.rammedearth.com) and another for a California company founded by David Easton, an early practitioner of the craft (www.rammedearthworks.com).

Rammed earth and adobe structures are made from earth, making these materials "sustainable" in the truest sense of the word.

A way out of this morass arrived in 2000 in the form of the Leadership in Energy and Environmental Design program (or just LEED for short), a set of specific, measurable building standards developed by the U.S. Green Building Council for commercial construction. By 2006, it had evolved into a pilot program called LEED for Homes that was headed for full-scale adoption sometime in 2007.

To date, LEED is the only national green building program that puts the exact requirements for earning green status in writing and requires independent verification that buildings are constructed that way. And this is key. Over time, consumers are almost certain to become far more educated and a lot less tolerant of slippery definitions of green building: "Is that house really green?" they'll ask. "Prove it." Without published standards that can be certified in the field by independent inspectors, it will be very difficult for builders to show homebuyers they're getting what they paid for.

In spite of, or maybe because of, the proliferation of green building initiatives and published guidelines, there is still ample room for confusion among builders who want to build green. Not only are there a number of programs to choose from, but their different criteria can compete with one another. For example, durability of building components is an important consideration because it's one way of reducing waste. Vinyl siding lasts a long time but there are concerns about dioxin and other dangerous by-products that result from the manufacture and incineration of polyvinyl chloride. So, can a house built to sustainable standards include vinyl products? If so, which ones are acceptable and which are not?

House size poses another such dilemma. Suppose a house built for two people includes a variety of recycled products and energy-saving building techniques or is even capable of operating completely off the grid—but it's 6,000 sq. ft. and cost $500 per sq. ft. to build. It uses far more resources than an

MYTH #1: GREEN BUILDING IS FOR TREEHUGGERS

Yes, committed environmentalists do like green building. But green building is not for extremists. It's going mainstream. According to an estimate from the Environmental Home Center in Seattle, the overall market for sustainable building materials is about $20 billion a year, and it's expected to grow more than 10 percent annually. That makes it big business.

Why are a growing number of consumers buying into green building? Rising energy prices are certainly a big reason. Consumers are beginning to realize that sustainably built houses mean lower heating and cooling costs.

Health is another major reason: Our health and well-being are notably affected by the large amount of time we spend indoors. According to the American College of Allergy, Asthma, and Immunology, more than 38 percent of Americans suffer from allergies. According to the U.S. Centers for Disease Control, the number of asthma cases grew by 75 percent from 1980 to 1994—to more than 17 million.

Since when is saving money and enjoying good health an issue for any particular cultural or political minority?

MYTH #2: GREEN BUILDING IS TOO EXPENSIVE

Some green building components do cost more. But many cost less. When thinking green is part of the initial planning process, it's easier and less expensive to incorporate features that significantly lower operating and maintenance costs.

For example, passive solar design coupled with high-performance insulation can make a conventional furnace or boiler unnecessary. Orienting a house to take advantage of solar energy does not in itself cost a penny more than standard construction. Adding a few windows and investing in insulation does cost money, but the rewards on the other side of the ledger are far more substantial, initially and over the life of the house.

Many builders have found that the real cost is in learning new techniques. Products themselves are becoming more readily available and more affordable as major manufacturers develop new lines to meet consumer demand.

MYTH #3: GREEN BUILDING IS UGLY

Green buildings do not have to look like yurts. True, a yurt can have its own beauty, but understandably not everyone wants to live in one. Uniformity or plainness of design is one factor that hampered wider acceptance of alternative building practices back in the 1970s (let's face it, some of those houses were just plain ugly). But a green home can look like any other house: colonial, modern, southwest, ranch—you name it. Even on the inside, green homes can be just as varied in design, just as stunning, as any conventional home.

On another level, green buildings are inherently more beautiful because builders and homeowners take the time to understand how the house works and what materials will work better than conventional products. Reclaimed wood, recycled glass, certified lumber—the list of beautiful green materials is very long indeed.

A green house that doesn't necessarily look it: This pleasant bungalow-style house in Hawaii uses long-wearing steel roofing made to facilitate the addition of photovoltaic panels at a later date. The bungalow design with deep overhangs and protected porches suits the climate perfectly.

GETTING BIGGER

In 1973, the average new single-family home in the U.S. measured 1,660 sq. ft. By 2005, the size had risen to 2,434 sq. ft.—an increase of 46 percent. That still may seem modest, but in some parts of the country, huge houses are the norm. In Boulder County, Col., for example, the average new house is 6,000 sq. ft. In Aspen, Col., it's 15,000 sq. ft.

average-size house, and certainly far more than is necessary for a single couple. Can such a house really be considered green?

There may be no perfect answer to these questions, only a process to balance competing interests. For builders and consumers alike, it can be a bewildering process.

Dealing with the World around Us

Political history and diversity aside, the nation's green building programs share a common goal—building houses that recognize some uncomfortable realities in the world around us.

Increasingly savvy home buyers want assurances that their new home is "green." A passive solar design with south-facing glass, formaldehyde-free cabinet components, and flooring from sustainable sources can contribute to certification.

Some of the most important fundamentals of sustainable building—energy and resource conservation and indoor air quality—are a reaction to a world very different than it was a decade ago. Seen in this light, sustainable building is a practical response to a variety of issues that affect us all.

Energy supplies are peaking

Let's start with something known as "peak oil," the hypothetical moment when the world has pumped the maximum possible number of barrels per day out of the ground. After that, oil production starts to decline. The U.S. hit its peak in the mid-1970s. Many oil geologists believe the world will hit peak production sometime in the next decade. Whether we reach that point in two years or 10 years, we are nearing the end of the cheap oil era. That's alarming enough on its own, even more so when you consider that buildings are responsible for at least 40 percent of all energy consumption in the U.S.

As recently as the mid-1990s, energy experts assumed there was enough natural gas to serve as the transitional fuel from a petroleum economy to a hydrogen economy. It is a near-perfect fuel—abundant, domestic, clean-burning, and relatively inexpensive. As a result, turbines that burned natural gas were built to augment many coal-fired plants in the U.S. Then the do-

Buildings contribute over 40 percent of the total greenhouse gases in the atmosphere, more than either industry or transportation alone.

mestic supply of natural gas began to decline. Gas wells stopped producing but demand kept growing with the construction of both buildings and power plants. From 2002 to 2004, natural gas prices doubled in much of the U.S. In some markets, prices went up even higher.

ENERGY SUPPLY GAP

With the end of the oil era in sight, energy planners had hoped that methane would bridge the gap between an oil-based economy and one fueled by hydrogen. But a sharp increase in demand for natural gas along with limited supplies has produced an energy gap that may spell shortages ahead.

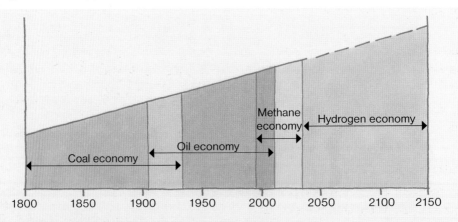

Adapted from J. Ausubel, 1996 "Can Technology Spare the Earth?" *American Scientist*, v. 84, p. 169.

The U.S. started to import natural gas from Canada and Mexico through new pipelines. Today, we are close to using the total volume of available gas from all North American sources. In some parts of the country, there are not enough pipelines to meet the demands of growing communities.

Oil is easily shipped in tankers. But natural gas must be compressed, liquefied, and shipped at very low temperatures in huge refrigerated tanks aboard a ship. Due to the potential danger in handling liquefied natural gas (LNG), there is tremendous resistance to installing off-loading facilities in U.S. ports. As a result, we don't have the capacity to import much LNG. It, too, will become increasing expensive and harder to get.

Because of these and other factors, energy conservation is a cornerstone of green building. Cutting energy use has an obvious and immediate effect on how much it costs to heat and cool a house. Not worried about how much oil is left in Saudi Arabia? OK, green building can be about your heating bill next winter.

Climate change means a tougher environment

Scientists may argue about the ultimate cause, but climate change is certainly upon us. Most people recognize it as "weird" weather. Everywhere in the world, local weather patterns change in unpredictable ways. There are more intense hurricanes like Katrina, longer droughts like those in East Africa, unheard of floods in New England and Ohio, and more violent weather events such as tornados.

This office was made from a variety of green building products, including structural insulated panels and engineered structural beams, but cost only $75 per sq. ft. Located in Colorado, its radiant floor heating is driven by a conventional water heater.

Most experts lay the blame on higher concentrations of carbon dioxide (CO_2) in the atmosphere. It's called a "greenhouse gas" because it traps heat that would otherwise be radiated back into space. And the problem feeds on itself. As more CO_2 builds up, it in turn traps more heat, which accelerates the process. Take, for example, what happens in the arctic when ice melts due to higher global temperatures. As the ice cap melts, more of the dark ocean is exposed and more heat is absorbed, which helps to melt more ice. This "positive feedback loop" is a cycle: more heat, less ice, and a faster rate of melting.

Green building's response is to cut the amount of carbon dioxide produced directly and indirectly by encouraging the use of renewable energy sources where possible and recycled products or products that take less energy to produce. The result is a smaller "carbon footprint." This is why zero-energy homes, houses that produce as much electricity as they consume, are springing up across the country.

GREENHOUSE GAS EMISSIONS

A steady increase in concentrations of atmospheric carbon dioxide is behind a sustainable building goal of reducing the "carbon footprint" of houses and their occupants. CO_2 has increased from 280 parts per million prior to industrialization to 381 ppm in 2005. The timeline in this chart is from 1958 through 2005 at the Mauna Loa Observatory in Hawaii and shows seasonal spikes even as overall concentrations rise.

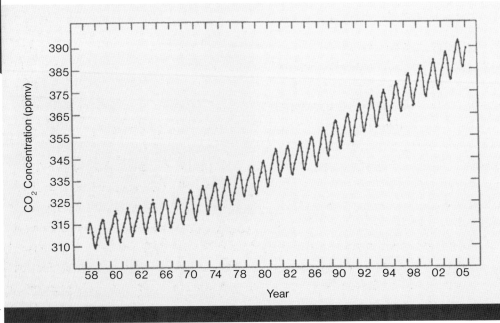

Adapted from: *Carbon Dioxide Information Analysis Center.*

Water isn't boundless, either

The U.S. uses water so flagrantly that many of us may not think of it as a finite resource. After all, two-thirds of the planet is covered in water and it's raining somewhere all the time. What few of us realize is that less than 1 percent of the planet's water is drinkable. Most of the earth's fresh water is frozen in the polar ice caps. What we have been living on is surface water, aquifer water, and fossil water.

Surface water, found in lakes, rivers, and streams, is confined primarily to the region where it is found—the Great Lakes, for instance, or the Colorado River. Aquifer water, replenished by rainfall that seeps into the earth, is what we tap into when we drill wells in drier areas. Fossil water is like oil: It will never be replenished. All three are being challenged from either pollution or overuse.

Roof-mounted solar panels are one way of reducing the consumption of fossil fuels and shrinking the "carbon footprint" of a house.

As climate change becomes more intense, rainfall patterns around the world will change. Some regions will get more, some significantly less. In the U.S., predictions are that the western U.S. will become increasingly drier over the next 20 years with the possibility of a drought to rival the one that produced the Dust Bowl in the 1930s. The huge but shallow Ogallala Aquifer under the Great Plains from the Dakotas to Texas is dropping at the rate of 30 ft. per year, and the less it rains the faster it is drawn down. Northwest China is one of the four largest grain-producing areas in the world

Many Americans have taken clean water for granted, but increasing pressure is taking its toll. Aquifers once thought to be nearly limitless are dropping rapidly as a growing population competes for a finite resource.

and feeds China today. But it runs on fossil water, which may be completely gone in the next five years. What happens then?

Decreasing water supplies, along with rapidly rising energy prices, will bring higher food prices. Competition for food will also lead to increased conflict over food-growing areas and water sources.

Seen in context, those 10-gal.-a-minute bathroom shower spas may not look quite as appealing. Water conservation becomes an obvious component of green building and goes a long way toward explaining an emphasis on water-saving toilets, low-flow showerheads, and landscaping that doesn't require much watering.

Other natural resources on the wane

Structures—residential, commercial, and industrial—account for 40 percent of all natural resources consumed in a single year. Yet construction of the average 2,000-sq.-ft. house also yields 50 to 150 cu. yd., or 8,000 to 12,000 lb., of construction waste. Most of that ends up in landfills.

MYTH #4: GREEN BUILDING DOESN'T WORK

The list of consumer concerns about how well a green building works is long: "The low-flow showerheads leak." "Bamboo flooring warps easily." "Zero-VOC paint doesn't cover walls as well as the paint I've always used." "Compact fluorescent lights give off a weird bluish glare." Some complaints have been justified, but these concerns tend to focus on exceptions rather than on the big picture.

In general, sustainably built houses tend to be more energy efficient, more durable, and less costly to maintain. That said, some green products have had quality issues. But keep in mind that conventional products have also had quality concerns, not to mention unacceptable effects on our health and the environment.

Many green products were designed to do something better than a conventional product, not specifically because they could be considered "green." Inevitably, if a green building product does not work, market forces will force it off the shelves, just as under performing conventional products are gradually abandoned in favor of something else. Today, manufacturers of low-flow showerheads, bamboo flooring, and low-VOC paint are creating reliable products. Although the industry has had some growing pains, in the end green building is simply better building.

Construction debris from a single house can be measured by the ton, but some builders are getting smarter about recycling waste and reusing building components. Dismantling this house provided a wealth of material that could be reused and kept recyclables out of the landfill.

RECYCLING PAYS

Builders may look on jobsite recycling as a pain in the neck. It's much easier, isn't it, to have a big Dumpster® dropped at the site? By the time the house is done, the Dumpster is full and everyone goes home happy.

That may be standard practice in many parts of the country, but finding ways to recycle waste at the jobsite can ultimately be much cheaper, as builders in some communities have already discovered. In Portland, Ore., disposal fees for garbage were about $71 per ton in 2005 (plus a $7.50 transaction fee). Most construction waste could be dropped off at a recycling center for fees that topped out at $35. In the very worst-case scenario, recycling cost half as much as throwing it in the Dumpster, probably less.

Too much lumber can compromise the resource efficiency of a house.

That rate of consumption simply isn't sustainable. It amounts to using 1.2 planets' worth of resources to take care of just one planet of about 6 billion people. When we hit 8.5 billion people in the year 2025 or so, those resources will have to be stretched a great deal thinner.

Wood is the most renewable of resources used in the building industry, and we use plenty of it for new houses. An increasing amount of it comes from tree plantations, not real forests, hence a green emphasis on making supplies go further and not converting natural forests to tree farms. Advanced framing techniques and the use of structural insulated panels, engi-

Americans make up 5 percent of the world's population but use 25 percent of the world's resources.

neered wood, and Forest Stewardship Council certified-lumber can all help. Those practices are explained in chapter 5.

A variety of metals are also used in building—copper pipe, steel framing and structural supports, aluminum flashing, and metal roofing. Three billion tons of raw materials are turned into foundations, walls, pipes, and panels every year. Using materials in their highest and best use is critical. Increasing the proportion of recycled materials helps reduce waste.

Green building is, above all else, applied common sense. Yet the building industry is agonizingly slow to change, partly because it takes time for new technologies and building practices to filter into the field and partly because builders, many of whom run small businesses, are reluctant to take risks on "new"

Landscaping that promotes natural plants and uses water wisely has twin benefits: houses look as if they fit the landscape more comfortably and water use can be cut dramatically.

ideas that have not been proven. They have their reasons: polybutylene pipe that sprang leaks, hardboard siding that rotted in humid climates, and a variety of other products that never quite lived up to the hype. They cost builders millions in claims and callbacks. Even so, sustainable building practices, designing and building homes using a whole system approach, and the products that go with them will eventually overcome those misgivings. It's not a gimmick. It's just good building.

As interest among consumers increases, so do the number of reliable and attractive green building products. Natural finishes, tile made from recycled glass, and cabinets constructed of bamboo contribute to the look of this kitchen.

The House as a System

Amory Lovins, one of the founders of the Rocky Mountain Institute, probably wasn't too far off the mark when he said, "People don't care where their energy comes from. All they want is hot showers and cold beer." That logic can easily be extended to the house as a whole. What many homeowners want is a house that's safe, comfortable, and easy to heat and cool—not a science course on how that's accomplished.

It's not that easy for builders. We can't build green houses until we understand how a house works as a system. To some builders this may seem like a long leap into unfamiliar territory. Many carpenters were taught how to build by older carpenters who themselves were following the footsteps of their own mentors. Very few of us go to homebuilding school to learn building science.

Yet science is what sustainable building relies on. Subsequent chapters in this book describe in detail how sustainably built houses can be oriented on the site, framed, insulated, plumbed and wired, ventilated, and landscaped. Those building practices didn't come out of thin air. They're based on principles that once understood will guide us every step of the way. Ultimately, green building begins with the fundamentals of designing and building the many parts of a house so they work together as a whole.

THE GREEN FACTOR

Sustainable building takes most of us back to the classroom for a refresher on the physical properties of energy, air, and water. It's much easier to build a green house when we understand how heat and cold move from one object to another, and how air and moisture move inside our houses. Green building practices, as well as the selection of appropriate building materials, revolve around a few basic principles of science. What's key:

- A house is a system of interrelated parts.

- Energy loses some of its potential each time it is converted from one form to another, which helps explain why passive solar heat is much more efficient than electric heat.

- Form follows function when it comes to design, meaning that construction should be tailored to the environment in which the house is built.

- Air leaks in the building envelope represent a significant loss of energy and open the door to moisture damage inside wall and ceiling cavities.

- Controlling the movement of heat, air, and moisture involves every part of the building and everyone on the building team.

How Heat Is Transferred

Nothing is more central to this notion of house-as-system than heat flow, or to get a bit more technical about it, the First and Second Laws of Thermodynamics (thermo = heat, dynamics = movement). Once we see how these principles are applied to building, we'll never look at a house the same way again.

Energy cannot be created or destroyed, only changed. That's the first law of thermodynamics. All the energy we have is in one of many forms: electrical, chemical, mechanical, solar. The second law says that every time you convert energy from one form to another it's degraded in the process.

Some forms of energy are more concentrated than others are. Electrical energy, for instance, can do all kinds of miraculous things, like make laptop computers work or turn heavy motors. Woodstoves, on the other hand, convert a lot of energy potential from the wood into heat, but you can't run a laptop with it. So there is a hierarchy of energy forms that we can con-vert to accomplish the work we want to do.

What the second law tells us is that each time we change the form of energy (chemi-cal to heat—heat to mechanical) it becomes less useful. This is called entropy. Efficiency is converting energy from one form to another with as little waste as possible. In the end, we can measure the "net energy" of any given process—the percent of the original energy potential versus the actual work we have ac-complished.

Does this have anything to do with build-ing houses? Actually, it does. Our challenge as designers and builders is to make the building as efficient as possible in all energy conver-sions—that is, to keep energy in its most useful form and not let it escape or degrade more than necessary. In other words, to create the least entropy. The closer the building is to the source—the bottom of the energy food chain—the better.

A classical example of high entropy ver-sus low entropy lies in the contrast between a

LAWS OF NATURE

Green building is based on building science. One key is understanding the flow of heat, which always moves from hot to cold. Heat transmits in three ways: conduction, convection, and radiation. All three principles can guide the selection of the most appropriate materials and practices for a green house.

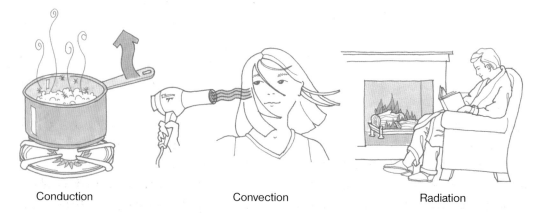

Conduction　　　　　Convection　　　　　Radiation

LOST IN TRANSIT

When energy changes from one form to another, some of it is lost. Take, for example, the energy potential in a lump of coal. Because of the different efficiencies of mining, transportation, and electrical generation, only 15 percent of its energy potential is actually delivered as usable power in a house.

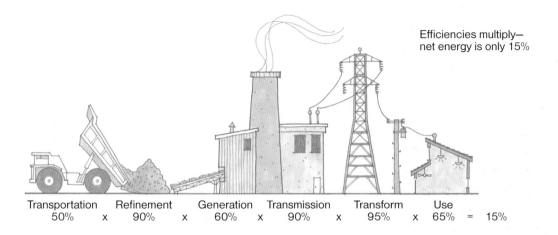

Efficiencies multiply— net energy is only 15%

Transportation		Refinement		Generation		Transmission		Transform		Use		
50%	x	90%	x	60%	x	90%	x	95%	x	65%	=	15%

house that is electrically heated and one that is designed to be passive solar. Electricity makes a long journey before it arrives at the baseboard heater. Suppose the electricity we use comes

By the time it reaches us, electricity has lost 85 percent of the potential energy of the coal used to make it. If we heat with electric resistance heat, we're getting only 15 percent of the energy the coal had to offer in the first place.

from coal. Coal itself is a very concentrated form of chemical energy that was created over millions of years in a process of photosynthesis that converted atmospheric carbon dioxide into a hydrocarbon fossil fuel. Enormous amounts of energy are required to run the extraction equipment, trucks, and processing equipment.

Then coal is transported to a power plant that burns the coal to boil water that creates steam. The steam spins a turbine that creates the electricity. The electricity then passes through a transformer to create 240,000 volts for high-transmission lines. As it runs through the lines there are line losses until it reaches its destination. It then passes through another transformer where it is stepped down to 240 volts that we can use in our homes.

Passive solar, on the other hand, uses radiant heat directly from the sun to heat a house. Here, the energy makes only one simple conversion from light to heat. The sunlight passes through south-facing windows, strikes a solid object, and turns into heat that is re-radiated to human bodies. There is only one energy conversion.

The efficiency of the process is determined by the transparency of the glass. At a minimum, we get 50 percent of the potential

heat and with well-designed glass, we can get up to 75 percent. And, it's all free. That's eating low on the energy food chain.

In green building, having an appreciation for entropy helps us select the best form of energy for the task at hand, using the most efficient appliances or designs that make energy conversions with the least amount of degradation (to heat) and retaining heat where we need it and in the form we want it. This is where the building shell comes in.

taking place on a more subtle level. All of these are important in a house for different reasons, and the principles help explain why some building techniques and materials work better than others do.

Thermal Transmission

Energy moves in three ways—conduction, convection, and radiation (see the drawing on p. 24)—and energy movement is always a combination of all three. While we refer to insulation in terms of its conductive resistance to heat movement, convection and radiation are also

Conduction

Heat moves through solid substances by this process. It is typically measured with an R-value (the higher the number, the greater resistance to heat flow). Anything that conducts electricity typically has a low R-value. Metals of all kinds fall into this category. Wood, not a good

Passive solar design sharply reduces the amount of energy a house will consume while still keeping occupants comfortable. Light-filled spaces are cheerful and inviting as well as energy efficient.

FEELING THE LOSS

The movement of heat is experienced in a variety of ways: by forced and free convection of air, by direct conduction through the floor, and by radiation to a cooler object, like a nearby window.

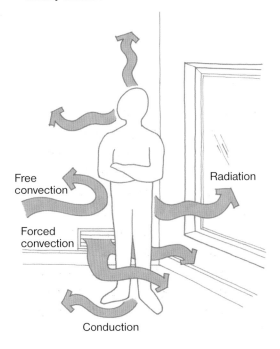

Free convection

Forced convection

Radiation

Conduction

conductor, has a higher R-value than metal. The insulation we use in houses works because it traps air, giving it a much higher R-value.

So in insulating a house from hot and cold, we look for materials that allow the least amount of conduction or take steps to shield conductive materials so they don't become energy transmitters. Light steel framing, for example, can move tremendous amounts of energy through the exterior walls of a house because it is such an efficient conductor. That's why a steel-framed house should be sheathed with rigid foam insulation. Cellulose, foam, cotton, mineral wool, and other types of insulation conduct very little.

Convection

Convection is the movement of liquids and gases because of differences in density. Convection explains why warm air ends up in the upper floors of a house while the basement stays cold, or why a chimney draws smoke up and out of the house.

Our houses are filled with convective currents, some of which we feel and some of which go undetected. Convection is more subtle than conduction, but when it's not controlled, it can result in a drafty, uncomfortable house. Worse, convection can carry moisture exactly where we don't want it—into wall cavities and attics where it condenses into water and encourages mold and deterioration.

When we become more aware of how convection works, we can take steps in building houses to reduce its impact on comfort and health.

Radiation

Radiation is the movement of energy from a hot object to a cooler one via waves. Think of the sun on a hot summer day. The air temperature is the same in the sunshine as it is in the shade, but we feel more comfortable when we get out of the sun and out of reach of all that radiant energy. A fireplace can keep us warm even as a great deal of hot air escapes up the chimney.

Radiant energy heats objects rather than air. That's why people are often happier with radiant-floor heat than they are with a forced-air furnace. Their bodies feel the heat directly rather than feeling the warm air.

Controlling Heat Flow

We build houses so we can stay comfortable, and to keep the weather at bay. Over time, we've gotten better and better at disconnecting our houses from the climate around them.

Houses today can look the same whether you're in Anchorage or Pensacola, and that doesn't make a lot of sense. More logically, houses in those vastly different climates would be designed to respond to the environment around them and thus have very different appearances.

Building science seeks to put the two back together. We want to understand the building well enough to take advantage of the environmental benefits of local climate and protect the occupants from undesirable climatic conditions (for more, see chapter 13).

Insulation is a key part of designing for climate. How much insulation we can get between outside and inside is partially determined by the structure of the building. Wood-frame buildings were once framed with 2x4s on 16-in. centers, an approach so common that architects and designers referred to this detail simply as "typical" or just "TYP." So this is the place to start with design.

In the framing chapter (see p. 83), we will discuss various options for building the structure, but the important thing here is to avoid "TYP" on construction drawings—it means that too little is being done to fit the house to its environment. A house should be designed to meet the requirements of the local environment. This means that insulation levels, or the overall R-value of the house, should be higher than the minimums required by the local energy code. In a good green home, the R-values of insulated floors, walls, and ceilings are often 50 percent higher than what the building code requires.

Air Leakage

Air leaks, or drafts, can be responsible for 25 percent of the heat loss in a new house, more in older houses. Moreover, when air moves through the house because of leaks it is often laden with moisture that can end up in wall cavities and condense, increasing the

Infiltration—unwanted air intake into a house—can account for 40 percent of the heating load in existing buildings. New homes are only slightly better at 25 percent.

likelihood of mold and structural deterioration. Air traffic control is the key. We have grown used to sealing the obvious problem areas with foam under bottom plates, expanding foam around window and door framing, and insulation stuffed into smaller wall cavities. It is the invisible and often convoluted paths of air leakage that need our attention. Because air leaks are so detrimental to the energy performance of a house, it is always a good idea to conduct a blower-door test after the house has been

An infrared photograph shows energy losses around a window. Areas shaded in red indicate sources of escaping heat—and wasted energy dollars.

UNCONTROLLED AIRFLOW ROBS ENERGY

Without an effective air barrier, a house is like a balloon peppered with pinpricks. Air leaks reduce energy efficiency, make the house less comfortable, and have the potential to cause mold and structural decay. Contributors range from recessed lighting to an unsealed chimney chase.

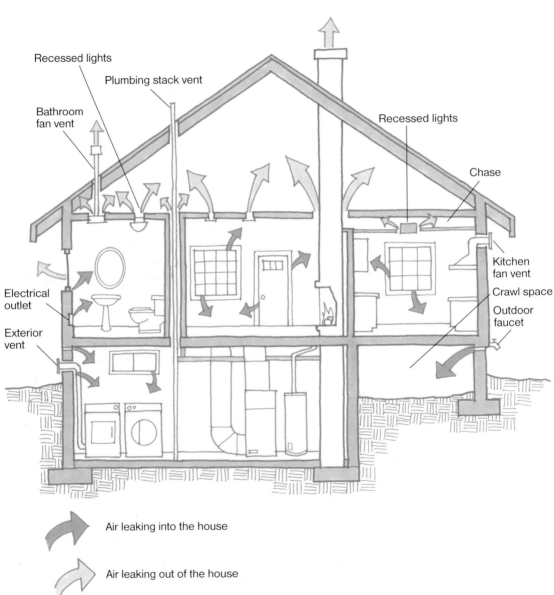

Recessed lights

Plumbing stack vent

Bathroom fan vent

Recessed lights

Chase

Kitchen fan vent

Electrical outlet

Crawl space

Outdoor faucet

Exterior vent

Air leaking into the house

Air leaking out of the house

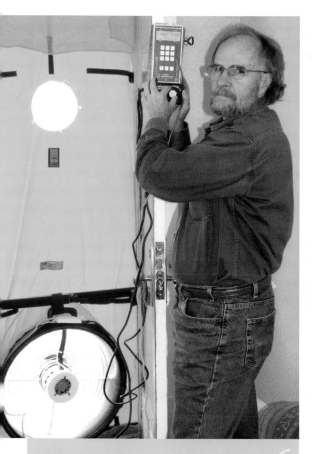

Sealing holes around electrical wires and plumbing pipes is an essential part of creating an effective air barrier. Expanding urethane foam makes a good sealant.

Doug Parker of Big Horn Builders is conducting a blower door test, an accurate way of measuring how effective an air barrier really is. It also provides a way to track down air leaks so they can be sealed.

ditioned spaces. Imagine a balloon with hundreds of tiny pinpricks in it. You can imagine that it won't be inflated for very long. The air barrier is the way we keep the conditioned air in the house and stop heating or cooling the outdoors.

There are many different materials assembled into the envelope of a house, and where these materials intersect should be the focus of air sealing. A stud doesn't allow much air to pass through it, but when there are studs nailed together, they form gaps that allow air to get through. When you install a window, you are creating a gap in the sheathing that can allow more air to escape. Pipes, wires, and ducts, as they intersect the structural members, also are places where air can leak. The integrity of the air barrier is one key to efficient heating and cooling.

Establishing and maintaining an effective air barrier is the responsibility of many members of the building team. From the start, the architect must understand where the air barrier will be. Framers should frame to meet that re-

sealed. A fan housed in a special door frame temporarily replaces the front door and pulls air from the house, "depressurizing" the structure so that air leaks can be detected with a smoke stick. Air leaks become visible so they can be corrected. The test shouldn't cost more than a few hundred dollars. It's a simple way of verifying that air-sealing has been successful.

Air Barriers

Controlling infiltration and exfiltration requires an air barrier between conditioned and uncon-

ACCOUNTING FOR WIND

When a house lacks an effective air barrier, air infiltration from wind becomes a problem. On the windward side, where pressure is higher, air blows into the house. On the leeward side, where pressure is lower, air is drawn through gaps and holes in the envelope. The result? A drafty house, wasted energy.

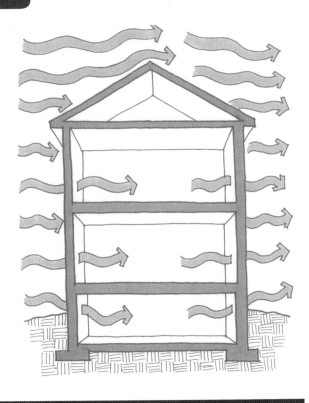

An air barrier on the outside of this house will help keep wind from washing through walls and lowering the efficiency of thermal insulation.

quirement, and the insulating contractor should be thorough. The superintendent or lead carpenter must be able to "see" the potential for air movement before the fact. In other words, everyone needs to be in the game.

Airflow Mechanisms

Wind speed and direction create pressure differentials on different sides of the building. The side facing the wind encounters higher pressure while the opposite side has a lower pressure. These differences cause air to move in the building. If there are cracks or penetrations on the windward side, air will be pushed into the building, through the insulation, and into the living space. That's often around doors and windows. Or the air may follow wiring and create drafts in unexpected places. Because

HOT AIR RISES

Conditioned air can vanish thanks to convection. As hot air rises through chimney flues, unsealed recessed lighting, and duct penetrations through the building envelope, it is replaced by air that enters the house elsewhere. Although the stack effect is an immutable law of nature, it can be controlled.

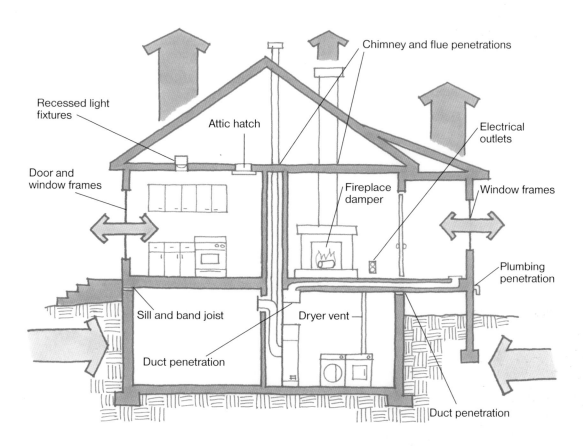

of the lower pressure on the leeward side of the house, air will be pulled out of the building and enhance the flow. This will always vary by season and microclimate conditions.

Stack effect

Basic convection pressures explain the stack effect. Cold air is heavier than warm air. It falls after coming into contact with cold window glass or poorly insulated walls, pushing warm air higher in the building. That, in turn, pushes

air out of the house. Warm air (under pressure) will find any way it can to escape into the attic or out through band joists. The higher the temperature difference, the greater the force. This causes infiltration from lower sections of the building. The remedy is to inspect the attic and seal all air bypasses well before insulation is installed. Also, pay special attention to how insulation is installed, and seal around wires, ducts, and pipes that penetrate the barrier between living spaces and the attic.

Flue effect

Any house with an atmospherically vented combustion appliance with a pilot light (furnace, water heater, fireplace) will have flues for combustion gases. They often run from the basement through the house and exit at the roof. Even when the furnace isn't running, the pilot flame is burning and causing a draft up the flue. This draft also carries conditioned home air with it so there is constant loss of conditioned air. All flues work this way, which explains why fireplace flues should always be closed when the fireplace is not being used.

Another way to defeat this energy-robbing phenomenon is to buy pilot-less appliances equipped with electronic ignition and to install direct-vent or sealed combustion equipment wherever possible. This type of appliance is typically vented through a sidewall of the house, not a chimney. It uses a double-walled pipe that introduces fresh air for combustion while safely venting combustion gases.

Tight Houses Need Ventilation

As we tighten up the house and seal all potential air leaks, we also have to provide a way to introduce fresh air and expel stale air with mechanical ventilation. Many builders wonder about the logic of tightening up the house so religiously only to install ventilation equipment that seems to undo all that effort. The reason is that it's much less expensive to control the flow of fresh air in a sealed house with mechanical ventilation than it is to depend on random air migration through the building envelope in a leaky house.

Barbara Harwood, an award-winning builder from Dallas, Tex., likes to say there is no such thing as a home that's built too tight. It's only underventilated. Long ago, there were subcontractors who specialized in HVAC (heating, ventilating, and air-conditioning). But somewhere along the line the "V" got dropped so that most are now "HAC" contractors. Too bad, because the ventilation part of their moniker is the most important one for good building performance.

Mechanical ventilation also helps us define the right pressurization of a house. Conventional homes with forced-air systems often create negative pressure inside the house because of leaky return ducts. They suck air from the house and draw in air from the outside. Add a dryer vent, a kitchen exhaust hood, and

KNOW YOUR CLIMATE

House design should start with a sense of place:

- What are the outstanding qualities of the climate (hot-dry, warm-humid, cold-windy, Mediterranean-mild)?
- What are the average high temperatures in the summer and average lows in the winter?
- How many months of the year MUST the house be air-conditioned?
- When the weather is mild (spring and fall) from which direction does the wind blow?

- What is the latitude of the site?
- What is the angle of the sun off the horizon on June 21 and December 21?
- How high is the water table?
- What kinds of insects in the area may affect the building (termites, carpenter ants) or the inhabitants (mosquitoes)?

a bathroom fan and the negative pressure can back-draft unburned gases from flues for the furnace or water heater. This can introduce carbon monoxide in the house, a potentially fatal problem (for more, see chapter 9, p. 173). A good mechanical ventilation system will create a slightly positive pressure in the house that resists infiltration and prevents back-drafting. At a minimum, the house should be pressure neutral.

Heat recovery ventilation

Heat recovery ventilation, which is discussed in more detail in chapter 9, brings in fresh air while exhausting indoor air. Heat recovery ventilators (HRVs) usually have two fans: one pulling in fresh air and the other exhausting stale house air. Air streams pass each other through an air-to-air heat exchanger that moderates incoming air by extracting heat from the condi-tioned air and conveying it to the incoming air stream (just the opposite when you're running an air-conditioning system).

Heat recovery ventilators are an effective way of taking the sting out of ventilation systems that expel conditioned air that has, after all, been heated or cooled at our expense.

The Many Faces of Water

If we think back to our high school physics classes, we'll remember that water can be a solid, a liquid, or a gas. In all of its forms—ice, rain, and vapor—water can be a challenge to control in a building. Ice dams forming on roof edges allow water to back up under shingles, get around the felt paper, and find its way into the house. In the form of rain, water can penetrate siding, migrate into wall cavities, and cause mold and rot. As vapor, it can enter wall

CAPTURING LOST ENERGY

A mechanical ventilation system is key to indoor air quality, and a heat recovery ventilator (HRV) is one way of ensuring that energy losses are minimal. An HRV tempers incoming air with exhausted air, which can be an effective energy saver in both heating and cooling climates.

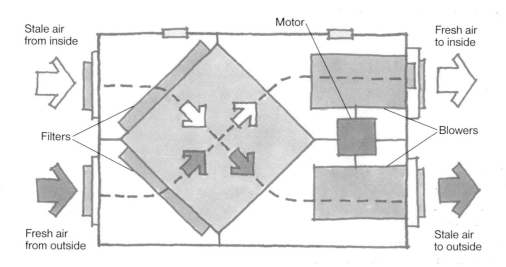

Stale air from inside

Motor

Fresh air to inside

Filters

Blowers

Fresh air from outside

Stale air to outside

cavities through switch plates and outlets or through any cracks in drywall (between base molding and drywall edge, for instance) and get into wall cavities. Prevention of moisture in all phases is our insurance of a durable house that will last 100 years or more.

Like heat, water wants to move. Understanding that process will help us design houses that are more durable.

Gravity

Water always flows downhill. Plumbers know that, which is why they make so much money. But many of the trades have forgotten that fact. We should always put felt paper on the roof from the eaves to the ridge with the upper course overlapping the lower course—just like the scales on a fish. This is also critical for

Whole-house mechanical ventilation keeps people healthy. A heat recovery ventilator reduces energy losses by extracting energy in outgoing air and using it to temper incoming air.

walls where either housewrap or tarpaper is used. Housewrap with holes or tears in it can't work as designed, and no seam should face uphill. This may seem painfully obvious, but the fact is that some builders don't follow these simple rules.

Diffusion

Water (like heat) always flows from areas of higher concentration to areas of lower concentration. That means if we have saturated

AIR MOVES MOISTURE

Moisture can be carried into wall and ceiling cavities in a process called vapor diffusion. Wall assemblies also need a way of drying out, even more difficult when a vapor barrier is placed on both interior and exterior surfaces (A). In the second instance, permeable interior finishes allow drying to the inside of the building (B).

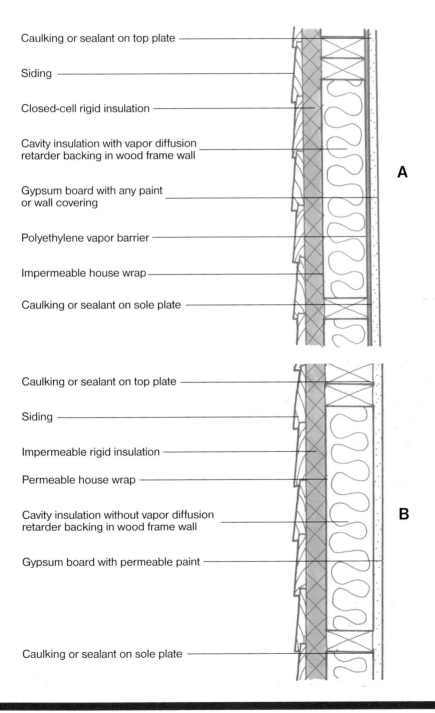

Caulking or sealant on top plate

Siding

Closed-cell rigid insulation

Cavity insulation with vapor diffusion
retarder backing in wood frame wall

Gypsum board with any paint
or wall covering

Polyethylene vapor barrier

Impermeable house wrap

Caulking or sealant on sole plate

A

Caulking or sealant on top plate

Siding

Impermeable rigid insulation

Permeable house wrap

Cavity insulation without vapor diffusion
retarder backing in wood frame wall

Gypsum board with permeable paint

Caulking or sealant on sole plate

B

soil on one side of a foundation wall and warm, dry conditions inside the house, water will try to find a way through the concrete to the drier side. This is why foundations should always be treated to block moisture and why perimeter footing drains and porous backfill around a foundation are important.

Capillary action

Capillary action is the ability of water to flow through a material, from wet to dry. Just like heat, moisture moves through materials based on their properties. Some are better at wicking moisture (remember that was wood's job when it was a tree), and some are more resistant (petroleum-saturated felt paper, for instance). We need to know which building components will be in contact with water and protect them with appropriate materials to resist the migration of moisture.

Airflow

Water vapor goes where air moves it. Think of it as a hitchhiker on molecules of air. If air can get into a wall cavity, so can moisture. It wouldn't be such a problem if the people inside the house would stop their bad habits that create a lot of moisture. But it seems we are committed to taking showers, watering plants, boiling vegetables, and, worst of all, breathing. So if we can't change our behavior we need to prevent that moisture from getting into walls and ceilings from the inside.

The most effective way to reduce interior moisture is to collect it at its source and get it out of the house. Installing good quality bathroom fans and range hoods (good quality so they work quietly and people actually use them) is one obvious step. Another is making sure that dryer vents are correctly installed and never terminate in a basement or attic.

Controlling Sound Transmission

Increasingly, Americans are becoming aware of noise pollution. Whether it is produced by a teen blasting music from his bedroom or a nearby freeway, noise can be an unpleasant intrusion. We may aspire to peace of mind at home, but that's hard to do when we're bombarded by loud and unexpected noises. It makes us irritable, distracted, anxious, and hostile, sometimes without consciously making the connection to noise. Good design and selection and installation of building materials can reduce the intrusions whether they originate in the house or from outside.

> **Carpet is not a cure-all for noisy houses. In fact, it is typically only 15 percent to 20 percent absorptive. It would take four times as much carpet to have the same impact as a typical acoustic material, which is about 80 percent absorptive.**

An acoustics expert might tell you that controlling noise at the source is usually the best solution. That works with your teenager's stereo but many environmental sources of noise—highways, trains, airplanes, nearby construction equipment—are beyond our control.

Windows are often the culprit

When noise from the outside is a distraction, windows are often to blame. Exterior walls will typically block at least 45 to 50 decibels of sound, but even a very high quality window might not be able to block 40 decibels.

Dual-pane windows with increased air space between the sheets of glass improve acoustic isolation. "Superglass" windows, in which glass is combined with a very thin layer,

MIGRATING WATER

Capillary action can move water into places it wasn't meant to go. In the first instance below (A), a polyurethane barrier and coarse gravel stop the migration of some water but the lack of a capillary break between the foundation wall and the footing allows moisture to migrate into foundation walls. A capillary break (B) reduces the problem.

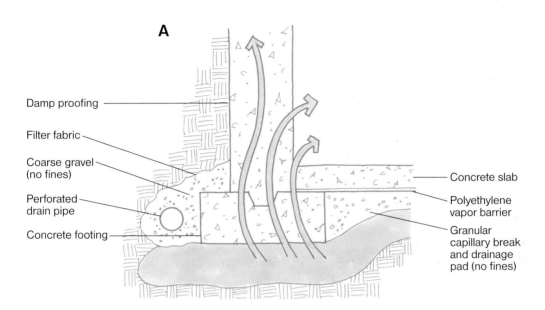

A

Damp proofing

Filter fabric

Coarse gravel (no fines)

Perforated drain pipe

Concrete footing

Concrete slab

Polyethylene vapor barrier

Granular capillary break and drainage pad (no fines)

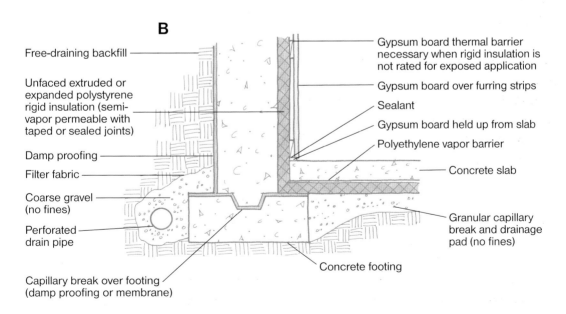

B

Free-draining backfill

Unfaced extruded or expanded polystyrene rigid insulation (semi-vapor permeable with taped or sealed joints)

Damp proofing

Filter fabric

Coarse gravel (no fines)

Perforated drain pipe

Capillary break over footing (damp proofing or membrane)

Gypsum board thermal barrier necessary when rigid insulation is not rated for exposed application

Gypsum board over furring strips

Sealant

Gypsum board held up from slab

Polyethylene vapor barrier

Concrete slab

Granular capillary break and drainage pad (no fines)

Concrete footing

or layers, of plastic are even more effective (for more, see p. 140). Noise, however, migrates through the weakest structural element, and that could be a door or ventilation duct as well as a window. The acoustic isolation provided by a door is only as good as the effectiveness of the door seal. If air can get around or under the door, so can sound.

Walls that reduce sound

Walls vary in their ability to reduce noise. A typical single-partition gypsum board/stud wall will have a sound transmission class (STC) in the mid-30s depending on such variables as the width of the stud and the amount and type of insulation in the wall cavity. Ideally, one would want to match this wall with a similar STC rating for the glass opening. Thinner laminated glass will equal a considerably thicker piece of plate glass.

Typical wall construction of 2x4s on 16-in. centers with fiberglass insulation is not very effective in reducing sound. Structural insulated panels or framed walls with exterior rigid foam are more effective. Cellulose and foam insulation do a better job of reducing noise than conventional fiberglass batts (although there are fiberglass batts explicitly designed for sound mitigation). The ideal combination for houses close to noise sources would take advantage of SIPs, sided with cementitious boards, along with Superglass® windows. This combination results in a very quiet house and, coincidentally, is a recipe for a very energy-efficient home.

Another option for homes close to environmental noise is the staggered stud approach, which has the added advantage of reducing thermal bridging. A further option is to add flexible C-channel to inside walls perpendicular to the studs. These are placed on 16-in. centers as backing for drywall. The C-channel absorbs some of the sound and isolates the drywall from the vibrations of the wall assembly.

Barriers and distance to block sound

Something as simple as increasing the distance from the source of noise or putting other materials between the sound source and the house can reduce unwanted noise. That can be a factor in deciding where to locate a house on the site, assuming the size of the lot provides some wiggle room.

Noise barriers are also a possibility. They can be earth berms, solid walls, or neighboring buildings. Vegetation, by the way, provides little if any reduction in noise. To be effective, barriers must block the line of sight between the noise source and the house. A density of 4 lb. per sq. ft. is enough, providing there are no openings in the wall. Barrier walls, however, won't reduce noise by more than about 10 decibels.

As cities and neighborhoods become ever more crowded and traffic increases, noise becomes more difficult to control. While specialized construction techniques and materials can be used to control noise transmission inside the house, we can't do much about urban sprawl and commuter traffic. If you can't reduce sound to a satisfactory level by any other means, you may have to combat noise with some of your own—an outdoor water feature, for example, that masks an unpleasant sound with a soothing one.

Putting It All Together

What building science tells us is that good design requires good thinking about the house as a system. By considering the thermal properties of the home from a building science

DECIBEL COMPARISON CHART

In the Ear of the Beholder

Noise is measured in decibels, a logarithmic not a linear scale. An increase of 10 dB, for example, is perceived as a doubling in sound. Choosing building materials carefully can reduce the impact of unwanted sound substantially.

Source	Level
Threshold of hearing (TOH)	0 dB
Rustling leaves	10 dB
Whisper	20 dB
Normal conversation at $3\frac{1}{2}$ ft.	60 dB
Busy street traffic	70 dB
Vacuum cleaner	80 dB
Train whistle at 500 ft.	90 dB
Large orchestra	98 dB
Walkman at maximum level	100 dB
Power saw	105 dB
Front rows of rock concert	110 dB
Threshold of pain	130 dB
Military jet takeoff at 100 ft.	140 dB
Instant perforation of eardrum	160 dB

ESTIMATED STC RATING

Keeping the Noise Down

Building materials can be deployed in a variety of ways to reduce sound transmission. How effectively a wall or window blocks sound is described as its Sound Transmission Class (STC). It's roughly equivalent to the sound reduction, in decibels, the building component provides. Loud speech, for instance, can be heard through a STC 30 wall but not a STC 60 wall. Walls should be STC 45 or higher where noise is a concern. These assemblies are typical for walls separating apartments or condominiums.

Wall Assembly	Estimated STC Rating
2x4 studs, two layers of $\frac{5}{8}$-in. gypsum, batt insulation	34–39
$3\frac{5}{8}$-in. metal studs, two layers of $\frac{5}{8}$-in. gypsum, no insulation	38–40
$3\frac{5}{8}$-in. metal studs, two layers of $\frac{5}{8}$-in. gypsum, batt insulation	43–44
2x4 studs, double layer of $\frac{5}{8}$-in. gypsum on each side of wall, batt insulation	43–45
Staggered 2x4 studs, two layers of $\frac{5}{8}$-in. gypsum, batt insulation	46–47
2x4 studs, two layers of $\frac{5}{8}$-in. gypsum, resilient channel and batt insulation	45–52
Double 2x4 wall separated by air space, $\frac{5}{8}$-in. gypsum and batt insulation	56–59
Double 2x4 wall separated by air space with a total of four layers of $\frac{5}{8}$-in. gypsum, batt insulation	58–63

- Look for designs that use energy as close to its source as possible to minimize conversion losses: passive solar heat, for example, over electrical resistance heating.

- Consider heat transmission in all its forms—convection, conduction, and radiation—in selecting building materials and building practices.

- Design and build houses so they are responsive to the environment around them rather than adopting standard or universal plans.

- Create an effective air barrier and make sure everyone on the build team understands their role in maintaining it through various stages of construction.

- Include some form of mechanical ventilation in house plans and strive for a "pressure neutral" interior as a minimum requirement.

- Make sure construction details are able to handle water movement via gravity, diffusion, and capillary action.

- In areas of high noise, consider window upgrades, sound barriers, and alternatives to conventional stick framing.

perspective, code becomes irrelevant—not irrelevant to getting a building inspector's blessing along with a certificate of occupancy but irrelevant in terms of good construction.

We can control how the house will perform. Determining the pathways for all forms of water is a cheap insurance policy against mold, mildew, and rot. Deciding where the air barrier will be makes it easier for the trades to do their part in building a tight house. Managing air pressure inside the house will keep it healthy for children as well as the rest of us. Paying attention to sound sources and building accordingly will keep your customers happy for as long as they live in the house.

Planning and Design

3

Early planning is good planning. According to estimates from the U.S. Green Building Council and the Department of Energy, by the time 3 percent of the design budget for a new house has been spent, 70 percent of the energy use over its lifetime has been set in stone. What do those numbers mean? That a tiny fraction of all design decisions—those made at the start of a project—largely determine how much energy will be required to operate the house. Forever. Getting religion about good building practices when you're well into the project can make a difference, but not nearly as much as taking care of the fundamentals from the start.

Building green *means integrating every part of the design and construction process, from siting the house so it can take advantage of the sun all the way through landscaping to suit the climate.*

Get the Team on Board

Getting the team together from the start has huge implications for the design process. It requires that we rethink how we design a home so that it can both operate efficiently and stand up to environmental conditions over its lifetime. One very effective (and very inexpensive) insurance policy is what's called a *design charette*. This is a pre-design meeting that includes the owner, the architect, the builder, and as many of the trade subcontractors as possible. Some guidelines:

- When choosing members of the design and build team, look for an open, positive attitude about green building techniques, not necessarily deep experience. "Experts" not open to discussion may be more trouble than

they are worth. What you want is to open a dialogue.

- Make sure there is a clear and shared understanding of goals for the project. What's high on the priority list—Energy efficiency? Good indoor air quality? An effective acoustic barrier? Low maintenance on the exterior? Low environmental impact? Possibly the list includes all of the above but whatever the objectives may be, everyone on the project should clearly understand them.

- Determine the performance goals for each of these objectives and how they can be measured.

- Builder and designer should create a detailed project design schedule (not to be

A meeting involving builder, architect, owner, and trade subcontractors may seem foreign to some builders but it's an excellent way of ensuring that everyone is on the same page. Strategy sessions may also help to cut costs.

confused with a construction schedule) that identifies decision-making paths and milestones. Things will go awry when the designer, builder, and subcontractors make decisions in isolation.

- Establish how the design and build team will determine whether the house performs as intended once it's completed. Feedback is essential. Plan a follow-up visit within a month and another in one year to check.

This last point is especially important because it encourages different subcontractors to talk with each other face-to-face. Each trade affects the other. What carpenter hasn't complained about the plumber who bores big holes through floor framing to run drain pipe? What plumber hasn't complained about the carpenter who frames a bathroom floor without regard for where the bathtub drain is to be located? What finish carpenter hasn't cursed the fact there is no blocking in the walls where he needs it

for trim or cabinets? Building a house often involves many such potential conflicts—and many of them could be avoided. Not only will these discussions help to minimize problems as the project moves ahead, but a group is also more likely to discover better overall solutions to common building problems than one person is working alone—no matter how smart that person might be.

Charettes probably will be foreign to builders who haven't tried them before. But approached with an open mind, they can yield surprising results.

Talking a good game is not enough

Measuring or quantifying performance is also key. Rising public interest in sustainable building is very similar to what happened with "natural" or "organic" foods some years back. Without guidelines that defined exactly what those terms meant, just about any food retailer could claim its sack of flour or carton of eggs was

EARLY CONVERSATIONS YIELD SAVINGS

I was the green building consultant on a project in Steamboat Springs, Col., for a couple who had a child with asthma. They wanted to build the healthiest house they could. The architect understood, the contractor was resistant but willing, and the trade contractors had never been invited to a meeting to talk about *how* to build such a house. They typically got a set of plans used to make a bid and didn't pay attention until they were scheduled to do the work. Because the design was somewhat complex and the green aspirations were new to everyone, the architect and I presented the project to the assembled team and I talked about how green approaches might affect their respective trades.

One thing that concerned the owners was the presence of formaldehyde in the fiberglass

insulation. Cellulose insulation didn't have that problem, but the builder balked because he had only used fiberglass in the past and was wary about trying something new. It was only when the insulation contractor offered to get training for installing cellulose as a way of expanding his services that the builder capitulated.

Then the plumber spoke up. If the architect would flip a closet and a bathroom, he said, it could save several thousand dollars in reduced labor and materials. And so it went. After three hours of lively conversation, the owners had racked up more than $10,000 in savings—and this was in addition to solving the original problem of keeping formaldehyde out of the house.

—DJ

A blower door test is one way of ensuring that a house meets standards designed to minimize air leaks. It should be part of an overall assessment that measures performance.

"organic" and "natural." Government rules now give consumers greater confidence they're actually getting what they pay for.

And so it is with sustainable building. "Greenwashing" is the phrase often used to describe inflated claims made by builders or manufacturers about the products or services they offer. It's easy to market something as "green" when the definition is squishy or poorly understood. But as consumers become more savvy, and measurable standards more widely deployed, fewer home buyers will be hoodwinked.

There are several sets of guidelines to help ensure that the house will perform as designed. A program called Leadership in Energy and Environmental Design (LEED) is one of them. Developed under the auspices of the U.S. Green Building Council, it targets big commercial buildings and has succeeded in changing the national market for office and municipal buildings. LEED for Homes, a newer program, outlines a number of specific requirements necessary for progressive levels of certification (see www.usgbc.org). On the other end of the spectrum is the National Association of Home Builders' Green Building Guidelines (see www.nahb.org/gbg). They are more general and are primarily geared for production home builders. In between are local guidelines developed specifically for local climates and market conditions such as the Build It Green guidelines for the state of California (see www.builditgreen.org). Regardless of which set of guidelines you choose, make sure the overall construction budget has enough money for performance testing once the house has been finished.

Siting a House for Comfort

Every building site offers a southern exposure. That seems obvious, but the invention of air-conditioning and the relatively low cost of energy (at least until recently) seem to have obscured that fact from many builders and architects. For thousands of years, humankind used solar orientation to keep whole cities warm in winter and cool in the summer. Builders of the Roman Baths included south-facing windows for warmth. At Mesa Verde, a pueblo in southern Colorado, occupants took advantage of south-facing caves with overhangs that allowed the low winter sun in for heat yet blocked the summer sun and thereby helped to keep their occupants cool. Today, we build very few passive solar homes. What happened?

There's nothing especially new about passive solar designs. During the energy crisis of the 1970s, the Department of Energy pioneered design tools for building passive solar houses that are as relevant today as they were

A pueblo in Mesa Verde, Col., is evidence that even early builders understood the importance of solar orientation in construction. In winter, sunlight penetrated into buildings for warmth; in summer, the hot sun was blocked by the lip of the cave and buildings stayed cooler.

FACE THE SUN

How the house is oriented on its site affects both energy efficiency and comfort. Simply rotating the house so that south-facing walls take advantage of solar gain during the winter can have a surprisingly significant effect on energy use.

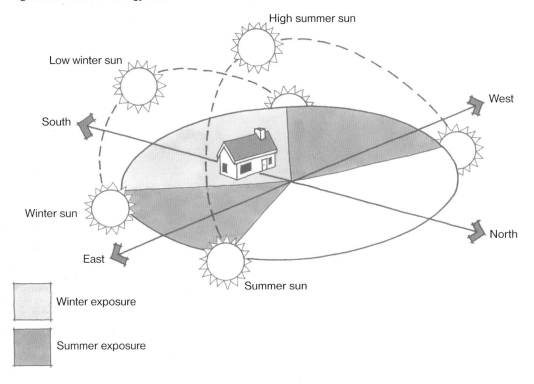

High summer sun

Low winter sun

South

Winter sun

East

West

North

Summer sun

Winter exposure

Summer exposure

LOOKING SOUTH

Ideally, major windows should face within 30° of true (not magnetic) south. The deviation between true and magnetic south varies depending on where you build.

North

30°

30°

True south

then. Given the energy future we face, passive solar (that is, non-mechanical means of using solar energy to heat homes in the winter and keep them cooler in summer) is the least expensive way to reduce fuel bills. And it can be tremendously effective, reducing heating costs between 30 percent and 50 percent in conventional homes. If you live in an area with tough winters, another consideration is to orient outdoor spaces to take advantage of the southern sun so they become pleasant microclimates that extend the outdoor season in both spring and fall.

Houses that combine solar orientation, *thermal mass to soak up heat, and the right number of south-facing windows can reduce heating costs substantially.*

South-facing houses *offer advantages outside as well as in. Porches and other protected areas become pleasant microclimates that extend the outdoor season.*

SAVING THE EASY WAY

One of my first projects for a production builder was to take a model the company had built hundreds of times and "green it." I was stuck with the floor plan—that couldn't be changed—but not the way the house was oriented. One wall of the house was mostly glass, and this typically faced west to make the most of mountain views.

The first thing I did was to rotate my project house 90 degrees so the glass wall could do a better job of capturing sunlight. Along with modifying the standard type of window glass the builder was using and extending roof overhangs, this simple change reduced the heating and cooling load by 40 percent. As a result, we started with a building that was 25 percent more energy efficient than government Energy Star standards.

—DJ

Even in winter, rooms with south-facing windows can be warm and comfortable. The key is balancing window area to the relative mass of floors and walls illuminated by sunlight.

Orient the house for energy savings

Every building has some passive solar potential. South-facing windows should be considered early in the design process so they can be integrated into the overall architecture of the house. In the late 1970s and early 1980s, the biggest mistake in designing passive solar houses was to include too many south-facing windows. Entire walls of glass cooked homeowners during the summer. Now, with better insulation in exterior walls, successful passive solar designs need many fewer windows—the equivalent of between 8 percent and 12 percent of the floor area in rooms with south-facing

Too much window: *Large expanses of south-facing windows can lead to overheating—even in winter (notice the drawn shades). Balancing window area to the square footage of south-facing rooms helps.*

CALCULATING WINDOW AREA FOR SOLAR GAIN

Just how much window area should be included in south-facing walls depends on the mass of surfaces directly and indirectly illuminated by sunlight. The higher the volume of mass, the more window area can be placed on the south wall. For example: if a 1-in. pine floor is replaced by a 4-in. concrete slab, 50 sq. ft. of glass can be increased to 250 sq. ft. of window area. The slab is much denser, which allows it to absorb more heat from the windows to release after the sun has gone down. Indirect or reflected light is much less effective at absorbing solar heat than mass that is directly illuminated, so more mass is required to have the same thermal storage properties.

Material Thickness	Mass Surface Area to Passive Window Area Ratio (Directly Illuminated)				
	Concrete	Brick	Gypsum	Oak	Pine
½ in.	–	–	76	–	–
1 in.	14	17	38	17	21
1½ in.	–	–	26	–	–
2 in.	7	8	20	10	12
3 in.	5	6	–	10	12
4 in.	4	5	–	11	12
6 in.	3	5	–	11	13
8 in.	3	5	–	11	13

Material Thickness	Mass Surface Area to Passive Window Area Ratio (Indirectly Illuminated)				
	Concrete	Brick	Gypsum	Oak	Pine
½ in.	–	–	114	–	–
1 in.	25	30	57	28	36
1½ in.	–	–	39	–	–
2 in.	12	15	31	17	21
3 in.	8	11	–	17	20
4 in.	7	9	–	19	21
6 in.	5	9	–	19	22
8 in.	5	10	–	19	22

Source: The Thermal Mass Patern Book, Author: Total Environmental Action p.3

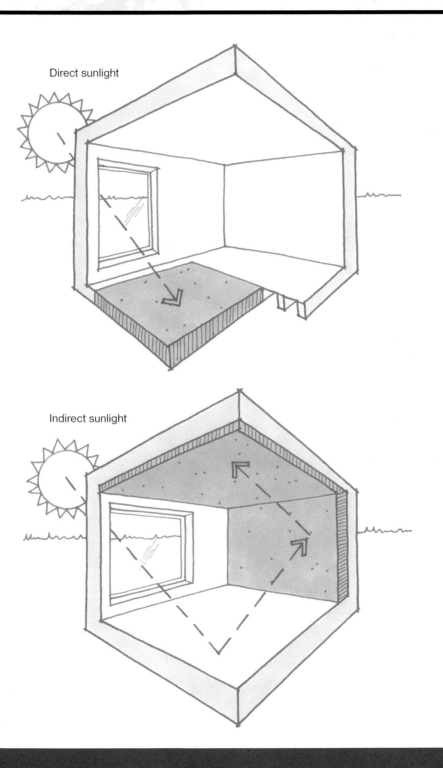

Direct sunlight

Indirect sunlight

GOOD GREEN HEALTH

Edward O. Wilson, a Harvard biologist, coined the phrase "biophilia," meaning "a love of nature" and, more broadly, "the connections that human beings subconsciously seek with the rest of life." Researcher Roger Ulrich later showed that these ties have a bearing on health: gallbladder surgery patients recovered faster and required less pain medication when they had views of trees rather than brick walls from their rooms. Similar benefits were found for heart surgery patients whose rooms were painted with landscape scenes. Abstract art, on the other hand, was so disturbing that experiments to compare the two were discontinued.

windows. That translates to only two or three additional (and strategically placed) windows on the south side of the house to increase comfort and energy efficiency.

Studies commissioned by Pacific Gas and Electric in California found that daylight has measurable benefits on learning rates. Students in classrooms with the most daylight showed learning rates as much as 26 percent higher than those in classrooms with artificial light.

There's another advantage: more daylight means less reliance on electric lights. In a house with sensible solar orientation, it may be possible to keep the lights completely turned off during the day and still see perfectly well. Besides, dogs and cats love nothing better than a patch of sunshine. (Solar energy is covered in much greater detail in chapter 13.)

Shading options for south-facing windows

Passive solar works only when south-facing windows are shaded during the summer. Shade prevents the house from getting too hot and, as a result, reduces cooling costs. In areas where oppressive heat is likely only for short periods during the summer, this strategy may be enough to tip the scales against mechanical cooling altogether, and that can mean sizeable savings in both construction and operating costs.

Two principal approaches to providing shade are with fixed overhangs and landscaping. Architectural elements that shade the glass are usually the best option. They can be designed specifically for the latitude of the house and incorporated into the overall design. The equation is simple. At any given latitude, determine sun angles for December 21 and June 21 (the dates on which the sun reaches the year's lowest and highest points in the sky, respectively). With these angles in hand, windows and overhangs can be placed so that on the winter solstice (Dec. 21) nothing blocks sunlight from coming in the window at noon. On the summer solstice, the opposite is true—the window should be completely shaded when the sun is at the highest point in the sky. In spring and fall, there is a mix of sun and shade.

WINTER AND SUMMER SOLSTICE

To take full advantage of the sun, determine the location of the sun on both the winter and summer solstice when the sun reaches the lowest and highest point in the sky for the year. In winter, let the sun in. In summer, keep it out with roof overhangs, window awnings, or trees and other plantings.

Winter
December 21

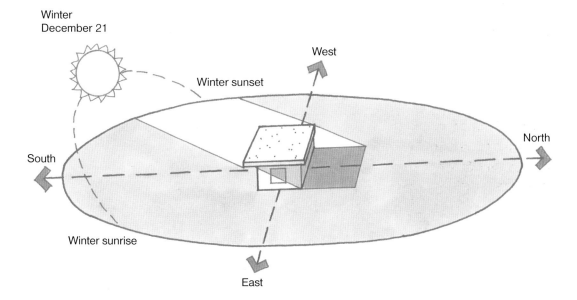

Summer
June 21

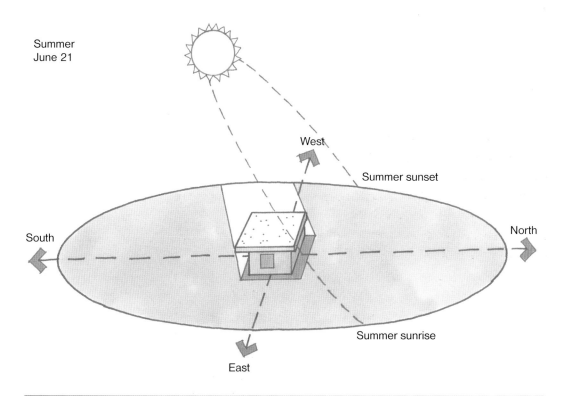

The overhangs help shade a large expanse
of glass, making the house cooler in summer
but still allowing filtered sunlight inside.

BLOCKING SUMMER SUN

Design roof overhangs over south-facing windows so sunlight penetrates the house in winter and is blocked in summer. Roof overhangs and window height are considered together.

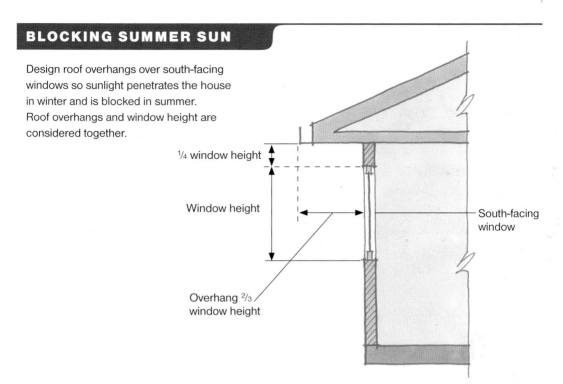

¼ window height

Window height

South-facing window

Overhang ⅔ window height

Window awnings can have architectural as well as practical merit.

Landscaping is another way of shading a home and preventing overheating. Good landscape design can greatly enhance a home's energy performance while connecting the house gracefully with its surroundings. Deciduous trees—particularly local species—leaf out just when the house needs shading. They are very good at shading the south side of the house, although it might be necessary to increase the overall glass area to compensate for tree trunks and branches. Vines and trellises are good for summer shading. But be wary of species that don't drop their leaves in the fall (like beech and most evergreens). They may block the beneficial winter sun.

Plants and trees can also be used to shade east and west windows. Windows on these walls are the greatest source of unwanted heat gain in the summer because they face the rising or setting sun low in the sky.

Trees not only create shade, but they also "evapotranspire," or sweat, thereby cooling air in the process. A mature shade tree can evapotranspire as much as 40 gal. of water a day, comparable to removing all the heat generated in four hours by a small, electric space heater. Mature tree canopies reduce the average temperature in suburban areas by about 3 degrees.

CHOOSING THE RIGHT TREES

Existing or planted vegetation can help heat and cool the house. To the north, a band of evergreens blocks the wind in winter. Toward the south, deciduous trees help shade the house in the heat of summer but let light pass in winter.

Plant evergreens on the north side.

Deciduous trees to the south let in winter sun but block the glare of summer light.

Deciduous trees on the south side of the house offer shade in the summer but drop their leaves to admit light during the winter. Heavily treed lots require some adjustment in window-to-floor ratios to compensate for trunks and limbs.

Make the layout work

Coming up with the right floor plan can mean a significant savings on home energy use. When rooms are arranged to track the sun, activities can take advantage of daylight, thereby reducing the need for electric lights. Plan for how the house will be used at different times of the day and take into account where the sun will be. For example, the kitchen should be in the southeast quadrant of the home, which makes for bright and cheerful mornings. The living room and den can be located in the south and southwest parts of the house because they are more likely to be used later in the day and can thereby take advantage of afternoon sun. A good spot for the master bedroom suite is on the west-northwest side of the house because it's typically not used during the day and doesn't need as much natural light as other parts of the house. That location also spares its occupants from blinding morning sunlight. Other bedrooms and baths, utility rooms, corridors, and the entry can be located in the core of the house or on the north side because they are rarely used during the day.

PLAN ROOMS AROUND THE LIGHT

Plan room layouts with the sun in mind: Rooms that need morning light and warmth should be located in the southeast quadrant of the house; locate rooms used later in the day facing west and utility areas on the north side. Careful orientation reduces energy use and makes occupants more comfortable.

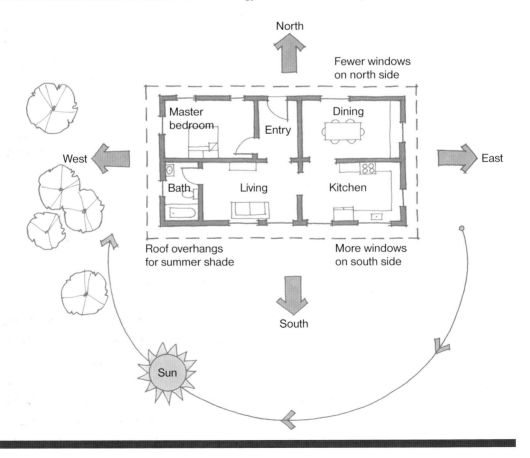

With careful planning, electric lights may not be needed in some rooms at all during the day. And by placing daytime activities on the south side of the building, the sun keeps the rooms warm, reducing the need for supplemental heat.

Arranging rooms to take advantage of the sun means more than saving a few bucks on the heating bill. Much like natural ventilation, natural daylight is something our bodies need. With it, we feel better, are generally healthier, and work more effectively. Research in Sweden has found that children who attend schools with natural lighting do better than children in windowless classrooms. Research also indicates that children in rooms lit with fluorescent bulbs have more cavities than those in naturally lit rooms. That's because our bodies produce

Careful floor plans can reduce heating and lighting costs. Rooms should be organized so activities taking place in them make the most of natural light and solar gain. During daylight hours, electric lights might not be needed at all in some rooms.

vitamin D with the help of natural sunlight. Who knows what other biological functions are inhibited when we rob ourselves of natural lighting.

With proper house orientation, attention to window placement, and the use of skylights and light tubes, we can create day-lit spaces even deep in the interior of the house. Only after we have designed the natural lighting in a home should we consider the electrical plan. At that point, the type of lighting, where it is

Animals always know the warmest spot in the house.

Light tubes bring sunlight into core areas of a house where natural sunlight isn't possible.

placed, and how bright it needs to be can all be weighed more carefully. That approach is a long way from mindlessly placing electrical fixtures where they have always been located: by habit.

Adding natural ventilation

Airflow through a house makes for both comfort and high indoor air quality. It's a little more complicated than opening a few windows, but it's not rocket science, either. As we learned in the building science chapter, warm air rises and cold air falls.

It's a simple concept that designers seem to overlook all too often, but it can easily be worked into plans for a house. Take the house shown in the photo below. The cupola allows hot air to flow out through the highest spot in the house. The cooler air from under the porch flows through the house as the hot air escapes. Cultures around the world have used just such a strategy for thousands of years. Only with the advent of air-conditioning have we lost our indigenous understanding of how to work with nature to stay comfortable.

Natural cooling or ventilation is great for swing seasons, but in cold weather, it is not sufficient. We still need fresh air in winter. Too often, we seal up the house and breathe stale

A cupola at the top of this house takes advantage of convection to rid the house of hot air during the summer. In some regions, natural ventilation may eliminate the need for an expensive central air-conditioning system.

hot air that has been cycled over and over in furnaces. It has no vitality left in it. So mechanical ventilation is necessary to maintain healthy air in the house. (Details about indoor air quality are covered in chapter 14, p. 273.)

Planning for Water Management

Water is another early planning issue. Indiscriminately shunting rainwater away from the house is a wasteful practice, particularly in parts of the country prone to drought and declining supplies of groundwater. Roofs are, in effect, large devices that catch water that can easily be used to irrigate lawns and gardens, flush toilets, and provide clean water for drinking and cooking. Instead, this water is often diverted to storm drains that are already filled to overflowing with runoff from parking lots and streets. When we want to water the lawn, we turn on the spigot and draw on diminishing supplies of water that have been pumped, treated, and piped to the house through expensive municipal water systems.

How much sense does this make? When you think about it, not much. In parts of the American Southwest and in island communities where fresh water is scarce, rainwater is captured and stored for irrigation and other purposes. The practice is not as widespread as it could be. Even in parts of the country with groundwater supplies that seem abundant, a rain barrel connected to a gutter downspout and used to water the garden is an easy way of making greater use of what comes naturally.

A large-scale water collection system probably isn't in the cards for most houses, but managing both rainwater and groundwater is something that should be addressed in the early stages of planning for any house. Key questions include:

- How high is the water table and does it change seasonally?

- What type of soil are you building on?

- Does the slope on the site allow for gravity drains for gutters as well as below-grade drainage systems to divert high groundwater or runoff?

- What is the annual rainfall and when does it occur?

A variety of other factors can also affect how water moves on or under a house site, including native plants that may be disrupted during construction, a neighbor's water management plan (or lack of one), and the design of the house itself. During design, the key decisions involve how and where below-grade drains should be installed. Water use as it relates to landscaping is something that can be addressed later, after the house has been built (see chapter 16). But any management plans that include below-grade work should be mapped out while the heavy site work is still ahead. A lack of planning can mean a seasonally wet basement, the increased likelihood of mold inside the house, and uncontrolled runoff that causes a host of problems on and off the lot.

Start by thinking like a water drop. If water is moving through the site, it will find a way into the house unless you create a path of lesser resistance for it to follow. Take, for example, a slightly sloping site in a rainy climate. During the wet season, water will move through the saturated soil in an invisible sheet. Perimeter drains at the base of the foundation may not have enough capacity to

Rainfall is a potential water bonanza in areas where groundwater is scarce. Large outdoor tanks can store thousands of gallons of water for use later in irrigation or, with treatment, for drinking and cooking.

handle the flow. It can be managed with a V-shaped swale on the uphill side of the house. This is a trench with a layer of crushed rock or gravel in the bottom. The rock is covered with a geotextile material, covered with soil, and then seeded. Instead of moving downhill toward the house, water is picked up at the bottom of the trench and diverted. If runoff is significant, 6-in. perforated PVC pipe at the bottom of the trench will help groundwater flow more easily.

- Schedule a "design charette" before construction begins and include architect, builder, owner, and all subcontractors.

- Orient the house so that the south wall faces to within 30 degrees of true (not magnetic) south.

- In rooms on the south side of the house, windows should equal between 8 percent and 12 percent of the adjacent floor area. Proportions can be adjusted according to the relative mass of walls and floors that are directly and indirectly illuminated.

- Shade windows on the south wall of the house from the summer sun, with either roof overhangs or awnings designed for the specific latitude where the house is being built.

- Find out the direction of prevailing winds (they may change seasonally), and specify casement windows on walls facing those directions. They do a better job of scooping up air for natural ventilation than do awning or double-hung windows.

- Locate rooms so they take advantage of natural light and heat at the times of day when they are most commonly used.

- Control storm water runoff on site with perimeter drains, gutters, and subsurface drainage systems that accommodate anticipated groundwater levels and average rainfall (and snowfall).

On flat lots, low spots are potential water collectors. These should be identified during site analysis (a transit is helpful before the soil is disturbed). Fill can be brought in to alter the grade, or these areas can be landscaped with hydrophilic plants and trees such as willows.

Runoff from gutters should be directed to the most appropriate spot on the site—that is, away from the house to a spot where it will do the least amount of damage. Gutter runoff should be kept a minimum of 3 ft. from the house. More is better. Installing underground drains now to take care of inevitable runoff problems is a cheap insurance policy. Don't, however, forget about your neighbors. Taking care of your own water problems without regard to the potential damage it's doing to adjoining property is only solving one problem to create another.

Foundations

Whether a new house is built to green standards or just built out of habit, it has to have a foundation. That's a given. Too often, a foundation is designed as if it has little effect on how the house will perform. In reality, a well-planned foundation can make a substantial contribution to controlling heating and cooling costs while eliminating potential moisture and mold problems.

Depending on where you live, a conventional foundation could be a concrete slab, concrete block on poured footings, or a full basement with 8-in.-thick concrete walls on concrete footings. All of these options will do the essential job of supporting the weight of the house. When made properly (and barring unplanned disasters), a foundation should not need any attention for the life of the house.

THE GREEN FACTOR

Foundations are a structural necessity, but they don't get the attention they deserve in terms of how they can contribute to the overall energy efficiency and air quality of a house. In sustainable building, there are three key issues:

- **Resource conservation.** Concrete footings, slabs, and basement walls consume a great deal of concrete, whose production is a significant source of greenhouse gas emissions. Using less concrete reduces energy use and costs to the consumer.

- **Energy conservation.** If basement or slab insulation is an afterthought, we're not as likely to make foundation walls a part of the conditioned space of a house. Uninsulated foundations can account for sizable energy losses, particularly in cold-weather parts of the country. Insulating from within at a later date certainly helps, but it's not as good a solution as making it part of the plan from the start.

- **Moisture control.** Uncontrolled moisture can lead to mold as well as wet basement floors. Damp-proofing a foundation may not be enough to keep moisture out of the basement over the long term. Along with perimeter drains, a more effective seal may be needed where groundwater is high.

Poured concrete foundations and slabs are standard fare for residential construction, but unless they are insulated, well drained, and sealed to prevent the intrusion of water they become a net energy drain and a potential source of mold.

Like insulation and basic framing, the foundation should be designed as part of the house as a system—it is costly and complicated to retrofit one when construction is finished.

From the point of view of sustainable building, conventional foundations, while amply strong, have one or more fundamental problems. First, they are often designed and built without regard to their potential for energy loss (or, looked at the other way, without regard to the contribution they can make to the overall energy performance of the house). Second, it takes a lot of energy to make cement, the critical ingredient in concrete. Substituting fly ash, a power plant by-product, for some of the cement not only recycles this industrial waste but also coincidentally improves the strength and durability of the concrete. Not all builders know they can order concrete with fly ash. Finally, the foundation may be stronger than it has to be, an unnecessary use of materials. Engineer-

According to the American Coal Ash Association, fly ash is the nation's largest single coal combustion product, amounting to nearly 71 million tons in 2004. In the same year, more than 14 million tons of this industrial by-product was used to replace portland cement in concrete. It not only makes for better concrete, the association says, but it's also cheaper than the cement it replaces.

Concrete slabs can mean cold rooms on the perimeter of the house unless the concrete is insulated with closed-cell foam insulation.

ing the foundation for the loads it will actually carry, and not simply to industry standards, is one way of conserving resources and making the house more affordable.

Foundations Should Be Insulated

Basements are often poured and then left unfinished. No doubt there are many reasons for this. Some jurisdictions don't tax unfinished basements, and some builders can market the square footage of the house to include

Concrete block foundations are more prevalent in some parts of the country than concrete, but the same principles of green building apply to both: insulate the foundation and use perimeter drains to help control moisture.

GET THE FOUNDATION RIGHT

A building is only as good as its foundation. My building mentor was a third-generation Colorado carpenter who had three ironclad rules for building: Plumb is plumb, square is square, and level is level. Period. "Good enough" wouldn't do.

If a foundation is off, it's very difficult to get the rest of the building right. Errors are compounded the further you go, and by the time you get to the roof you can be in real trouble. I learned that on one of the first houses I built, on Orr's Island in Maine. We poured the stem walls late one afternoon, and as we did, one of the forms blew out. Concrete oozed through the opening like lava. We worked some plywood into the break but it was a mess and by then too dark to see what we were doing.

When we started framing, we realized the foundation in that area was about 3 in. low. We cemented in some stone to make up the difference, covered the repair with mortar, and kept on framing. We thought it would be good enough but the walls were never quite level. By the time we began framing the hip roof, nothing fit. We finally had to get a "real" carpenter on the job to finish framing the roof.

And that was just the beginning of the nightmare. The plywood sheathing had to be ripped on an angle to fit the corner, as did the drywall. Exterior trim was never quite square, and baseboard had to be coped to fit. Problems went on and on. It was a hard lesson to learn, but I never forgot plumb, level, and square.

—DJ

the basement even though they leave it to the home buyer to finish the space. In some markets you can't sell a home without a basement, so the builder puts one in but doesn't try to make it a finished part of the house. Whatever the reason, in regions where full basements are the norm, it's often just an uninsulated concrete box when home buyers move in. In time, basements become recreation and entertainment zones, playrooms for the kids, home offices, and guest rooms.

What's forgotten in all of this is the amount of heat lost through foundation walls, crawl spaces, and concrete slabs. Foundations are thermally connected to the rest of the house, but too often they're not designed as part of the thermal envelope. How much this common oversight actually adds to the cost of heating a house obviously depends on a variety of factors, yet insulation can add up to considerable annual savings.

One obvious solution is to insulate the exterior of the foundation wall before backfilling. In most heating climates, 2 in. of closed-cell extruded polystyrene, which is more moisture resistant than expanded polystyrene, should be the minimum. This should be applied over the moisture-proofing on the outside of the foundation wall. The insulation helps to keep the basement at a steady temperature. And warmer basement walls minimize condensation and the mold and mildew that go along with it when the basement is made into a finished space.

An insulated foundation becomes part of the house's thermal envelope, contributing to energy conservation and creating a more comfortable environment.

INSULATING A FOUNDATION

Foundations should always be insulated, preferably on the outside to reduce the risk of condensation and make the mass of concrete or block walls part of the conditioned space. Two inches of closed-cell rigid foam insulation extending from the top of the foundation wall to the footing is a good start; increase to 3 in. in extremely cold areas (those with 6,500 heating degree days or more per year). Check local codes for requirements on termite barriers.

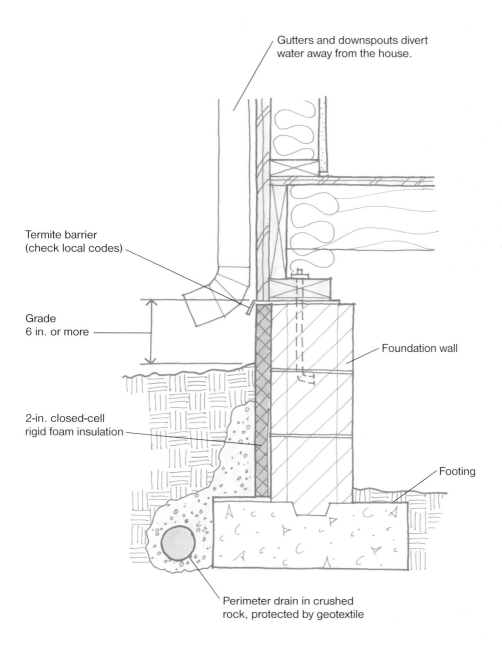

Gutters and downspouts divert water away from the house.

Termite barrier (check local codes)

Grade 6 in. or more

2-in. closed-cell rigid foam insulation

Foundation wall

Footing

Perimeter drain in crushed rock, protected by geotextile

Insulate the slab, too

Slabs are rarely insulated, which means they constantly wick heat or cold to the inside of the house. In areas where the number of cooling degree days is very high, heat gain at the edges of a slab foundation can account for as much as 15 percent of the cooling load. In heating climates, a lack of insulation often means cold floors in rooms at the perimeter of the house. Edge insulation is an easy answer. It should be installed inside the forms before the concrete is poured.

The thickness of slab insulation should be determined by climate, but use a minimum of 1 in. of closed-cell rigid foam. When the forms are removed, the insulation sticks to the concrete. When siding is installed over the framing, z-channel flashing can be installed over the foam to protect it. Any foam that's exposed after the foundation has been backfilled can be covered with cement board or a parge coat of stucco.

Radiant floor heat, in which tubing of cross-linked polyethylene heats the floor, is increasingly common. It requires different thinking about how heat flows. Not only should the edges of the slab be insulated with rigid foam but also the entire underside of the slab.

Insulating the entire slab with rigid foam insulation is a better approach than insulating only the perimeter, even if intial costs are higher. This is especially important when using radiant-floor heat in a slab.

PREVENTING HEAT LOSS AT SLAB PERIMETER

Rigid foam insulation on the inside of the footing for a slab foundation doesn't do much to prevent the loss of heat at the slab perimeter, making rooms there less comfortable and adding to energy costs. Adding 2 in. of closed-cell foam insulation beneath the slab, and at least ¾ in. on the interior of the frost wall, is a more effective thermal break and reduces heat loss.

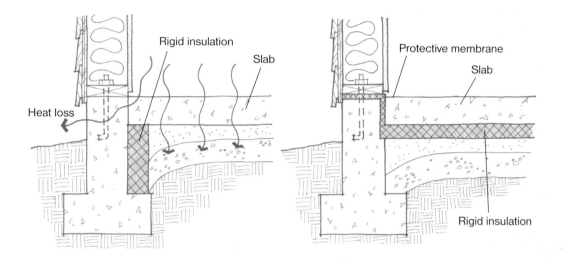

Rigid insulation

Slab

Heat loss

Protective membrane

Slab

Rigid insulation

THINK BEFORE YOU POUR

In some parts of the country, where full basements have come to be expected, foundation walls are typically 8 in. thick and rest on a 12-in.-wide concrete footing. Builders don't think about those specifications because they're deeply embedded in tradition. Like oversized headers and unnecessary framing members, these heavy-duty foundations may simply be a waste of money and resources.

Fernando Pagés Ruiz is one builder who thinks twice about the real value of building conventions and often finds a less expensive, more efficient way of getting the job done. His book *Building an Affordable House* (The Taunton Press, 2005) details a variety of ways to reduce the cost and complexity of construction. By applying value engineering to foundations,

he's found a number of options that are worth exploring:

• Reduce the thickness of concrete walls, at least for some parts of the foundation.

• As soil conditions permit, skip the footing altogether.

• Consider foundation alternatives, such as treated wood foundations and pre-cast foundations.

• Reduce the thickness of slab foundations.

Some of these alternatives may require soil tests or special engineering, and there's no guarantee that all of them will be embraced by local code officials. Yet the effort can pay off handsomely in the form of lower costs and a more efficient use of materials.

Shallow frost-protected foundations

The National Association of Home Builders' Research Center has developed a unique way to save concrete in foundations. Rather than pour footings below the frost line in cold climates, researchers placed footings just 2 ft. below grade and then insulated the slabs in two ways. Walls were insulated conventionally with 2 in. of rigid foam closed-cell extruded polystyrene. Then, horizontally, a section of rigid foam 2 ft. wide was placed around the perimeter of the slab 24 in. below grade (see the drawing below).

These added layers of insulation keep frost from being driven deep into the ground where it could crack the slab. Model building codes have recognized frost-protected shallow foundation design principles for more than a decade. In most regions of the continental U.S., these foundations can reliably be placed as shallow as 16 in. below grade. Performance has been proven in Europe, and frost-protected foundations have been used in very cold climates in the U.S.—in North Dakota, for instance—with perfect results.

FROST-PROTECTED SHALLOW FOUNDATIONS

Frost-protected shallow foundations require less excavation and less concrete than conventional slabs. Perimeter footings as shallow as 16 in. can be used successfully even in severe climates. A combination of heat migration through the floor and year-round geothermal heat in the ground is trapped by rigid foam insulation at the perimeter of the building, protecting the slab from cold-weather damage.

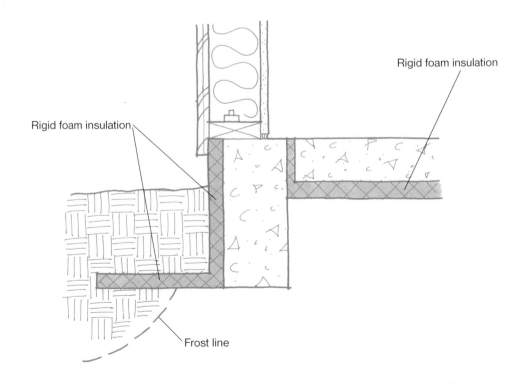

Rigid foam insulation

Rigid foam insulation

Frost line

It takes a lot less concrete to form one of these slabs when compared to the more conventional approach of placing concrete stem walls below the frost line before the slab is poured. That not only means a savings for the buyer but the use of less energy and materials—all without sacrificing performance.

Insulated concrete forms

Insulated concrete forms (ICFs) are a great family of green products introduced over the last decade. Made in several variations, they all share a design that combines insulation and concrete to form finished walls. Some types are made with 2 in. of closed-cell extruded polystyrene on both sides of the wall, with spacers in between to hold the form together as the concrete is placed. The spacers do double duty by serving as screw bases for the

attachment of finish wall materials on the inside and outside to cover the foam. Other types of ICFs are stacked like blocks. Their internal cavities are filled with concrete. In all cases, there is insulation on both sides of the foundation wall that keeps the basement warm and makes the wall water-resistant. The exterior surface in contact with the ground should still be coated with a waterproof membrane.

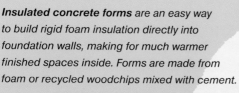

Insulated concrete forms *are an easy way to build rigid foam insulation directly into foundation walls, making for much warmer finished spaces inside. Forms are made from foam or recycled woodchips mixed with cement.*

The U.S. Department of Energy estimates that in Minneapolis, Minn., basement walls insulated to R-10 save $400 a year in heating costs. That number is lower in less extreme climates, but even in Washington, D.C., the annual savings add up to an estimated $250.

When using rigid foam insulation on foundation walls, keep in mind that the foam can provide safe passage for insects—particularly termites—that can make their way into the house without being seen. If termites are a problem in your area, protect the house with a metal termite shield installed between the top of the foundation wall and the mud sill. (Check local codes for specific requirements on using foam in contact with the ground.)

RECYCLED WOOD FOR FOUNDATION FORMS

If you don't like the idea of the plastics that go into many types of insulated concrete forms, consider blocks made from cement-bonded recycled woodchips—Durisol Wall Forms® are one such product. They can be installed above or below grade, come in several widths, and are available with inserts of mineral wool to boost insulating values.

One advantage of the wood-block forms is their ability to absorb and release high levels of moisture in the air without damage and without supporting the growth of mold. Some or all of the wood fiber used to make them comes from post-industrial waste. From an insulating standpoint, they are also attractive, ranging from R-8 for an 8-in. block to R-20 for a 12-in. block that has a 3-in. mineral wool insulating insert. Blocks are dry-stacked and then filled with concrete. Moreover, the blocks don't give off any toxic emissions.

These insulated concrete forms are made with cement-bonded wood fiber and contain no plastics. Durisol Building Systems, the manufacturer, claims that insulation inserts can boost the R-value of the wall to R-20.

Insulating interior walls

When a homeowner wants to turn an unfinished basement into living space, the usual
approach is to build new interior walls. One
way is to glue and nail 2x2s to the concrete
and fill in the spaces between the strapping
with rigid foam insulation. There are two caveats to this method. First, the wood should
be pressure-treated so it won't be affected by
moisture migrating through the concrete, and
second, the foam should be closed-cell extruded polystyrene, which also resists moisture
penetration.

An alternative is to use 2x4s to build a
conventional wall, usually insulated with fiberglass batts. If this is the approach, the sole
plate should be pressure-treated and a vapor
barrier should be applied to the inside of the
framed wall. Fiberglass insulation isn't very
effective at stopping air from moving through
the wall cavity, and along with the air comes
moisture. During the winter, warm, dry air will
pull moisture from the foundation wall into the
framed wall. In the summer, warm humid air
will move toward the foundation wall. In both
cases, moisture can become trapped and

INSULATING A BASEMENT ON THE INSIDE

Although exterior insulation offers more
advantages, basements can be insulated
from the inside, too. Connecticut builder
Andy Engel uses this approach to convert an
unfinished basement into a dry, comfortable
part of the house. The key is controlling the
movement of moisture and mold-inducing
condensation as warm air migrates to a cooler
surface. Engel uses rigid foam to isolate the
concrete on both walls and floors.

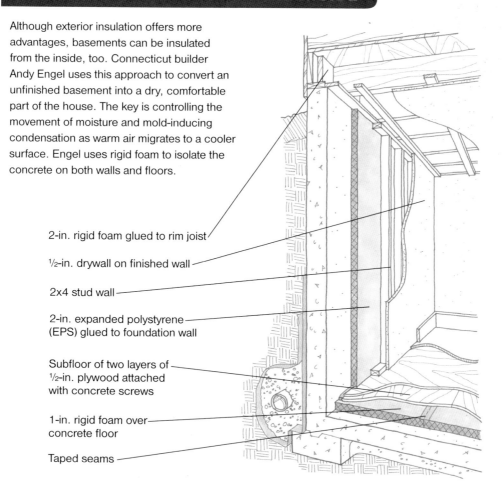

2-in. rigid foam glued to rim joist

1/2-in. drywall on finished wall

2x4 stud wall

2-in. expanded polystyrene
(EPS) glued to foundation wall

Subfloor of two layers of
1/2-in. plywood attached
with concrete screws

1-in. rigid foam over
concrete floor

Taped seams

cause mold and, eventually, rot. A barrier of polyethylene plastic will retard the movement of moisture, as will fiberglass insulation enclosed in a plastic jacket. Airtight drywall installation will also help to keep moisture out (for more on this technique, see p. 116).

Although both of these approaches are better than uninsulated concrete, the foundation is not part of the thermal envelope. That reduces its ability to hold heat and keep the basement temperate. And interior framing also reduces floor space that could be useful. Overall, insulation on the outside of the foundation is a better choice.

Forming Foundations with Wood

Wood form material is one of the largest sources of wood waste in building a house. Dedicated plywood or metal forms for full-basement concrete walls and stem walls can be used many, many times. But slab-on-grade foundations are often formed with 2x12s, which by definition come from old-growth trees. They may hold up through three or four foundations, depending on how carefully they are removed from the previous slab, but eventually the boards become unusable. By then, they are covered with concrete and permeated with the chemical release agents that keep the concrete from sticking, so they can't be recycled, either. A sad waste of good lumber.

Although the initial cost of alternatives such as plywood and metal forms is higher, they save the trouble and expense of replacing forms made from dimensional lumber. The fact that they also save good lumber from needless destruction is another advantage.

Then there are the release agents themselves. They're often a petroleum-based product or simply diesel oil, a waste of oil when

Using wide dimensional lumber to form the edges of concrete slabs is a waste of a diminishing resource. Metal or plywood forms are more expensive initially but last much longer. After a few uses, this lumber will have to be tossed—a combination of residual concrete and release agents render the boards unusable even for recycling.

today there are more natural oils available that do the job just as well for little additional cost.

Improving Concrete with Fly Ash

Concrete production produces 8 percent of global-warming carbon dioxide worldwide. That's an astonishingly high number when you think about it, and one way of reducing this huge outpouring of greenhouse gas is to combine concrete with fly ash, a waste product from coal power plants. Using fly ash has a double benefit: It not only provides a way of recycling fly ash but also reduces the amount of portland cement required in the concrete.

Fly ash is a difficult by-product to dispose of. What makes this marriage interesting is that fly ash bonds chemically with cement to make the concrete stronger, more water resistant, and more durable than a batch that uses portland cement alone. Typically, 15 percent fly ash is added to the mix to yield concrete with a compressive strength of 3,500 pounds per square inch—500 psi greater than a conventional concrete mix. In some parts of the country, fly ash is added to concrete automatically

Fly ash is a by-product of coal-fired energy plants produced by the millions of tons. Replacing some of the portland cement with fly ash makes superior concrete and recycles this waste at the same time.

MIX FOR FLY ASH CONCRETE

Concrete that uses a high volume of fly ash has a number of benefits. It diverts the waste from landfills and reduces carbon dioxide emissions by cutting the amount of portland cement in the mix. Moreover, the concrete is better: It has a higher compressive strength, is more durable and less permeable, and shrinks less so it reduces cracking. Here's a formula with 30 percent fly ash that yields concrete with a compressive strength of 4,000 psi.

Portland cement	490 lb.	Kaiser type I–II (59% Tri Calcium Silicate)
Fly ash	210 lb.	ISG—26% residue on 325 mesh
3/8-in. gravel	821 lb.	Estimated free moisture—2%
Top sand	2167 lb.	Estimated free moisture—6%
Water	250 lb.	Total (includes the estimated free moisture in aggregates)
Type C or E water reducer	24.5 oz.	(Preferably Type E for faster set)

at the ready-mix plant. The builder doesn't even have to ask for it. Builders in California are experimenting with mixes that contain as much as 50 percent fly ash and 50 percent cement and find they are working very well.

Concrete containing fly ash does have some drawbacks. It sets up slowly, meaning that construction might be delayed a day or two after the pour, depending on weather. That is what makes it more water resistant, however. In cold weather, it may require other admixtures to accelerate the set-up time.

Controlling Moisture around Foundations

Water can be a problem for foundations, and consequently for the rest of the house, in several ways. Water pressing on the outside of the foundation can exert tremendous pressure, enough to crack an 8-in.-thick wall. Moisture can also seep through the foundation wall and condense on the inside. When a basement has a musty smell, it's a good bet that moisture has been a chronic problem and is probably supporting the growth of mold.

Stopping moisture starts on the outside. Builders typically spray or brush on an asphalt-based damp proofing before backfilling the foundation, but that's not enough. These coatings are inexpensive, and they can be slopped on quickly by the least experienced member of the building crew. But they don't span cracks that can develop in the concrete, and over the long-term they are not as effective at blocking

Asphalt-based damp-proofing is often used to coat the foundation of walls, but the product offers little long-term protection against water migration through cracks that may develop. A better option is to use one of several commercial products that help water drain away from the foundation wall to perimeter drains at footing level.

A corrugated membrane applied over the outside of the foundation wall creates a reliable drainage plane that diverts water to perimeter drains.

Membranes conform to any changes in foundation height. They will be mostly covered when the foundation is backfilled and the site finish-graded.

moisture as some alternatives. Rubber-based coatings last longer and there are also several types of membrane coverings, such as sheets of dimpled plastic that work much better.

An essential detail is a drain that runs the entire perimeter of the footing. This consists of perforated 4-in. pipe in a bed of crushed stone, covered with filter cloth to keep the drain from clogging. Used in conjunction with an effective waterproofing system, the drains carry water away from the bottom of the foundation wall and help to keep basements dry and mold free.

Make Crawl Spaces Generous

Crawl spaces are common in many parts of the country. They keep the house off the ground enough to allow for the installation of wiring and plumbing. Building codes typically call for a minimum distance between grade and the floor framing of 18 in.

One issue with crawl spaces is how to insulate them properly. Increasingly, energy codes require floor insulation and 18 in. doesn't allow much room to get around and work. At a minimum, the floor should have as much insulation as the walls. More is always

Building codes may require only 18 in. of clearance in a crawl space, but increasing that to at least 24 in. makes it easier for workers to move around. Either the floor or the crawl space walls should be insulated.

- Foundations, including concrete slabs, should be insulated to reduce heating and cooling loads. Insulating the outside of the foundation is better than adding insulation on the inside. If you do insulate inside, use rigid foam instead of fiberglass batts.

- When planning a slab-on-grade house, switch to a frost-protected shallow foundation design. It uses less concrete and requires less excavation.

- To combine structure and insulation, consider insulated concrete forms.

- Foundation forms made from dimensional lumber waste material. Use plywood or metal forms instead.

- Make sure the concrete you order contains fly ash. That makes good use of an abundant industrial by-product, and makes for better, more durable concrete.

- Use moisture-proof coatings and perimeter drains to keep moisture out of foundation walls and lower the risk of mold while making basements more comfortable.

- Raise crawl space height to 24 in. to make access easier and include the crawl space in the conditioned space of the house.

better. To facilitate the installation, raising the height of the crawlspace to at least 24 in. will keep all the trades happier.

Installing insulation between floor joists keeps the floor warm, but it makes the crawl space an unconditioned space. If ductwork runs through an unheated space, heat loss and the risk of condensation and leaks increase. A better method is to insulate the exterior of concrete walls with 2 in. of rigid foam insulation, just as a foundation is insulated. This creates a heated or conditioned crawlspace and makes it easier to get to plumbing, wiring, and ducts in the future.

Building codes that require vents in a crawlspace can be a problem. Here, code hasn't kept up with building science. It's better to keep air and moisture out and make the crawlspace part of the insulated envelope, and it's worth having a heart-to-heart with your local building official if vents are still required. In any case, the ground should be covered with polyethylene 8 mils to 10 mils thick and sealed at the perimeter wall. A layer of sand under the poly can keep stones from puncturing this layer as plumbers and electricians crawl around. Seams should be sealed with polyethylene tape. If there are piers in the crawlspace, plastic should be sealed around them as well. This keeps the moisture out of the air under the house. The only exception to this approach is when a high water table periodically pushes water into the crawlspace. In that case, venting will be necessary. Power vents or fans along with a sump pump might also be required.

5

Framing

There's a tremendous diversity in the materials, techniques, and traditions that go into building the frame of a house. Some approaches, like rammed earth, adobe, and straw-bale construction, are by now well-established if still slightly offbeat alternatives to more mainstream techniques. Other materials are newer: blocks of aerated concrete developed in Europe, structural insulated panels that combine polystyrene or urethane foam insulation in a sandwich of oriented strand board, and hollow blocks formed with a mixture of cement and recycled polystyrene.

These materials all have their advocates, and they all have something to offer sustainable building. With the exception of structural insulated panels, or SIPs, which are described

THE GREEN FACTOR

Resource conservation, energy efficiency, and durability are key factors in framing a house to sustainable standards. Here are the basics:

- Stick-framing a house with dimensional lumber has ample potential for waste.

- Engineered lumber uses wood fiber more efficiently that dimensional lumber.

- Light-gauge steel framing may contain recycled material, a plus, but using it on outside walls significantly lowers energy efficiency. Used on interior partitions, however, steel goes up quickly and produces straight walls.

- Alternatives to stick-framing may be very attractive from a green standpoint, providing products are readily available and crews can be trained to work with unfamiliar materials.

- Structural insulated panels combine frame and cavity insulation in one and produce comfortable, energy-efficient houses.

- Timber-framed houses can be elegant testaments to traditional joinery, but they also consume a lot of wood.

Conventionally framed houses use more lumber than they actually need for structural integrity. Advanced framing techniques save money while providing more room for insulation.

later in this chapter, many of these products and techniques are not yet widely available or practiced. A number of these products hold intriguing possibilities for new ways of building and we do not intend to discount them. But for most residential builders in the U.S., wood is still king.

Wood is one of the best suited and most renewable materials used in construction. It has low embodied energy, natural durability, high strength, and (when untreated) low toxic-

ity. Ninety-five percent of single-family houses built in the U.S. today are stick-framed.

Advanced Framing Reduces Waste

Most wood-framed houses are assembled one piece at a time at the construction site. And that's part of the problem. Virtually every carpenter working on any given house learned on the job from someone who also learned on the job. Labor unions with formal training programs that turn apprentices into well-schooled journeymen carpenters historically have been most active in commercial, not residential,

Wasted lumber in unnecessary framing around door and window openings adds up. Much of this dimensional lumber serves no practical purpose and makes the building less energy efficient.

SAVING LUMBER WITH ADVANCED FRAMING

Optimum Value Engineering, or just advanced framing, eliminates unnecessary framing members without compromising the structural integrity of the building. The resulting cost savings can be significant, and the house will be better insulated. Although advanced framing normally calls for a single top plate, it makes more sense to include two. If nothing else, this makes building inspectors happier.

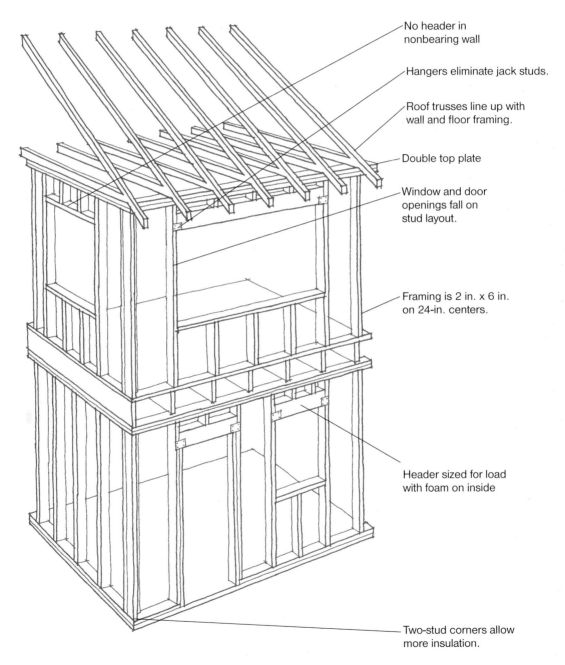

No header in nonbearing wall

Hangers eliminate jack studs.

Roof trusses line up with wall and floor framing.

Double top plate

Window and door openings fall on stud layout.

Framing is 2 in. x 6 in. on 24-in. centers.

Header sized for load with foam on inside

Two-stud corners allow more insulation.

construction. And so we have very few PhD framers working in the field these days. It is conventional wisdom that prevails; whether it's the best way to build is another question.

Many conventionally framed houses share a common problem. There is often too much framing—too many studs placed too close together, headers that are too big for the loads they carry, framing that gets in the way of insulation. Call it habit, tradition, or insurance on the part of the builder, but the bottom line is that these and other wasteful practices make building envelopes more expensive and less efficient than they could be.

In the late 1970s, during an energy crisis that was no doubt a practice run for what's to come, the National Association of Home Builders' Research Foundation conducted studies to identify what structural configuration was necessary to maintain superior strength and

yet allow the maximum insulation in wall cavities to improve energy efficiency. The result was called "Optimal Value Engineering" (OVE). Research showed that on average as much as 20percent of the framing material used in traditional construction could be removed without compromising structural integrity. Today, OVE is just referred to as advanced framing.

It's easy for framers to throw another stud in the wall or to beef up a door header just to be on the safe side. After all, an extra piece of material here and there can't make that much difference. Or so it would seem. But it all adds up. Advanced framing brings order to this haphazard system, reducing the amount of materials used in the shell of a house and simultaneously allowing greater energy efficiencies when the house is insulated. Both are cornerstones of sustainable building.

ADVANCED FRAMING BASICS

Optimum Value Engineering—or simply advanced framing—has two main benefits. First, it eliminates framing members that serve no structural purpose, thereby reducing waste as well as unnecessary costs for the buyer. Second, it makes more room for insulation and eliminates cold spots, making the house more comfortable and less expensive to heat and cool.

Virtually every part of the frame is affected, and while some of the techniques may seem like small potatoes the cumulative savings can be substantial. Advanced framing, however, is different, and for that reason it often challenges the long-held views of builders who aren't familiar with it. Change takes time, but advanced framing works. Here are some of the basics:

• Walls are framed with 2x6s on 24-in. centers rather than 2x4s on 16-in. centers to increase

insulation depth and reduce thermal bridging.

• Corners are made from two studs rather than four to allow more room for insulation and to eliminate cold spots.

• Headers are sized according to the load they actually carry, not to conform with an arbitrary formula or building traditions.

• Roofs are built with trusses rather than framed conventionally, reducing the amount of lumber that's needed.

• Floors are framed with I-joists rather than sawn lumber, making for stiffer floors that use less material.

• Insulating sheathing replaces conventional plywood or oriented strand board, reducing thermal bridging and making the house cheaper to heat and cool.

TWO-STUD CORNERS

One detail that is especially beneficial to the thermal performance of a house is a modified, two-stud corner that allows more insulation and blocks much of the thermal bridging in a conventionally framed corner. With less cold air inside the wall cavity, the chance of condensation and mold declines. Adding a layer of insulating sheathing to the outside of the building is an added benefit. Drywall clips or an extra piece of 1 in. x 4 in. catches the edge of interior drywall.

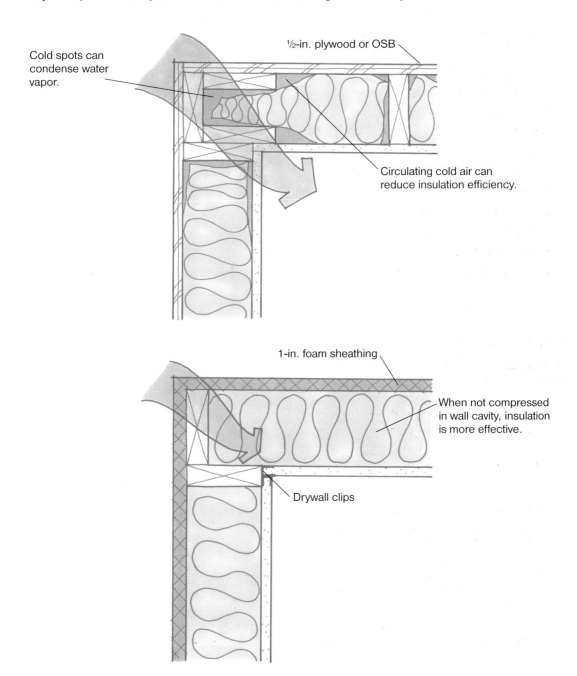

Cold spots can condense water vapor.

1/2-in. plywood or OSB

Circulating cold air can reduce insulation efficiency.

1-in. foam sheathing

When not compressed in wall cavity, insulation is more effective.

Drywall clips

PULTE'S HIDDEN LAKE STUDY

In 2004 Pulte Homes, one of the largest home builders in the country, conducted a study on advanced framing at its Hidden Lake development in Tracy, Calif. Pulte built test homes to determine how much money advanced framing would save in construction and to study its effect on heating and cooling costs. The work was supported by the Department of Energy and the California Energy Commission. The results were impressive:

- Using 2x6 wall framing on 24-in. centers cost $1,632 versus $2,749 for a conventionally framed house, with 2x4 studs on 16-in. centers.

- Advanced framing saved a total of 738 studs, amounting to more than 2,100 board feet of lumber.

- Energy costs in the advanced framing house were a total of $710 (both heating and cooling) a year, compared with $1,003 per year for the conventionally framed 2x4 house.

- Whole-wall R-values jumped from 9.4 to 15.2 by switching to advanced framing.

A study conducted by Pulte Homes found that advanced framing saved money and produced a better insulated building with lower heating and cooling costs.

Improving on conventional framing

If advanced framing seems like too much of a change all at once, there are significant ways to improve frames made the conventional way: that is, from 2x4s on 16-in. centers. Building Science Corporation, working with the Building America program of the Department of Energy, found that wrapping the frame of a house with rigid foam insulation increased the overall R-value of the walls and reduced heat loss. This added layer of insulation makes detailing, especially around doors and windows, more complicated. But there are ways to accomplish this—by switching from conventional ¾-in. trim to deeper brick mold, for example.

Some builders have switched from 2x4 to 2x6 construction on the theory that it allows for deeper stud cavities and therefore more insulation, which is true. If you're using fiberglass batt insulation, the nominal R-value of wall insulation jumps from R-13 (R-15 for high-density batts) to R-19. But when builders continue to space 2x6 framing on 16-in. instead of 24-in. centers the result is structural overkill.

Moreover, all that extra wood in the wall increases thermal bridging while decreasing space for insulation. You only frame a house once so it is best to create an envelope that's as energy efficient as possible.

We Have Tree Farms, Not Forests

Wood has attractive advantages as a building material, but the stupendous volume of material that goes into residential construction creates a variety of interrelated problems. And one of the biggest controversies in the world of green building is over how trees are forested.

More than 95 percent of the original forests in the United States have been cut down. Yet, according to the American Forest and Paper Association, there are more trees in the U.S. now than there were when the Pilgrims landed in Massachusetts nearly 400 years ago. On the surface, that seems like a good thing: Forests have bounced back and continue to be productive. But once we dig deeper into the issue our views may be more tempered.

A clear-cut forest where all of the trees, and the ecosystem that went with it, have been removed.

During the expansion of European-American culture, forests seemed endless and empires were built on what could be harvested. Replanting was unnecessary because there were so many trees yet to cut. As the resource became more depleted and the National Forest Service was created, tree farming became good business practice and tree plantations began springing up across the country. Today, most of the forests in the Pacific Northwest are tree plantations, not natural forests.

It is only when we visit the tiny pockets of indigenous forest that we realize what a profound difference there is between a tree plantation and true forest ecology. It takes hundreds of years for a forest to regain its complex interconnections of life-forms and the inherent sta-

Elk, deer, and bear are killed in the spring and fall by large forest products companies to protect their agricultural investment. According to the State of Oregon Forest Service, in 2004 alone 163 bears were killed by hired hunters to protect the trees from being "marked" or scratched by hungry bears looking for food. The practice is common in the Pacific Northwest.

True forests are complex systems that support a variety of plants and animals, but they are growing more scarce as demand for forest products intensifies.

Tree plantations have replaced native forests in some parts of the country. They provide the raw material for many lumber products, but they also have transformed trees into an agricultural product.

Western Forest Products
WFP PLANTED
1946

bility that goes along with them. Clear-cutting all living things in a forest only to replant with a monoculture like Douglas fir or some other single species completely destroys the ecosystem that we call a forest. Trees are turned into an agricultural commodity like corn or radishes—and that requires pesticides, fungicides, and herbicides that kill everything but the trees.

Trees are planted in rows to make harvesting easier 25 to 40 years down the road.

There are lots of trees, yes, but a monoculture is not a forest. Lost habitat forces animals that lived in the forest to find another place to live. Because they are artificial environments with a lack of natural diversity, tree farms are not places where people want to backpack, hike, or fish. So people flock to our overrun national parks, now so overcrowded they are barely managing the flood of people looking for a glimpse of the real thing.

Real forests are complex ecosystems, not just stands of trees. The conversion of many of our native forests into tree farms is a compelling argument for being frugal with this resource and using engineered wood products instead of large-dimension sawn timbers.

Replanted Douglas fir in a clear-cut zone will become a managed woodlot.

Hebel block is made from auto-claved aerated concrete (AAC), which is manufactured with en-trained air to boost R-values. It's laid up much like ordinary con-crete block but it has a number of green benefits.

ALTERNATIVES TO WOOD

Wood is still the predominant material for creating the shell of a house, but a number of builders have abandoned wood in favor of a variety of newer materials. Among them are North Carolina passive solar builders James Cameron and Kathleen Jardine (www.sungardenhouses.com), who have switched to blocks made from autoclaved aerated concrete (AAC).

AAC blocks take the place of a number of components used in a standard stick-frame—wood, insulation, house wrap, and drywall—all in a single product. The result, as these builders will tell you, is a house that's fire-proof, mold-proof, insect resistant, hypoallergenic, sound-absorptive, and engineered to withstand hurricanes and earthquakes.

AAC is an interesting product. Aluminum powder added to a mix of sand, lime, water, and cement creates a five-fold increase in volume while trapping insulating air bubbles. It's hardened in a mold and then processed in an autoclave to produce blocks 8 in. or 12 in. thick, 8 in. high, and 24 in. long. Blocks can be cut on-site with a specialized handsaw or bandsaw and laid up somewhat like conventional concrete block.

Walls made with AAC block (Hebel is one trade name) have far less air infiltration than conventional 2x4 constructions, the builders say, with insulating values for the 8-in. block as high as R-21 (less in colder climates). Although building with AAC is more expensive than standard 2x4 construction, the company offsets higher costs in other ways to remain competitive with wood-framed houses.

AAC blocks aren't the only alternative. Rastra is a type of insulated concrete form (ICF) made mostly of recycled polystyrene with some cement to form a material the company calls "Thastyron." It's made into hollow-core blocks that are relatively lightweight, can be cut with ordinary handsaws, and glued into place. Once stacked into walls, the blocks are reinforced with steel and filled with concrete to form finished walls. The company reports that

10-in.-thick walls have an R-value of 36.

Durisol is yet another option. These hollow-core blocks are made from mineralized wood shavings and portland cement, stacked into walls and then finished with reinforcing steel and concrete. The company says the material is noncombustible, sound absorptive, and dimensionally stable—and is made of 78 percent recycled content. It's also 100 percent recyclable.

Products like these share many green benefits and give builders interested in exploring new avenues considerable leeway. They are not as widely available as wood building products and may make the most sense in areas with local or regional suppliers. One more consideration: there is a learning curve in working with new materials. Converts will tell you it's well worth it.

Hebel block is lighter than a conventional CMU, making them somewhat easier to work with. They can be cut on-site.

Mechanized clear-cutting begins with stripping away most of what made the forest a real forest. It will be replaced with a tree plantation that can be managed like farmland.

Reduce waste and use certified wood

Does that mean we should stop using wood to build houses? No, that's not the point. But the relationship between building and the world around us shouldn't be ignored, either. What we can do is make sure this resource is used carefully. There are consequences to wasteful framing practices, not only in the impact they make on the world's forests but also in higher costs to the buyer. Careful framing results in better insulated, more comfortable houses—a

clear benefit to the customers paying the bills. One house at a time, it all adds up.

There's something else that can help. As concerns have mounted over how forest resources are being used, a number of programs have popped up to certify that lumber harvesting is causing no long-term damage to either the environment or the people who live nearby. There are two principal forest certification programs operating in the United States: the Forest Stewardship Council's (FSC) certified sustainably harvested wood program and the American Forest and Paper Association's Sustainable Forest Initiative, or SFI.

FSC is an international nonprofit organization that protects forests around the globe. Lumber certified by the FSC must meet certain standards designed to protect the forests in

The FSC logo identifies products that contain wood from well-managed forests certified in accordance with the rules of the Forest Stewardship Council. © 1996 Forest Stewardship Council A.C.

which it was cut, as well as the people who live there. The standards were adopted internationally in the mid-1990s. They include strict requirements for how wood is harvested, how much can be clear-cut, and how the existing forest ecology is to be protected. The program also determines whether indigenous people are affected by lumber harvesting. (Canada, for example, doesn't set aside reservations for native peoples as the U.S. does, and as a result many tribes lose their livelihood when forests around their communities are clear-cut.)

FSC relies on something called "chain of custody," a way of tracking wood from the stump to the point of sale, much like protecting evidence in a police investigation. Each forest, mill, distributor, and retailer must be certified to preserve the integrity of the lumber's sustainable sources.

Even though it does not include all of the protections built into the FSC system, SFI aims to protect endangered and fragile forests. As good as this sounds, the major forest products companies do not have a comprehensive program to protect all the lands they convert from forests to tree plantations. Only FSC protects the existing forests from conversion to monocultures. FSC certification is the only way you know the wood you are buying is from sustainably harvested forests, and certified products

FSC-certified lumber is becoming increasingly available in the marketplace as consumers start asking for it more often.

are becoming increasingly available in the marketplace.

In all, there are more than 50 different forest certification systems in the world, each claiming to monitor a certain amount of acreage. In addition to SFI (135 million acres) and FSC (195 million acres), those in North America include the American Tree Farm System (3.15 million acres) and the Canadian Standards Association (170 million acres). A new program, the European Programme for the Endorsement of Forest Certification (PEFC), is being developed to compare systematically all the certification programs globally so there is a common reference for wood procurement.

In all, the number and variety of these programs can be confusing. But the many programs are at least a step in the right direction, and the benefits of specifying FSC-certified lumber will continue to make new converts among home buyers.

Engineered Lumber Makes Sense

Using engineered lumber is another way to make sure that wood resources are not wasted—and engineered products often result in a better house. Once the exclusive domain of commercial buildings and high-end houses, engineered lumber is now commonplace in conventional construction. Two things makes this family of products green: engineered products use wood fiber more efficiently than solid sawn lumber, and they can be made from wood species that regenerate themselves.

Wood I-joists use only half the fiber to perform the same structural function as solid timber. And they do the job better because I-joists have longer allowable spans than solid

Wood I-joists are made mostly from engineered wood products and produce flatter, stiffer floor systems that are not subject to the same dimensional changes as solid lumber.

timber of the same depth. In addition, they can be made from aspen trees or a related species. These trees are really the fruit that springs from an underground root system, undamaged when a tree is harvested. When you cut an aspen tree, the following year the root system sends up a new shoot that matures quickly. When you cut a pine, fir, or hemlock tree, it's dead for good.

All engineered wood uses a binder to hold the wood or wood fibers together. Any engineered product with an APA stamp on it uses a phenolic resin as a binder (the APA-The Engineered Wood Association is an industry

Finger-jointed studs *have been embraced by carpenters in some parts of the country because they are predictably straight, eliminating a host of problems associated with warped dimensional lumber.*

trade group). This is an entirely different adhesive than urea-formaldehyde. Urea is a water-soluble glue that is used for indoor products such as particleboard and medium density fiberboard (MDF). The binder off-gasses formaldehyde for up to five years and is a major source of poor indoor air quality that can have a detrimental affect on health. Phenolic resin off-gasses a mere 4 percent of the formaldehyde that urea does and is not nearly as much of an issue. (See chapter 14 for more detail.)

Finger-jointed studs and glue-lams are another type of engineered lumber. Both are made from solid pieces of wood glued together to make larger pieces. Finger-jointed studs have an important advantage over sawn lumber in that they come straight. And they stay straight. Conventional studs are milled from fast-growing farm trees. They're famous for twisting, splitting, warping, and checking, making it increasingly difficult to frame a straight wall. Crooked walls cause problems for everyone from the crews that hang drywall to cabinet installers and trim carpenters. No one, least among them the homeowner, is very happy. Because straight framing lumber is increasingly harder to find, a significant number of builders in some markets—Seattle, for instance—have switched to finger-jointed material.

Glue lams are 2x4s or 2x6s that are glued together face-to-face to create a beam. Laminated veneer lumber (LVL) is like plywood but in the dimensions of beams. Parallel laminated lumber is made from long strips of aspen trees that are glued together lengthwise to create beams stronger than the tree itself. These replace large-dimension timbers used for long spans—over a garage door, for instance. Increasingly popular, they save old-growth trees and do the job better, stay straighter, and are typically less expensive.

Laminated veneer lumber *is one type of engineered beam that can be used in place of solid material. It is straight, stable, and strong.*

Using Steel Studs with Recycled Content

Steel framing members also have a place in the green construction world. On the plus side, they can be made with recycled materials, a central tenet of sustainable building. They're also dead straight, so walls and ceilings are true, and they're easier on the back because they're lighter. The problem is that steel is a marvelously effective conductor of heat—just think of the handle of a cast-iron frying pan that's been on the stove for a while.

When steel framing is used to build exterior walls, all of the sheathing as well as window and door frames have to be screwed on. Inside, drywall is also attached to the framing with screws. By itself, steel framing is a good heat conductor and all those thousands of fasteners just make it even better. The result is a thermal bridge that circumvents insulation used in wall cavities and conducts heat in or out of the house depending on the season.

The conductivity is substantial. The Oak Ridge National Laboratory found that steel framing reduces the effectiveness of cavity insulation by 50 percent. The only way around this is to attach a layer of rigid foam insulation to the outside of the building. In 2x6 steel-framed construction, the cavity insulation of fiberglass batts nominally rated at R-19 actually provides an insulating value of only R-10. Adding 2 in. of rigid foam insulation boosts the

Light-gauge steel framing is lighter and straighter than studs sawn from solid lumber, but when used on outside walls it can result in thermal bridging and lower energy efficiency unless the frame is wrapped in rigid insulation.

Wood blocks in the ends of this steel stud allow it to be attached easily to wood top and bottom plates.

overall rating to R-20. But that's about what you get with 2x6 wood framing on 24-in. centers. The only advantage is that the rigid foam insulation blocks a potential thermal bridge that also affects wood framing, though less dramatically. But this incremental improvement in performance adds substantially to the cost of the wall and the labor required to build it.

If there are disadvantages to using steel framing on the outside of a house, using it for interior partitions can save time and materi-

als. A crew proficient in framing with steel can knock out all the interior partitions in an average-size house in a couple of days, maybe less.

Steel framing is more common in commercial construction, and carpenters used to working with wood may slow way down when they get to steel. One option for builders in larger markets is to hire a commercial crew to build interior partitions. Let the regular crew frame the shell during the day. When they knock off, in comes the next crew to put up the

Wrapping a conventionally framed house with at least 1 in. of rigid foam insulation has a number of benefits: less air infiltration, higher wall R-values, a reduction in thermal bridging, and less chance of mold and water damage in wall cavities.

steel framing. Many of these crews are already used to working nights, and they will get the job done quickly.

Structural Insulated Panels Are Fast

Structural insulated panels (SIPs) are a sandwich of insulating foam and oriented strand board that can be used for floors, walls, and roofs. SIPs are a green building product on every level. They combine insulation and structure in a single product. Because they are engineered and cut to size off-site, houses go up very rapidly, minimizing the length of time that building materials are exposed to the weather. Houses built with SIPs are highly efficient, comfortable, and have virtually no air infiltration. Operating costs are half or less of a conventional house.

When using SIPs, speed and accuracy are everything. The savings come from rapid enclosure of the envelope, especially when building in cold weather. Once the frame is up you are in an insulated space—and that means jackets come off and productivity goes up. When the job is finished you have an airtight,

This combination of steel studs on interior partitions and wood studs on outside walls is a marriage made in heaven.

CASE STUDY

Structural insulated panels are a combination of foam insulation and skins of oriented strand board. They combine insulation and structure in a single component.

SIPS MAKE SENSE

I have a bias toward structural insulated panels (SIPs). My former company, Lightworks Construction, had a relationship with a SIPs manufacturer in the '80s. We sold panels and also used them on our remodeling jobs.

We started using SIPs because of a disastrous experience we had building a second-floor addition on a bungalow. The client wanted to stay in the house while we built the addition. We obliged and built the addition over the existing roof by cutting the roof back at the top plate of the first floor and framing up from there.

We worked around the clock to get the addition framed and weather tight. Toward the end, we had the addition wrapped in tarps and planned to roof the next day.

As Murphy's Law would have it, a huge thunderstorm blew in that night and ripped the tarps off the building. Rain driven sideways soaked everything. Plaster fell off the ceiling downstairs and drenched the first floor. Unfortunately, the top was up on a grand piano sitting on an ancient Oriental rug and it filled with water.

The client called at 2 a.m. and when I arrived I was horrified at what I saw. The ceiling was on the floor and the house was drenched. When I saw the piano I thought I'd have a heart attack. Suffice it to say I blessed our insurance company when it paid to clean, de-mold, and repair the first floor.

After that, we started using SIPs. A second-floor addition that would have taken weeks to frame conventionally took four days from start to dry-in. We could keep the crane moving from the pile of panels to the installers without stops in between.

Fifteen years later, I used SIPS to build my own office in Boulder, Col. I ripped the roof off a free-standing two-car garage and added a second floor. Because I was starting construction in January, speed was important. By the time we had the foundation ready, it was al-most February, traditionally one of our snowi-est months. The flatbed truck showed up early Monday morning with the panels, followed by the crane. By Thursday night we were un-der roof. On Friday the roofer came and we covered the window openings with polyethyl-ene. On Saturday a blizzard moved in and it snowed off and on for the next six weeks. If we had stick-framed the addition, it would have extended the job by months.   —DJ

One advantage to using SIPs is that workers are out of the weather quickly, meaning that comfort and productivity for the crew goes up. The author's office was up and tight to the weather in a matter of days, weeks before a conventionally framed building could have been dried in.

SIPs can be assembled rapidly by well-trained crews using a crane. They make for fast dry-ins and comfortable houses. Even roofs and floors can be made from the panels.

highly insulated envelope that also helps cut noise inside. The house performs extraordinarily well, and you don't have to worry about moisture and mold accumulating inside wall cavities because they're completely sealed.

Panels must be kept dry

There are several cautions when building with SIPs. First, and most important, the oriented strand board on the faces of the panels must be protected from water. The two simply don't make good bedfellows. The OSB gives the panels structural strength and if it gets wet and stays wet, it loses its integrity. Careful flashing is key.

The second issue is running electrical cable. Panels are made with channels in the foam to accommodate wiring—horizontally 18 in. off the floor for outlets and vertically

for wires leading to switches. When ordering panels it is imperative to provide an electrical plan so the manufacturer knows where to run these chases. Unfortunately, not all electricians are familiar with SIPs and they may make the mistake of hacking their way through the OSB to make room for wires without knowing the chases are there. Plumbing should never be run in an exterior wall so typically there are no chases provided for that purpose.

There also is a concern that insects may burrow into the foam. According to the Structural Insulated Panel Association, termites

The oriented strand board faces of structural panels would be damaged by water. A continuous waterproof membrane and careful flashing details are essential.

Wire chases built into panels make it easy to run electrical wiring for switches and receptacles.

won't feed on the foam core but they may nest there. As a result, manufacturers offer borate-treated panels and the SIPA suggests termites can also be discouraged by a steel mesh barrier.

Rigid foam insulation is a vital component of structural insulated panels. Many people wonder whether using a petroleum-based product like that can really be green. In reality, the amount of oil used to make insulating foam (which is primarily air) is very small and at least the petroleum committed to this product will serve a useful purpose for many years.

Comparing costs is difficult

Manufacturers are located all over the country, so you may have a local source for SIPs. Even if that's not the case, panels are shipped flat so transportation is not unduly expensive. Typically, there is a lead time of two to three weeks.

There is a significant learning curve associated with installing SIPs. Most suppliers today will sell the panels installed, meaning they provide the crew, you provide the crane. The primary advantage is the speed at which the building can be enclosed. If you try to do it yourself, you may not have the specialized tools and fasteners.

It's difficult to generalize about how the cost of SIPs compares with conventional stick-building. Panel prices vary by manufacturer and region, and there is the added complication of labor—a few months compared with a few days to get the shell up and weather tight. Building with SIPs can be more expensive than stick-building when you just compare material costs of a frame house built to minimum standards, but maybe not when you compare houses of equal performance.

Timber-Frame Construction

Timber-framing, or post-and-beam construction, is where carpenters become craftsmen. It is a very old building technique that has seen a resurgence in the last 25 years. Unlike a frame made from dimensional lumber, a timber frame is beautiful in its own right—one reason why major parts of the frame are left exposed. Mortise and tenon and dovetail joints are typical, with wood pegs holding pieces firmly together. This helps make the frame more like a fine piece of furniture than what we think of as a building.

This timber frame is made from reclaimed standing dead wood, making it appealing from a sustainably built point of view as well as just plain beautiful.

The large amount of lumber that goes into a timber frame is a disadvantage if the source is old-growth timber taken in a clear-cut. Better that FSC-certified, salvaged, or dead wood is used.

The roof of this timber frame is made from structural insulated panels for good looks and high performance.

Timber-frame construction provides the structure for the building, and insulation is then added between the posts. SIPs, straw bales, and more conventional insulation can be used to seal the envelope. The advantage is that the frame can be erected quickly to get the building under cover and the infill added once the weather protection is in place.

One of the important considerations with post and beam is where the wood comes from. The ideal is that timbers be chosen with care—FSC certified, salvaged, or milled from standing dead trees. Otherwise there is the possibility that the large-dimension lumber has been taken from old-growth clear-cuts. Using local lumber that is certified or reclaimed is a great option. It reduces transportation costs and supports the local economy at the same time.

The other green issue here is simply the amount of wood that goes into a timber-frame house. There's a lot of it, certainly more than would be used for a conventionally framed house or one that makes significant use of engineered lumber. Because a key element of green building is an efficient use of materials, there is an argument to be made that timber-framing is inherently a lesser choice than a house built with advanced framing techniques. Should the frame be made from certified wood, or locally harvested wood, this argument loses some of its punch. But it is typical of how hard it can sometimes be to weigh one green factor against another. There is no perfect answer.

6

Roofs and Attics

There's more to a roof than meets the eye. Although only the uppermost layer is visible from the outside of the house, what we think of as a "roof" is actually an assembly of materials that together control the flow of air and moisture, protect the house from fire as well as the elements, and insulate the house from temperature extremes. We want the roof to add to the curbside appeal of the house, and we might consider using it to collect water or as a base for solar panels.

Roofing is one of the most climate-specific materials that go into a house. Where you live can have a major influence on the type and color of the roofing materials as well as on how they're assembled—light colors and a radiant barrier to minimize solar gain in hot climates, steep-pitched roofs and plenty of room

THE GREEN FACTOR

A roof is a system of interdependent components that protects the house from the elements, buffers it from outdoor temperatures, and controls the flow of air and moisture.

• Roofing materials should be durable, able to withstand local climatic conditions that might include hail, wind, rain, and snow as well as ultraviolet light.

• The surface should be nonflammable, especially in regions with a high fire risk.

• The roof should have a long lifespan with a minimal need for maintenance.

• Roofing should not be a source of toxic runoff.

• Where possible, roofing should contain some recycled content.

Roof pitch is determined by climatic conditions, particularly rainfall and snow loads. The lower the pitch, the slower the rain runs off the roof. Steeper roof pitches—6 in 12 and greater—are best for areas that get a lot of snow. Flat roofs are more appropriate in drier climates and are great candidates for a green roof.

for insulation in snow country, resilient roofing materials where hail is common.

So what makes a green roof? Some roofs are literally green. Live vegetation can take the place of shingles, tile, or sheet metal. We'll discuss that type of roof later in the chapter, but among the most important considerations for a sustainably built house is durability. The longer the roof lasts, the greener it is. Roofing materials in many new homes won't last as long as the mortgage. Yet when installed with care, a number of roofing materials perform reliably for decades.

PLANNING FOR SOLAR PANELS

When a considerable area of the roof faces south, it makes sense to prepare for the future installation of solar panels. Most solar panel racks are lagged directly into rafters or trusses and flashed appropriately to prevent leaks. The internal preparation consists of installing two 1-in. insulated pipes and one 1¼-in. conduit from the attic to the utility room while the house is under construction. It saves the owner money when solar panels are installed.

Even if original construction plans don't call for roof-mounted solar panels, it makes sense to rough in conduit and insulated pipes so both can be added in the future.

In addition to seeking out the most durable materials we can find, we should look for materials that don't need much maintenance, are easy to clean, and pose a low threat of toxicity from water runoff.

Frame with Trusses

How the roof and attic ceiling are framed has a big impact on how the attic can be insulated, and what the roof is framed with has a direct bearing on resource conservation. Both of these issues are important in sustainable building.

Engineered beams—laminated veneer lumber, I-joists, glulams, and trusses—are all more attractive options than solid dimensional lumber. As we discussed in the framing chapter, you get more mileage from the same amount of wood fiber in an engineered building part than you do in sawn lumber, and the components are often lighter, easier to handle, and less likely to have defects. In some cases, they are also less expensive and save money by speeding up construction.

But conventional roof trusses (or rafters made from dimensional lumber for that matter) don't allow the full thickness of insulation near the eaves. This can promote the growth of mold in cold corners where warm, moist air from inside the house encounters roof sheathing and framing that's below the dew point. That causes condensation, a possible catalyst for mold. Moreover, in snow country, the repetitive freezing and thawing of snow along roof edges forms ice dams that allow water to back up beneath the shingles and get inside the house. Not having enough room for air to circulate underneath the sheathing can also cause moisture problems in the roof.

The answer is to specify raised-heel trusses (also called energy-heel trusses), which have more room at the eaves for insulation (see the drawing on p. 112). In addition, be aware of where the air barrier starts and stops to prevent air movement from the house into the attic.

Make sure to install baffles to keep air from the soffit vents from flowing through the insulation, which will reduce the effective R-value. It's a good practice to extend sheathing up to the top chord of the truss to serve as a baffle before adding soffit returns. If you use batt insulation in the attic ceiling, install two layers: first, a 3½-in. R-13 layer parallel to the trusses, and then a 12-in. R-38 layer perpendicular to the trusses. Layering two courses in opposite directions minimizes air leaks. Blown-in fiberglass or cellulose, however, is better at filling voids and makes it easier to get the exact quantity that you want for high R-values.

A "green" roof should be durable and low in toxicity and framed with engineered lumber or roof trusses to make the most of wood resources.

Finally, consider using wood I-joists or parallel-chord trusses in place of 2x10s or 2x12s to reduce the amount of lumber that comes from old-growth trees. I-joists from 12 in. to 24 in. deep are readily available. Trusses are custom designed and available in any depth you want.

Attic Ductwork

Another consideration is whether heating and air-conditioning ducts will run through an unconditioned attic, a common practice in many new homes even if it doesn't make a lot of sense. It's certainly convenient, but it's also antithetical to systems thinking. Consider a house built with

RAISED-HEEL TRUSS MEANS MORE INSULATION

Trusses save time in the field and require less dimensional lumber to make than a conventionally framed roof—both strong points. But standard trusses don't leave much room at the eaves for insulation. Switching to a raised-heel truss solves the problem by allowing full-depth insulation to extend all the way to the outside of the wall.

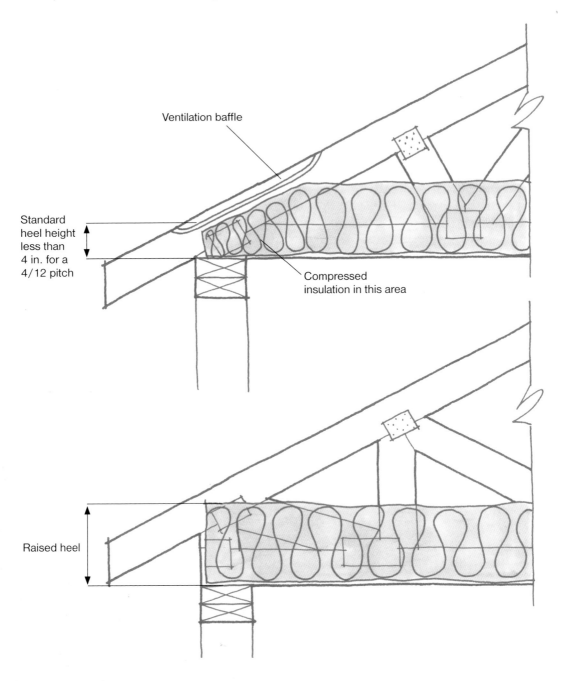

Ventilation baffle

Standard heel height less than 4 in. for a 4/12 pitch

Compressed insulation in this area

Raised heel

roof trusses in which the ceiling is insulated and the attic is unheated. During the heating season, the attic will approximate the outside temperature. Ductwork running across the attic will be hung from rafters or laid on top of the ceiling joists. Ductwork is insulated in the R-4 to R-6 range. So we have the hottest air in the house running through the coldest space in the house with the least insulation between the two. What's wrong with this picture? Lots.

The reverse is true in the summer. In the Southwest, attics can reach 160° in summer. We run 60° air through cooling ducts—that's

Substituting I-joists *for wide dimensional lumber is a smart use of wood resources. I-joists provide equal or superior performance using less wood fiber and relieve pressure on remaining forests of big trees.*

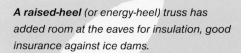

A raised-heel *(or energy-heel) truss has added room at the eaves for insulation, good insurance against ice dams.*

100° of temperature differential. Even with R-6 flex duct, the heat gain is enormous—no wonder people living in such houses complain they can't keep the house cool.

Superinsulated Attics and Roofs

Insulating the roof and attic is of the utmost importance. Depending on where you live, R-values for attic insulation should range from R-38 to R-50 (U.S. Department of Energy recommendations by region can be found on p. 211). There are a couple of ways to reach the upper range of these R-values. In houses where ductwork must run in the attic, one approach is to insulate both the roof and the attic ceiling. That makes the attic a semi-conditioned space and a better buffer between inside and out because the temperature difference between the attic and the floor below is not as extreme. Because this is conditioned space, the ventilation for the shingles should be at the sheathing level rather than in the attic.

One product that can prove helpful in building a roof like this is Nail Base made by Atlas Roofing. It consists of a layer of polyiso insulation laminated to a sheet of OSB. Insulation directly under the OSB is grooved to encourage air to flow up and into the ridge vent.

Ventilation ducts should be run in a conditioned space to reduce heating and cooling losses from the ductwork. The ducts themselves should be insulated and carefully sealed with mastic.

Substituting this for ordinary roof sheathing adds a layer of insulation at roof level to reduce heat loss through ducts. It also has the benefit of reducing the risk of condensation on attic framing and sheathing.

Another option is to use structural insulated panels on the roof. They provide high R-values, as discussed in the insulation chapter, and they can be cut to size at the factory to speed installation on the jobsite.

Stopping Air Leaks at the Ceiling

Intersections between interior partition walls and ceilings hold a lot of potential for air leaks, which in turn allow warm, moist air into the attic. For a variety of reasons, this is something to avoid. Here are two approaches that can help.

Sealed drywall air barrier. When hanging drywall on the ceiling, don't run screws any closer than 6 in. to the edge. You don't really need fasteners here because the ceiling will be supported by drywall on the walls. By allowing drywall edges to float, any movement in the trusses or joists will be less likely to crack corners and allow moist air to leak into the attic. This is particularly important when tight drywall joints, not polyethylene sheeting, are the prin-

Nail Base, a product made by Atlas Roofing, consists of polyiso insulation bonded to oriented strand board with the option of an air space for roof ventilation. When used instead of standard sheathing, it turns an attic into a semi-conditioned space that's friendlier to heating and cooling ducts.

Structural insulated panels combine framing, insulation, and sheathing in one product, and because they are cut to size at the factory on-site installation is speedy.

cipal ceiling air barrier. When ceiling joists or trusses are parallel to the wall and the edge of the sheet may not land on solid support, provide solid backing for the ceiling drywall with blocking or use drywall clips. But don't attach the drywall directly to them. Attach wall panels firmly at the top plate after applying a bead of caulk or drywall adhesive. Carefully taping the joint will provide an effective air barrier.

Poly air barrier detailing. Install 6-mil polyethylene sheeting over the ceiling before you frame any interior partition walls to create a continuous air barrier. This is the best approach with the fewest opportunities for air leaks. If you can't get the entire ceiling in advance, wrap a strip of plastic over the top of each partition wall before tipping it in place. Then install poly on the ceiling and seal the edges of the plastic together with poly tape.

After going to all this trouble to create an effective air seal at ceiling height, it would be a shame to ruin it by failing to seal other potential leaks. At any point that a cable, conduit, drain line, vent, or anything else penetrates the air barrier, take care to use expanding polyurethane foam to seal any gaps or cracks. Recessed

USING DRYWALL AS AN AIR BARRIER

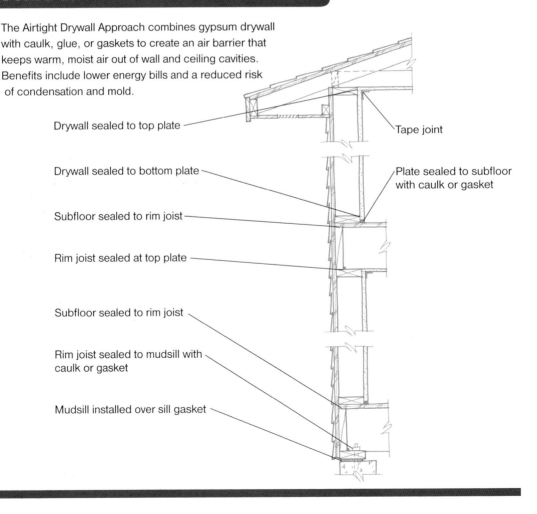

The Airtight Drywall Approach combines gypsum drywall with caulk, glue, or gaskets to create an air barrier that keeps warm, moist air out of wall and ceiling cavities. Benefits include lower energy bills and a reduced risk of condensation and mold.

Drywall sealed to top plate

Drywall sealed to bottom plate

Subfloor sealed to rim joist

Rim joist sealed at top plate

Subfloor sealed to rim joist

Rim joist sealed to mudsill with caulk or gasket

Mudsill installed over sill gasket

Tape joint

Plate sealed to subfloor with caulk or gasket

BETTER SEAL: POLYETHYLENE SHEETING

A very effective air barrier is provided by a continuous sheet of polyethylene attached to the ceiling before interior partitions are built. If that's not possible, drape the top of the partition with poly before tipping the wall into place. Another sheet of poly should be stapled to the ceiling and the two pieces sealed with poly tape.

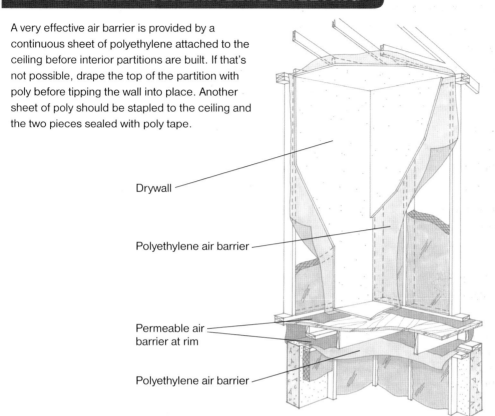

Drywall

Polyethylene air barrier

Permeable air barrier at rim

Polyethylene air barrier

CAPPING AIR LEAKS AROUND LIGHTS

Recessed lights in the ceiling can produce air leaks. They should be capped with insulation or an insulated box to provide a seal. But make sure the box is made from noncombustible materials and is big enough to dissipate heat from the light. Otherwise, the "fix" becomes a fire hazard. An alternative is to use air-sealed fixtures rated for contact with insulation (IC-rated).

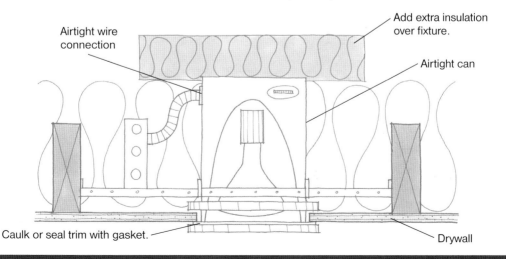

Airtight wire connection

Add extra insulation over fixture.

Airtight can

Caulk or seal trim with gasket.

Drywall

lighting is a great source of unintended leaks, and can lights should get a protective cap made from rigid foam insulation to prevent hot air from migrating through the top of the fixture into the attic (see the bottom drawing on p. 117). Or use the newer type of sealed recessed lighting.

Sheathing and Roof Membranes

Each layer of a roofing system—sheathing, tar paper (or other membrane), and the finished roof covering—has its own role to play as part of the roofing system. The roof deck itself is usually plywood or oriented strand board, and sometimes tongue-and-groove planks; of the three, OSB is the winner from the standpoint of sustainable building. It has one big advantage—it's made from wood fibers instead of whole medium- to large-diameter trees. Some exterior grades of OSB are extremely weather resistant and come with very long guarantees.

If you choose plywood, use exterior-grade labeled with "exterior 1" or "HUD approved." Phenolic resins make these panels moisture resistant. If they're available in your area, buy FSC-certified panels or plywood that's produced regionally.

After sheathing, comes a membrane that forms the primary weather barrier to protect the sheathing from water that might make its way through nail holes in the finished roofing material. This is usually 15-lb. or 30-lb. tar paper installed in overlapping courses from eave to ridge. However, products that are more specialized can replace tar paper. Among them

Roof sheathing made from oriented strand board is a better green choice than plywood because it makes efficient use of wood resources.

Cedar Breather is a 1/4-in.-thick nylon mesh applied over roofing felt that promotes air circulation behind wood shingles, prolonging the life of the roof.

are self-adhering bituminous membranes such as Grace Ice and Water Shield® and uncoated spun-bonded polypropylene barriers that work well with metal roofs.

Self-stick membranes have become very common, particularly in areas where ice dams are a potential problem. They are self-sealing around nails so that even when water backs up under roof shingles at the eave the roof won't spring a leak. One 3-ft. strip along the edge of the roof protects this vulnerable area from leaks; another strip can be used in valleys. The rest of the roof can be covered in tar paper. In high-wind or coastal areas, some builders cover every square inch of the sheathing with this membrane. It's good insurance against wind-driven rain.

Whatever type of membrane is used, it should be applied only on a dry roof deck and layered correctly (top course overlapping bottom course). Tar paper along the eaves should overlap the top of the drip edge—that is, put the drip edge on first here—but along rake edges the drip edge is put on after the membrane. Any water driven in along the edges will drain harmlessly away.

A detail where a roof abuts the sidewall of a house also helps prevent water damage.

Grace Ice and Water Shield, a self-adhering membrane, is an excellent weather barrier along eaves and in roof valleys. In areas where wind-driven rain and snow is a threat, it's sometimes applied to the whole roof deck.

Forming the bottom-most piece of step flash-ing to divert water away from the house (called kick-out flashing) protects this vulnerable spot for heavy rain runoff. A simple step pays big dividends. All wood trim and siding should be held at least 1 in. above the roofing to prevent rot.

Roofing Materials

Roofing materials include a wide range of manufactured and natural products—wood, slate, concrete, tile, and sheet metal among them. So what's important on a sustainable built house? Roofing should have a long service life with minimal maintenance and without contributing to any environmental degradation, either in how it's manufactured or in what it might leach into water runoff.

Asphalt shingles

No roofing material is more widely used than asphalt shingles, one of the least expensive options on the market. But buying cheap three-tab shingles rated for only 15 or 20 years is not a good green option. That's not a very long time in the life of a house, and shingles are rarely recycled. Buying shingles that you know will have to be replaced relatively quickly is simply adding unnecessarily to our already overburdened landfills and guarantees an expensive re-roofing job for the owners.

KICK-OUT FLASHING

This flashing detail at the intersection of a sidewall and the base of a roof helps prevent water damage and infiltration. It kicks water out and away from the building.

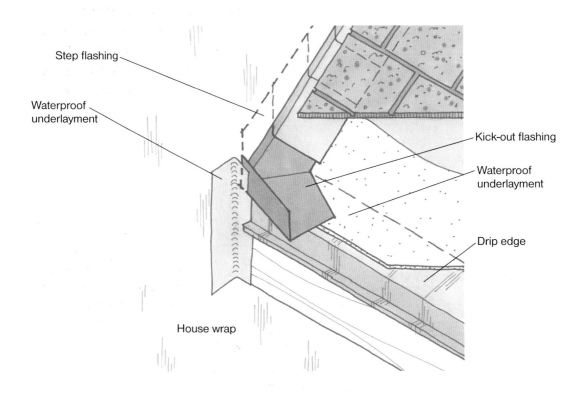

Step flashing

Waterproof underlayment

Kick-out flashing

Waterproof underlayment

Drip edge

House wrap

GUTTERS AND DOWNSPOUTS

There are all kinds of gutters to choose from—PVC, copper, galvanized steel, aluminum, wood—in both half-round and profiled versions. What's important is not so much what the gutter is made from but what it does to keep moisture away from the house. A roof without gutters dumps a tremendous amount of water right next to the house. If the foundation damp-proofing fails, the soil used to backfill around the house isn't porous enough, or the perimeter drains are missing or have failed, water may end up inside the basement. If nothing else, water dripping from the eaves can kick up a good deal of mud or sand on the sidewalls of the house, hastening decay.

Gutters help eliminate this potential for damage. Ideally, downspouts should be connected to an underground drain that runs to daylight. If that's not possible, slope the grade away from the house to help channel water away.

The diversity of materials used to make gutters makes it easy to get something that works with the house aesthetically. Seamless aluminum, made to order on the site, has no connections to leak and the aluminum can be recycled. That's a plus. Because the dies used to make the gutter are very expensive, most gutter installers are likely to offer only the ogee profile called K-style.

Spending more initially gets you a top-grade asphalt shingle that is thicker and heavier and will last more than twice as long (you can now find shingles with 50-year guarantees). Asphalt shingles are one of the most hail-resistant roofing materials available, a big plus in parts of the country susceptible to this kind of weather, and some are made with recycled or reclaimed material.

There is, of course, the concern that asphalt shingles are made with petrochemicals, some of which may leach from the roof with water runoff or escape as volatile organic compounds as the roofing sits in the sun. However, we have not found definitive studies on this question. As with other products that use petrochemicals, such as insulation, it is a judgment call as to whether you can consider

High-quality asphalt roofing shingles will last for many years and they perform well in regions where hail storms can damage other types of roofing materials.

asphalt roofing "green." At least in this case, using petrochemicals in a product designed for a long life seems more appropriate than burning them up in your car in a matter of minutes.

Some 11 million tons of waste asphalt roofing shingles are generated in the U.S. every year, according to an estimate from the California Integrated Waste Management Board. While there are efforts under way to recycle asphalt roofing shingles, they are slow in developing and not nearly as widespread as recycling for metals, plastics, and glass. Buying top quality shingles with a 50-year warranty is one way to minimize the problem.

Cedar shakes and shingles

Wood roof shingles share many of the same drawbacks as shingles used for siding. The best ones are manufactured from the sound heartwood of a rot- and insect-resistant species, often cedar—the very old-growth trees that we're trying to protect. Shingles are an expensive option, not only in terms of the material itself but also in the labor required to install them. Shingles are also made from southern yellow pine, which doesn't carry the same sustainability baggage as cedar. Yellow pine shingles have long warranties, but they are usually treated with preservatives, moss inhibitors, and fire retardants, raising the potential for chemical-laden water runoff and making disposal more problematic. Finally, there is the fire issue. Wood shingles are not permitted in some jurisdictions, even when chemically treated to have a Class A fire rating.

On the plus side, top grades of wood shingles can last a long time when installed properly. They are happiest when they can breathe. In an earlier day, builders promoted air circulation by laying shingles over "skip sheathing," which consisted of sheathing boards nailed to the rafters or purlins with an air space in between. Because of these gaps, shingles could dry to the inside. These days, we use panel products like plywood or OSB for roof decking and consequently shingles have a lower drying potential. It's good practice to use a breathable layer between the felt layer and shingles. One such product is Cedar Breather®, a 1/4-in. thick nylon mesh that aids air circulation and prolongs roof life (see the bottom photo on p. 118).

As long as you choose the material carefully, wood shingles can make a durable and attractive roof without the potential for chemical runoff. Make certain they are FSC-certified.

Metal roofing

There's a lot to like about metal roofing: long life; fire resistance; innovative coatings that resist fading, chipping, and chalking; and, in lighter colors, high reflectivity, which helps control heat gain. Steel roofing can contain up to 50 percent recycled content, while the lighter-weight aluminum roofing contains nearly 100 percent recycled content. Some designs work particularly well with solar photovoltaics (see p. 262). It's a relatively expensive but long-lasting choice.

Take care to maintain the finishes. On steel roofing, scratches that penetrate the coating and uncover bare steel will rust. In aluminum roofing, look for products with an anodized finish, which is environmentally preferable. It is baked on, not painted, so it's more durable.

All the pluses aside, stay away from copper and zinc-coated roofing materials. The production of copper is extremely polluting, and

copper leaches from roofs into streams where it is toxic to aquatic life. Galvanized steel's protective layer helps prevent rust by continuously releasing zinc, which is carried away by rain. It, too, is toxic to aquatic life. Some green building advocates are also concerned with the possibility that a polymer used to make Kynar® and Hylar® coatings on metal roofing is hazardous, although it is not clear whether this is a potential problem during manufacture, at the time of disposal, or during the service life of the roofing.

But on balance, as long as it's not copper or galvanized steel and pending more research on the toxicity question surrounding certain coatings, metal roofing has many green benefits.

Fiber cement composite

Typically made to look like slate or shingle, fiber cement consists of portland cement and

Cedar shingles and shakes make a beautiful and long-wearing roof, but the wood may come from sources that are not FSC-certified. Wood roofs are not permitted in all jurisdictions because of fire hazards.

cellulose fiber added for reinforcement and to reduce weight. Fiber cement shingles have shattering problems in regions with extreme temperature variations and frequent hail. If you don't live in hail country, fiber cement can be a good option. Just keep in mind that walking on

Overhangs help protect exterior walls. Many building scientists recommend a 2-ft. overhang around the entire building to make sure water stays away from the intersection of walls and soffits.

the roof tiles can crack them so replacement or maintenance is a little more challenging.

Clay tile

Clay tile (terra-cotta) is durable, attractive, and very popular in parts of the country such as California and Florida. The corrugated design has a cooling effect on the roofing system, as air is able to flow underneath the tiles. However, hail can shatter clay tile, so it is not the best option for northern climates, and it is difficult to walk on to repair for this same reason. Because they tend to outlast the buildings they protect, clay tiles may be reused depending on how they were installed. Clay tiles do not leach pollutants into runoff, making them water-friendly, but they can be heavy and require additional structural support.

Metal roofing has many green attributes, including low maintenance, high fire resistance, and durability. But avoid copper and zinc-coated roofing because rain runoff may be toxic to aquatic life.

Concrete

Concrete tile roofing reduces heat buildup, increasing occupancy comfort and decreasing air-conditioning bills. Made from portland cement and sand/aggregate, these tiles resemble clay tiles, shakes, or slate but cost a lot less. Although they require a large amount of energy to produce, concrete tiles offer a long life expectancy and require minimal maintenance, both key environmental benefits.

Slate

Slate is minimally processed cut or split rock that makes a very durable and attractive roof.

Slate poses no pollution threat from water runoff, has a good fire rating, and once installed requires little maintenance. Slate is a natural resource extracted from the earth, and it can easily be reclaimed and reused in other building projects. In areas where slate is readily available, it's not uncommon to strip slate from a dilapidated barn or outbuilding and reuse it on a brand new structure and still get many years of life out of it. The downside is that slate degrades in the presence of acid rain (sulfuric acid from coal-burning power plants). This can reduce the life expectancy of the material dramatically in areas like the Northeast.

Despite its many advantages, slate comes with a few caveats. Skilled installers can be tough to find. Slate is an expensive option, and walking on a slate roof can crack individual tiles so repairs, as well as installation, can be a challenge.

Recycled content roofing

Recycled synthetic shingles offer an alternative to materials such as cedar shingles and shakes, natural slate, clay or concrete tile, and

Clay tile is non-polluting and so long-wearing that it can outlast the building on which it's originally installed. But tiles are heavy, and because they are somewhat brittle not a good choice in hail country.

Concrete tiles have at least two green attributes— a long life and low maintenance. They can be made to look like slate or clay tile and they are less expensive, another plus.

standing-seam metal roofs. Recycled synthetic shingles have high ratings for hail and wind resistance, are good seismic and sound insulators, and are thus considered a very durable roofing option.

Shingles are made from various materials such as recycled plastic and cellulose fibers, tires, and industrial rubber. Not all of them have been tested for their impact on water quality, so keep that in mind if you're using a roof to harvest rainwater. A substrate of cementitious board, such as tile backer, improves fire resistance.

EPDM rubber

EPDM (ethylene propylene diene monomer) rubber is one of the most common, low-slope roofing materials in the United States, primarily because it is relatively inexpensive to install.

Slate makes an extremely durable roof and is a completely natural product, two very big green advantages. On the downside, it's very heavy and can crack under foot, making maintenance and roof work problematic. It's also expensive.

During and after installation it doesn't release odors and fumes as some other roofing materials do. It should be coated with a light-colored or reflective sealant to reflect heat and improve long-term performance.

Light Colors Reduce Heat Gain

In hot climates, a roof should minimize heat gain in the attic. Light-colored metal roofing with high Solar Reflectivity Index ratios

(SRI) acts as a radiant barrier to reflect the sun's rays. Raising the metal roof above the roof deck encourages airflow and prevents excess radiant heat from entering the building envelope. A layer of building felt acts as a vapor barrier underneath. Combined with a well-sealed insulated attic, this "shell" keeps out hot outside air and moisture, requiring less work on part of the air conditioners that may be located in the attics. A light-colored roof also tends to last longer because it doesn't expand and contract thermally as much as darker colors.

Using light-colored roofing also addresses an issue called "heat island effect." Heat from the sun that is soaked up by roofing and other building components can make dense urban neighborhoods warmer than undeveloped areas. Using light-colored roofs, or cool roofs as they are sometimes called, with a high SRI can offset the heat island effect and help mini-mize this phenomenon, a plus for animals as well as human occupants (for more information visit www.coolroofs.org).

Really Green Roofs

Another way to beat the heat island effect is to install green or vegetated roofs. Also known as living roofs or eco-roofs, they typically consist of a low-pitch roof with various roofing layers topped with a soil-like growing medium and

plants chosen for their ability to withstand a roof's extreme conditions. These roofs replace heat-absorbing materials with plants, shrubs, and small trees that cool air through evapo-transpiration (or evaporation of water from leaves). They act as an additional insulation layer to reduce summer heat gain and winter heat loss. The soil captures, filters, and slows roof runoff, and it extends the life of the roof itself by protecting the waterproof membrane from sunlight and punctures.

Vegetated roofs have a lot of green appeal—after all, what could be any greener than planting a field on top of your house? Aside from the high cost of this type of roof, the other complicating factor is making sure the vegetation and soil work are well suited to local conditions. It's not as simple as going down to the local garden center and buying flats of plants and sacks of growing medium. Both

A metal roof with an air layer separating it from the roof sheathing lowers heat buildup in the attic and makes the house easier to keep cool. A metal roof with a high reflectivity index also reduces solar gain.

- Use raised-heel trusses. If framing the roof with dimensional lumber, install a rafter plate to allow sufficient insulation at the eaves.

- In a cooling climate, use radiant-barrier roof sheathing.

- If ductwork runs through the attic, treat the attic as conditioned space by insulating both the rafters and the ceiling.

- Choose the most durable roofing material available that's appropriate to the climate. Avoid copper and galvanized metal roofing as well as inexpensive asphalt shingles.

- In cold-weather regions, protect the lower 3 ft. of the roof and valleys with a self-adhering bituminous membrane.

- Install an effective air barrier between any ceiling and an unconditioned attic. Seal any penetrations.

plants and soil must be matched very carefully to local climatic conditions. Soil depth can also be key. A shallow soil layer may not be enough to protect root systems from intense cold or may not hold enough moisture in dry areas to keep the roof healthy without additional watering. That can add dramatically to summer water use—a maintenance and resource conservation issue.

Yet there are big pluses as well. If the soil-plant layer has been chosen correctly, this vegetative layer lasts more or less indefinitely. With a layer of soil keeping out the sun's UV radiation, the EPDM membrane typically used as the base is protected against degradation. Cooling and heating loads will be somewhat less, and the roof undeniably adds some curb appeal to a green house.

A vegetated roof is green in many ways and when properly designed and constructed should last indefinitely. But selecting the right plants and soil is critical to success.

7

Windows and Doors

Windows and doors are our portals to the outside world. Their design and placement helps determine what our houses look like, and in that sense they represent an important marketing decision for builders and a design tool for architects. At the same time, windows in particular have a significant impact on energy efficiency and comfort. From a green-built standpoint, they rank second only to the design of an HVAC system in overall technological complexity.

Manufacturers have made tremendous strides in improving window technology. Today, windows are capable of providing energy performance we could only have dreamed of a decade ago. State-of-the-art windows incorporate high-performance glass, low-emissive

THE GREEN FACTOR

Doors and especially windows are technologically complex building components that make a big energy, as well as aesthetic, contribution to a house. Green building can take advantage of these technologies to make houses more comfortable and more energy efficient while reducing maintenance.

- Single-pane windows, common just a generation ago, have been replaced by a variety of new designs that incorporate multiple layers of insulating glass with reflective coatings.

- Frames made from aluminum- and vinyl-clad wood, extruded PVC, and fiberglass are more durable than frames made from plain wood and need less maintenance.

- Carefully chosen windows can make an energy contribution to the house.

- Installing windows and doors correctly will help eliminate air infiltration and water leaks, contributing to a longer life for the building and greater comfort.

Like insulation, windows are rated for their ability to resist the flow of heat. Instead of the familiar "R values," windows get "U values," the inverse of an R value (U = 1/R). As a result, the lower the number, the more energy efficient the window. Plain glass has a U value of 1, but the best-performing glass assemblies now rate at U 0.07, the equivalent of an R-14 wall.

coatings, insulating spacers, and improved frames with built-in thermal breaks to reduce energy losses. In fact, properly placed high-performance windows can be viewed as an energy asset rather than as a liability. Some have the insulating equivalent of an insulated 2x4 wall, and most fixed high-performance south-facing windows will actually gain more heat over the heating season than they lose. Windows, like insulation, are rated for their insulating value—a real help in choosing the right ones. Only in this case, the best of them have very low numbers.

The keys to reducing heat loss from windows and doors (and optimizing solar gain) are to select good quality, energy-efficient units and to ensure that installation minimizes air and water leaks around the outside of the frame.

There are three primary factors in a window's energy performance: frame construction, glass, and the spacer material that separates

Windows are generally not as energy efficient as walls, but the many improvements in glass and frame technology increase potential solar gain while minimizing air leaks and energy loss. Careful installation is key for both windows and doors.

HOW WINDOWS STACK UP

In both heating and cooling climates, windows can make a big difference in energy costs. Key factors include the U-value and the solar heat gain coefficient of the glass and whether the frame is insulated. With the right windows, savings can amount to hundreds of dollars annually.

HEATING SEASON

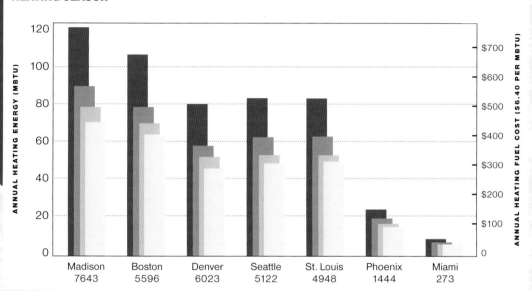

Madison	Boston	Denver	Seattle	St. Louis	Phoenix	Miami
7643	5596	6023	5122	4948	1444	273

WINDOW TYPE

 Single pane, clear
Aluminum frame
U = 1.30 • SHGC = 0.79

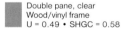 Double pane, clear
Wood/vinyl frame
U = 0.49 • SHGC = 0.58

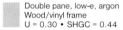 Double pane, low-e, argon
Wood/vinyl frame
U = 0.30 • SHGC = 0.44

Triple pane, low-e, krypton
Insulated vinyl frame
U = 0.15 • SHGC = 0.37

COOLING SEASON

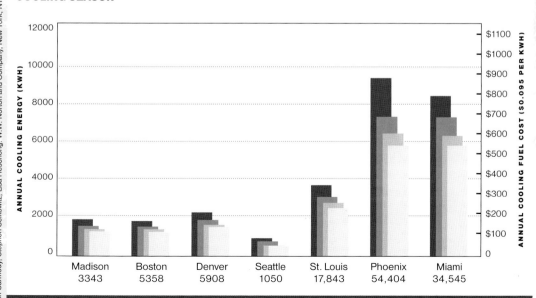

Madison	Boston	Denver	Seattle	St. Louis	Phoenix	Miami
3343	5358	5908	1050	17,843	54,404	34,545

Adapted from: *Residential Windows: A Guide to New Technologies and Energy Performance.* John Carmody, Stephen Selkowitz, Lisa Heschong. W.W. Norton and Company, New York, NY 1996. p.160

individual panes of glass. There is a potential for heat loss through windows in four ways:

- Through the glass (by radiation).
- Across the spacer material that separates the two glass layers at their edges and through the frame of the window (by conduction).
- Through the movement of air in the space between the glass (by convection).
- Between the moveable or operable frame components (by air leakage).

Choosing the right windows for a green home amounts to finding ones that minimize all of these potentials for energy loss. Although good windows aren't cheap, they are an important investment in long-term energy efficiency and comfort as well as lower maintenance and less frequent replacement.

Just as placing windows to maximize solar gain is a fundamental part of passive solar design, placing windows so they encourage natural ventilation is a benefit for indoor comfort.

RATING WINDOWS FOR PERFORMANCE

The National Fenestration Rating Council (NFRC) was formed to standardize the claims of energy efficiency by window manufacturers. Since "center of glass" U-values can be compromised by edge spacers, frame types, and air leakage, the NFRC created standard protocols for testing the whole window. The NFRC labels affixed to windows tell the whole story:

U-factor for the entire window, distinct from a center-of-glass rating.

Solar heat gain coefficient represents the amount of heat that is transmitted through the glass. The lower the number, the less heat transmittance.

Visible light transmittance is the "sunglasses" effect. The lower the number, the darker things will appear through the glass.

Air leakage is rated in cubic feet of air passing through a square foot of window area. The lower the number, the less air will pass through cracks in the assembly. This may be left blank by manufacturers of lower-quality windows.

Condensation resistance measures the ability of the window to resist condensation on the inside of the glass. The higher the number the better.

World's Best Window Co.	
Millennium 2000+	
Vinyl-Clad Wood Frame	
Double Glazing • Argon Fill • Low E	
Product Type: **Vertical Slider**	
ENERGY PERFORMANCE RATINGS	
U-Factor (U.S./I-P)	Solar Heat Gain Coefficient
0.35	**0.32**
ADDITIONAL PERFORMANCE RATINGS	
Visible Transmittance	Air Leakage (U.S./I-P)
0.51	**0.2**
Condensation Resistance	
51	**—**

National Fenestration Rating Council®
CERTIFIED

Manufacturer stipulates that these ratings conform to applicable NFRC procedures for determining whole product performance. NFRC ratings are determined for a fixed set of environmental conditions and a specific product size. NFRC does not recommend any product and does not warrant the suitability of any product for any specific use. Consult manufacturer's literature for other product performance information.
www.nfrc.org

NATURAL VENTILATION

Doors and windows that encourage airflow keep rooms more comfortable without the use of mechanical cooling equipment. Understanding prevailing winds on the site can help locate windows correctly. Casement windows are effective in scooping up breezes and directing them inside.

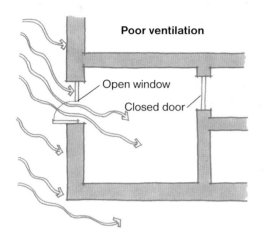

Poor ventilation

Open window

Closed door

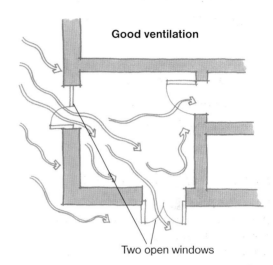

Good ventilation

Two open windows

Window Frames

Until fairly recently, wood was synonymous with residential window frames. It has a high warm and fuzzy quotient and a long architectural history. Problems include the potential for decay when exposed to harsh weather and sunlight. Manufacturers have addressed those problems by cladding the exterior part of the frame with aluminum or vinyl (a good use of both materials). Some wood windows today incorporate engineered materials like oriented strand board or particleboard for the core and wood veneer for the interior surface. That, too, is an advance, making the window more stable over time.

Wood windows are still a sign of quality and performance. But are relatively expensive and not a necessity when there are other options that perform as well at a lower cost. Depending on materials, quality of construction, brand, and where you buy them, wood-framed

Wood casement windows reduce heat loss through the frame and have good weatherstripping that reduces drafts.

windows can be two or three times as expensive as windows made with different kinds of frames.

Vinyl and composites

Cost-conscious builders make vinyl windows their first choice. Vinyl frames are extruded in many forms to create a wide diversity in style and energy efficiency. Vinyl has a similar energy efficiency or frame R-value as wood, so the two materials are competitive in that regard. The real difference lies elsewhere. Most vinyl windows expand in summer and contract in winter due to changes in outside temperature,

Windows with extruded vinyl frames can deliver high performance at a reasonable price. Look for weatherstripping that will compensate for vinyl's characteristic shrinking and expanding with changes in temperature.

Wood is a traditional material for window frames, but it's susceptible to decay and needs periodic maintenance. Frames clad in vinyl or aluminum are less prone to weather damage.

just like other plastics, which is exactly the opposite of what we want in a window frame. When the window frame contracts in the cold, weatherstripping can be pulled away to create drafts. A good-quality window will have two forms of weatherstripping to overcome this problem. If you live in a cold climate and your window supplier shows you a window with only one form of weatherstripping go somewhere else.

Composite materials address some of these issues. Andersen®, for example, uses vinyl scrap from its wood cladding line to create a proprietary material that is more stable that pure PVC. Milgard® makes a unique type of vinyl that offers high UV protection and resists the powdering that can affect standard PVC after years of exposure to the sun.

ARE VINYL WINDOWS GREEN?

That's a question with no definitive answer. Hard PVC products, like window frames and pipe, don't have the same plasticizers that make soft vinyl (flooring and shower curtains, for example) undesirable. In service, vinyl windows are not an environmental problem. Moreover, vinyl windows are durable and reasonably priced, which makes high-performance windows available to more homeowners. In those respects, good quality vinyl windows are green.

Manufacturing PVC, however, creates hazardous by-products, such as dioxin, and disposing of PVC at the end of its useful life is somewhat problematic because the material should not be incinerated. In the end, there is no black-and-white answer to the question of vinyl's "greenness." Like many other building products, it has characteristics that fall on both sides of the fence. Builders and homeowners have to weigh those factors and decide what works best for their own circumstances.

Fiberglass

Relatively new to the window market, fiberglass is a material tried and proven weather-worthy in the boat and car market. Window frames made from fiberglass are stable and energy efficient, and because they are made from spun glass they expand and contract exactly like the glass they hold. This reduces window failures due to extreme heat and cold. Some Canadian manufacturers even fill the hollow frames with urethane foam to increase the R-value, making them the best of the breed for cold climates. Fiberglass windows are often available with highly efficient glass so they are super energy efficient. There is a wider choice of colors in fiberglass than vinyl.

If there's a downside, it lies in the actual production of fiberglass, where workers handle solvent-based resins. But in service the windows are inert and overall they make an excellent green choice.

U-FACTORS FOR WINDOW-FRAME MATERIALS

FRAME MATERIAL	U-FACTOR
Aluminum (no thermal break)	1.9 to 2.2
Aluminum (with thermal break)	1.0
Aluminum-clad wood/reinforced vinyl	0.4 to 0.6
Wood and vinyl	0.3 to 0.5
Insulated vinyl/insulated fiberglass	0.2 to 0.3

Fiberglass window frames come in more colors than vinyl and the material has a history of durability in auto and marine markets. Frames show nearly the same thermal expansion and contraction as glass, an advantage.

Aluminum

Because aluminum window frames are so susceptible to thermal bridging, they are only appropriate in the mildest of climates. The primary market for aluminum windows is in commercial buildings and very inexpensive manufactured housing. At a minimum, the window frame should include a thermal break, an epoxy bond between the inner and outer layers of the frame to reduce heat loss via conduction. But even thermally broken windows don't come close to the energy performance of other materials. Avoid them.

Aluminum window frames should be avoided in all but the mildest climates. Thermal bridging reduces their thermal efficiency.

Glazing

What the industry calls glazing is really just glass, but coming up with energy-efficient designs has been anything but mundane. Enormous progress has been made in transforming a seemingly innocuous material into something that makes an energy contribution to a green house—as long as you know what you're looking for.

A single pane of glass has the insulating equivalent of R-1. It is the next best thing to an open hole in the wall. Millions of homes built before 1985 still have single-glazed windows, many of them in metal frames. They may stop the wind from whistling through the house, but contribute nothing to energy efficiency. In an existing home, they're a prime target for a window upgrade.

An obvious question for both builders and homeowners is whether the wealth of new technology in windows is worth the extra money. In a word, yes. But the many variables in pricing and distribution of high-performance windows make it hard to predict how much you're going to spend. At a minimum, a green house should have low-e, double-glazed, gas-filled windows. If the budget allows, go up a grade and buy windows with more advanced glazing and better insulated frames. In general, you should buy the best windows you can afford. Over time, the improved performance and greater indoor comfort they provide will prove a good investment. Remember, it's not hard to upgrade an inexpensive door but that's not the case with windows—they're built in. Make the right purchase the first time. You won't regret it.

Double-glazed windows

Double-glazing—often called sealed insulated glass—separates two panes of glass with an air space for better energy efficiency. On average, they are about R-2 (U-0.50) at the center of the glass, a measure of how well the glass itself reduces the flow of energy from one side to the other (the spacers that separate the glass at the edges of a window are another issue, which we'll deal with shortly). In a cheap

Double-glazed windows are much better thermal insulators than single-paned windows, but look for air space of ½ in. between sheets of glass.

window, the airspace is ¼ in., which doesn't really allow the window to take advantage of its double-pane construction. To get an R-2 rating, glass panels should be at least ½ in. apart.

Gas-filled windows

Although separating pieces of glass with airspace is a definite improvement over a single pane, the air can create a convective loop that lowers efficiency. Air on the hot side of the window rises while air on the cold side falls, creating a thermal conveyor that helps channel heat in or out of the house. To reduce this effect, argon and/or krypton gas is used to fill the space between the panes. These gases are heavier than air and less likely to create convective loops. As a result, insulating values are higher.

Low-e coatings

In the late 1970s, a revolutionary coating called spectrally selective glazing was introduced. For some wavelengths of light, the coating is transparent. In the lower part of the light spectrum, where infrared is found, the coating acts like a mirror. In practice, the coating reflects infrared energy back toward the warm side of the glass and transmits light in the visible band of the spectrum. Eventually, the coating became known as low-emissive glass, or just low-e for short.

LOW-E GLASS

Low-e coatings represented a big boost in window performance when they were first introduced. Coated glass allows the passage of visible light but reflects infrared energy toward the warm side of the glass to keep people more comfortable.

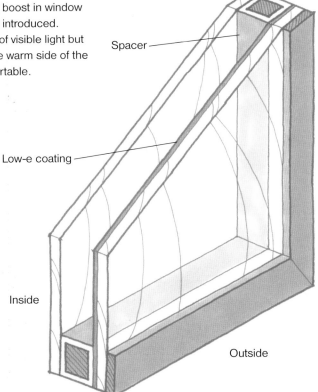

Spacer

Low-e coating

Inside

Outside

It was a breakthrough. Low-e coatings increase window R-values to 3 (U-0.33). Even though it has taken almost 30 years for low-e coatings to become mainstream, many manufacturers now offer low-e glass as standard and make non-coated glass available only as a special order. In almost any climate, low-e makes absolute sense. Beyond the improved U value, low-e makes the glass more comfortable for occupants. Stand in front of a window with non-coated glass on a cold night and you will feel the heat sucked out of your body as warmth is radiated to the colder surface of the window. A low-e window reflects body heat back at you, and you feel warm standing next to the window.

Today there are many forms of low-e coatings: low-e squared (two coatings of low-e) and now low-e cubed (three coatings). More sophisticated, high-performance coatings allow more visible light to pass through the window while blocking UV radiation. Cardinal Glass Industries, for example, says its low-e cubed 366 glass blocks 95 percent of UV to reduce solar gain and help glass stay warmer on the inside during winter.

BENEFITS OF ADVANCED GLAZING

Heat moves through windows from the hot to the cold side via radiation, convection, and conduction. Low-e coatings are designed to reduce heat loss through radiation while an air space between panes of glass in a double-glazed window reduces loss by conduction. Adding an inert gas, such as argon, to the center of the window reduces convection.

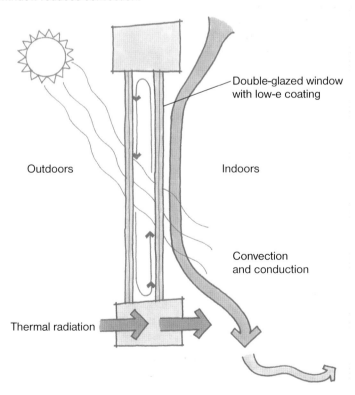

Double-glazed window with low-e coating

Outdoors

Indoors

Convection and conduction

Thermal radiation

Super energy-efficient windows

Double-glazed windows with low-e coatings and gas infill have gradually become more commonplace. They are a baseline choice for a green house. There are, however, higher-performing types of windows that offer superior energy efficiency.

Heat Mirror®

One high-tech improvement comes in the form of a thin film of high-transparency plastic suspended between two panes of glass. The technology was developed in the late '70s by a company called Southwall Technologies and is sold in a variety of forms as Heat Mirror. The film, in effect, creates triple glazing and provides two more surfaces for low-e coatings, raising the R-value of the window up to 7 (U-0.14). This starts to open up great architectural possibilities because it allows more wall area to be turned into glass without com-promising energy performance and without making the house uncomfortably hot. The proprietary film is produced regionally. Local production is key for cost-effectiveness.

Super windows

"Super windows" is a term for windows that go a step above the double-glazed, low-e windows. They integrate a variety of energy-efficient improvements with foam-filled fiber-glass frames and high-tech glazing. These windows start to approach the R-Value of a wall; prototypes are now available with center-of-glass R-values of 14 (U-0.07). You could install one in a shower and never have it steam up on the coldest of days while the fiberglass frame would prove impervious to rot.

If you can afford to incorporate these windows in the house, do it. A window with nearly the same R-value as the adjacent wall is absolutely worth it.

SUPER WINDOWS

Super windows combine a variety of advanced features, including highly insulated glass and foam-filled frames. R-values are as high as R-14.

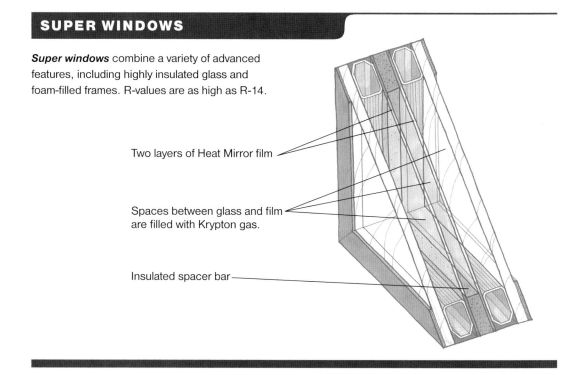

Two layers of Heat Mirror film

Spaces between glass and film are filled with Krypton gas.

Insulated spacer bar

Window spacers

Spacers that hold panes of glass apart, or serve as the frame for stretched plastic film, also play a role in the overall energy efficiency of the window. A spacer makes the seal that traps air or gas between the panes. In early double-pane windows, spacers could fail and allow air, moisture, and dust to collect on the inside of the window. That's rarely a problem today.

"Center of glass" U-values measure the thermal performance of the glass only. Windows also have U-values for the entire unit, which take into account heat loss through the edge of the windows as well as the frame. It's similar to the difference between an R-value of a given amount of insulation and the R-value of an assembled wall.

Spacers that separate panes of glass in multipane assemblies are generally made from metal or some kind of epoxy or composite. An epoxy type of spacer allows for thermal breaks and reduces heat loss at the edge of glass. Heat Mirror windows use an aluminum spacer to stretch the plastic film. This has greater heat loss, reducing the overall U-value of the window unit.

Metal window spacers *between panes of glass are more conductive than epoxy or composite materials, increasing thermal bridging and reducing window efficiency.*

ENERGY LOSS IN WINDOWS

Three factors largely determine the energy efficiency of a window: its frame, the insulating value of the glazing measured at the center of the glass, and the edges of multipane assemblies. High-quality windows minimize energy losses with a combination of glazing with low U-values, spacers with low conductivity, and a frame that reduces air leaks.

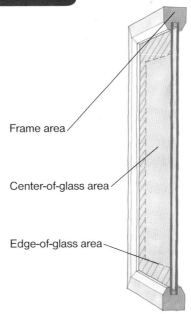

Frame area

Center-of-glass area

Edge-of-glass area

We don't shop for windows based on what type of spacers they incorporate, but if given the choice look for something with low conductivity. When installing fixed-pane super glass in a frame on-site or in a shop, cover the edge of the window with wood or urethane foam trim to help reduce heat loss from the spacer.

Canadian fiberglass triple-glazed

The frigid climate of our northern neighbor has encouraged Canadians to manufacture the best windows in North America. They have taken the best of fiberglass frame technology, filled the frames with foam insulation, and incorporated multiple low-e coated triple glazing for a window that outperforms 99 percent of U.S.-made windows. U.S. manufacturers have noticed, and they're starting to produce similar designs.

One disadvantage of triple panes of glass is that the increased number of layers affects solar gain through the window. For example, a triple-glazed window with ordinary glass reduces solar gain by 40 percent or more compared to a single-glazed window with the same glazing area. A double-glazed unit reduces solar gain by between 10 percent and 15 percent. This is fine for east, west, and north windows but starts to inhibit passive solar gain on the south side of the home where we want it. South-facing glass with a Solar Heat Gain Coefficient of 0.3 or lower requires twice as much glass to capture the same amount of heat. In other words, windows should be "tuned" for their specific orientation.

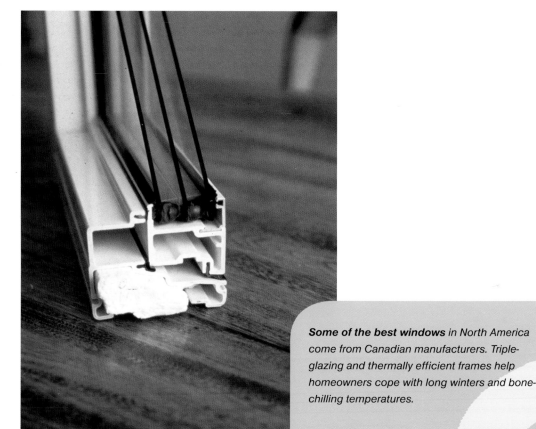

Some of the best windows in North America come from Canadian manufacturers. Triple-glazing and thermally efficient frames help homeowners cope with long winters and bone-chilling temperatures.

WINDOW TUNING

Window glass is increasingly designed for low solar heat gain, which can present challenges for a passive solar builder. A builder trying to "tune" a house with windows would choose high solar heat gain windows on the south side and low solar heat gain on east and west walls. The reason? South-facing windows with high solar heat gain allow the interior of the house to soak up more of the sun's heat, reducing heating costs, while low-gain windows on east and west walls tame morning and afternoon sun in summer. Northern exposures aren't as critical for solar gain, but the best choice here is the lowest U-value possible. High solar heat gain windows are often a special order these days.

MORE GLASS, LESS LIGHT

More glass usually means better thermal insulation and more places to add low-e coatings. The corollary, however, is less visible light transmittance and a lower heat gain coefficient. For south-facing windows in a passive solar design, windows with high solar heat gain should be specified so the house can take advantage of potential solar energy.

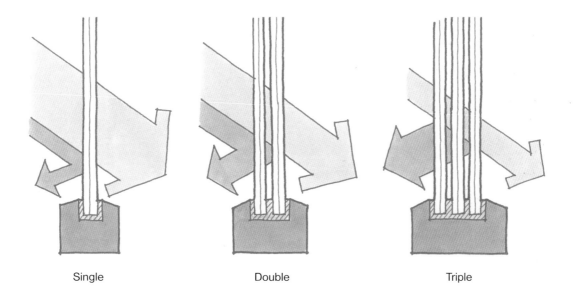

Single   Double   Triple

Preventing Air and Water Leaks

Air leaks in the building envelope waste energy and make a house drafty and uncomfortable, which is why we spend so much time and effort creating an effective air barrier. Why blow that with the wrong windows? The object in a green house is to choose windows with a low potential for air leaks and make sure they are installed correctly. Windows with the lowest leakage rates, regardless of type, tend to be *fixed* windows, that is, windows you can't open. Operable windows come in many types but those with the fewest leaks are awning, casement, and similar types that have a closure mechanism that pulls the sash against a compression gasket.

Air leaks can also be a big problem if a window is poorly installed in the rough opening. If the space between the window frame and the rough opening isn't sealed with caulk or foam insulation, air will leak through the gap. This space should be insulated and sealed before the window trim is attached.

If the house is going to spring a leak—of either air or water—it's most often going to be around doors and windows. Flashing details discussed in the roofing and siding chapters apply especially to windows. Common practice is to install housewrap first and the windows later. But this can leave the top flange of the window over the housewrap, presenting a lip that will catch water that then gets behind the siding. Once inside, the water can flow behind the window into the framing and create a watering device for mold colonies. Eventually, this causes rot.

Window and door flashing is available from DuPont and Grace Building Products, among others, that's designed to prevent this kind of problem. These specialized tapes seal the top flange to the housewrap to prevent

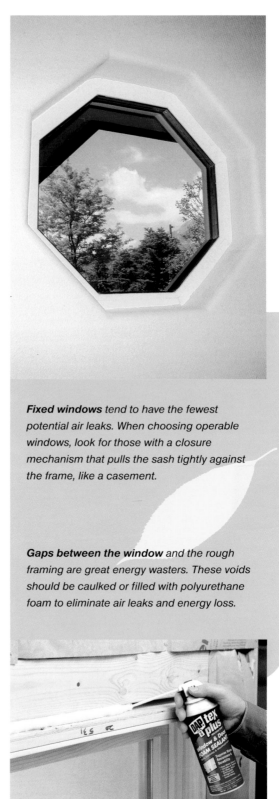

Fixed windows tend to have the fewest potential air leaks. When choosing operable windows, look for those with a closure mechanism that pulls the sash tightly against the frame, like a casement.

Gaps between the window and the rough framing are great energy wasters. These voids should be caulked or filled with polyurethane foam to eliminate air leaks and energy loss.

INSTALLING A WINDOW

Even the best window will perform poorly if it's not installed to keep out water. Installation is a four-step process that guarantees that any water that finds its way past the siding will be directed out and away from the building.

STEP 1

Sill flashing folded over the bottom of the rough opening and up at each end

Fasten the top edge of the flashing to the wall sheathing below the sill but leave the lower edge unattached for now.

Wall sheathing

Extend flashing horizontally 16 in. beyond the edge of the rough opening.

12 in. minimum

STEP 2

Fold jamb flashing around the side of the rough opening and over upturned sill flashing.

Jamb flashing on both sides of the rough opening should extend beyond the sill flashing and above the point where head flashing will intersect it. Lap jamb flashing over the sill flashing but leave the bottom edge unattached.

STEP 3

To seal the window frame to the opening, apply a continuous bead of caulk on the back of the window flange near its outer edge, or apply the bead on the opening so it contacts the flange when the window is installed.

After installation, seal all corners that are mechanically joined.

Shim and adjust window so it's plumb and level.

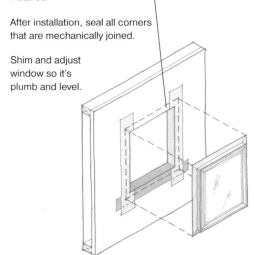

STEP 4

Install drainage plane over head flashing and over the top of window flange.

Slip drainage plane beneath jamb flashing and sill flashing at bottom of window.

4-in. minimum horizontal laps

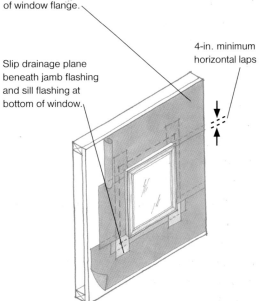

water infiltration at this vulnerable intersection. Good custom builders have been using it for years. Production builders in many parts of the country still treat it as a luxury product and skip that step. It's also best practice to lap the housewrap or tarpaper over the top edge of the window flange (or window head flashing) by cutting a horizontal slit in the house wrap at the right height to accept the flange. This makes a water-shedding connection that will be effective even if the tape fails.

Metal windows in basements

Putting windows into concrete basement walls typically means forming a metal buck, or frame, into the concrete and filling it with a single-pane steel window—a sorry excuse for a window and a hole in the concrete that exhausts heat. And because many homeowners finish their basements at some point, these windows become a very cold and unpleasant element in a children's playroom, the TV room, or a guest room.

Self-adhering flashing is an excellent hedge against water infiltration that can lead to structural damage. It should be standard.

The thermal quality of windows installed in a basement wall should be of the same quality as in the rest of the house. Single-glazed windows with metal frames waste energy.

REPLACEMENT WINDOWS

Old windows can suffer from a long list of problems—single glazing that wastes heat, inadequate weatherstripping that lets in drafts, wood frames that are cracked or degrading from exposure to weather and sunlight. It's no wonder that a whole industry has sprung up around replacing old windows with new ones. From a green standpoint, window performance rather than aesthetics should be the driving factor in selecting new windows.

Depending on the type of existing window and its original installation, it can be difficult to get access to the head flashing or to seal air leaks between framing members and window jambs. Rot around window openings may be difficult to see.

The best bet is to identify a test window, then remove it to explore conditions around the opening. A north window is often a good choice because it must endure the most challenging weather conditions without the benefit of direct sunlight that would dry out damp wood. Removing trim and carefully examining framing, jambs, and flashing should make it clear whether problems can be corrected by replacing only the sash. It's some-times better to replace the entire window—frame and all—even if it means a more extensive repair.

All new windows in any climate should be low-e. Selecting a frame type will typically be driven by aesthetics or budget. But avoid the least expensive vinyl windows. You get what you pay for, and they may not hold up after several years of duty.

Older windows with leaky weather-stripping and single glass panes are good candidates for replacement.

So the greenest thing you can do is to avoid that approach. Anything else is better. Preferably, use a wood form that can serve as the frame for a window of the same quality as in the rest of the house. At a minimum, use a low-e vinyl window because it will stand up to the moist conditions near grade. Double-glazed models are a minimum. Make basement windows big enough so they meet code requirements for egress in bedrooms so that option is open to homeowners in the future. Get as much natural light into the basement as possible, which means going beyond a C-shaped steel window well and looking at the variety of other products on the market designed to open the angle of view to the outside.

Insulating Windows Themselves

One of the best ideas to come out of the solar age of the late '70s and early '80s was moveable window insulation. The idea is to let in light and open up views during the day while you're using the room, then close off the window with an insulating layer when the room is unoccupied or at night. Heavy curtains can help in any house, but this works best when the edges are sealed to the window casing to reduce convective currents behind the curtains. Otherwise, air is cooled as it makes contact with the window, falls to the floor, and feels like a draft at your feet. Then it rises as it warms to repeat the process.

Hunter Douglas® makes a product called Duette® that incorporates an insulating airspace between two layers of fabric. Other approaches include moveable panels of fabric, covered rigid foam, and exterior motorized shutters that automatically open and close depending on sunlight and temperature with a manual override. Products like these are great. No matter what type of windows you install,

Insulated window coverings are an excellent way of reducing energy losses, particularly at night when temperatures are low or when rooms are unoccupied.

they will have greater heat loss than adjacent walls. Anything you can do to reduce that heat loss when the window isn't actually in use will keep people in the house more comfortable and lower energy costs. This is especially true in a retrofit where outright window replacement is not in the cards.

Skylights and Light Tubes

Essentially, a skylight is an R-3 hole in an R-30+ roof. On a pitched roof, skylights allow only diffuse light into the house during the winter and direct light in the summer—just the opposite of what's best in a heating climate

Tubular skylights get natural light into rooms without exterior walls. Tubes that pass through unconditioned spaces should be insulated.

and just the opposite of what south-facing vertical windows can do. That said, the natural daylight that skylights provide takes the place of electric lighting that would otherwise be needed during the day. At a minimum, skylights should be the type that are made with low-e glass, never the "single bubble" variety.

Light tubes direct daylight to areas like bathrooms and hallways in the core of the house and have the potential to reduce the heat loss associated with skylights. The outside is still connected to the inside, however, by a metal tube that can act as a thermal bridge. If light tubes run through an uninsulated attic, the tube itself should be insulated with duct insulation to reduce heat loss and gain. Typically, light tubes are less expensive and more energy efficient than skylights and therefore a better bet for a green house.

Doors

Doors come in almost too many styles to count and in a wide range of materials—fiberglass, wood, wood composites, vinyl, and metal. Because in-service conditions are so different for entry doors and interior passage doors, criteria for making the best green choice vary. But, in general, choosing the best door is similar to evaluating any other building material. The best of them are durable and made from materials that don't adversely affect the human or natural environment. In the case of exterior doors, weather-tightness, insulating value, and installation are additional considerations.

Entry doors

Entry doors are more ornamental than they are energy efficient. A solid-core door is about R-1 per inch and sometimes less when composition material is used. Seen in that light, entry doors have about the same insulating potential as a double-glazed window but with more opportunity to leak air. By adding a storm door, the efficiency goes to R-3 but doors still lose eight times the energy of an R-24 wall. Given the fact we have to have doors that may seem tolerable, and because doors aren't usually adjacent to sitting areas in the house the impact of this inefficiency is lower. But if we are going for all the conservation we can get, entry doors represent an opportunity to do better.

Insulated steel or fiberglass entry doors are several times more energy efficient than a solid wood door. Of the two, fiberglass is more impact resistant and less likely to show dings

A wood entry door, though attractive, will not have the same insulating value as a good quality window and represents a real potential for energy loss. Insulated fiberglass or steel doors are more efficient.

and dents and conducts less heat than a metal-skinned door. Manufacturers have learned to give fiberglass door facings realistic wood-grain patterns that when stained look surprisingly like the real thing. If you're going the traditional route with a solid wood door, look for one that's made from wood that's reclaimed or sustainably harvested.

Even a well-insulated entry door with high-quality weatherstripping is not as energy efficient as a well-insulated wall. One solution is to include a mudroom or entry "airlock" that helps buffer the rest of the house from the relatively low thermal performance of the door itself. Houses in northern climes often include mudrooms where you can take off your boots, hang up hat and coat, and jump into a pair of cozy slippers before entering the house. A mudroom also serves a wonderful thermal purpose: When you open the door to the outside, only the conditioned air in the mudroom escapes. It functions as an airlock. That's why revolving doors make so much sense in commercial settings.

Sliding glass doors

Sliding glass doors are just windows that are large enough to walk through. All of the considerations for choosing windows apply here. Wood frames clad with vinyl or aluminum will stand up in the long term and offer greater comfort; low-e glass should be standard. The biggest variable is how well the weatherstripping between the doors actually works. Sliders are notorious for letting in cold air. There should be a positive seal between the fixed and sliding units, and a double weather seal inside and out along the track and the jamb that captures the door when closed. Sliding doors with super glass from Canada are also available in northern markets.

Mudrooms offer practical storage for coats and muddy boots while providing an "airlock" that helps to minimize energy losses and drafts.

Sliding glass doors are essentially big windows, so using the same benchmarks for choosing them will help conserve energy and make the house more comfortable. Effective weatherstripping is key.

Installing doors

Doors are most vulnerable at the sill where they are more exposed to water and snow. Typically, a door is installed so the sill rests directly on the subfloor with a bead of caulk or construction adhesive providing a seal. It's better to install doors more like windows; that is, with a sill pan to protect the subfloor from water and flexible flashing at the jamb to protect the wood. The head of the door flashing should be tucked under the house wrap to provide a positive drain for water. In this way, the entire opening is water-proofed. Spray foam should then be applied between framing and door-jambs to eliminate any air infiltration.

SEAL POTENTIAL LEAKS

Installing a door takes the same care as putting in a new window. Urethane foam between the jamb and rough framing eliminates potential air leaks.

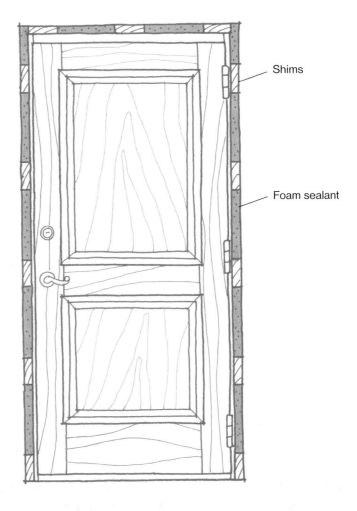

Shims

Foam sealant

Doors should be installed like windows to reduce the risk of moisture infiltration and air leaks. Use a sill pan beneath the door, self-adhering flashing at the jambs, and expanding urethane foam to seal the door in the rough opening.

Interior doors

Interior doors come in many styles and materials, from solid wood to hollow-core flat panel. When buying solid wood doors, look for ones made with FSC-certified wood. Many are now imported from offshore and manufactured from wood of unknown origins. This is a global problem because in places such as Indonesia, Borneo, and Vietnam, wood is illegally harvested and sold on the black market. Although the wood is beautiful when finished, these tropical trees rarely regenerate once the forest has been devastated.

Luan is a classic example. It has been used for so many years as a skin for hollow-

core doors that we don't think twice about where it came from. Harvesting this species has led to thousands of square miles of clear-cuts, mountain sides denuded and ravaged by erosion. Erosion has turned once-clear rivers into seas of mud, which not only destroys the ecosystems where the trees were cut but also ocean habitats where rivers empty into the sea. Typically, U.S. markets drove this type of operation for decades. But on moral grounds, a luan door has no place in a green home.

Another undesirable feature of hollow-core doors is that they are glued together with urea formaldehyde adhesives, one more product that contributes to low indoor air

In choosing interior doors, stay away from hollow-core doors made with luan mahogany and medium-density fiberboard that uses urea-formaldehyde as a binder.

quality and a growing health challenge for our children.

Another option for interior doors is medium density fiberboard (MDF), which can be made to look just like a paneled wood door that's been painted. MDF doors are heavy, so they have a solid feel when they're open and closed, and they're dimensionally stable. But conventional MDF is made with urea-formaldehyde binders that are detrimental to indoor air quality. Avoid MDF doors unless you can find ones that are manufactured with a different type of binder.

8

Plumbing

What could be green about plumbing? We all know that liquids flow downhill and cold should always be on the right. There may have been a day when a plumber's life was that simple, but no longer. Plumbing systems are often complex, fixtures and materials more varied, and the potential for water and energy conservation greater than ever.

Those twin conservation issues are really at the heart of a plumbing system in a green-built home. Heating water for domestic use accounts for as much as 30 percent of residential energy consumption—an almost incomprehensible number on a national scale. Yet lots of that energy goes right down the drain because conventional plumbing systems make people stand by the shower or sink and wait for hot water. Water heaters themselves are another area where making the right decisions can add up to substantial savings in energy use over the life of the appliance.

Water conservation is no less important. The availability of clean water is becoming a critical issue for the planet. Only 1 percent of

THE GREEN FACTOR

Plumbing is more than a network of pipes, drains, and fixtures. What makes plumbing worthy of attention in a green-built home is the potential for water and energy savings:

• Changing climate and weather patterns, along with a steady increase in the demand for clean water, are powerful incentives for plumbing systems that are more efficient and waste less water.

• Potential savings in water in an average household amount to thousands of gallons per year—with no loss of performance or convenience.

• Energy for domestic hot water makes up a substantial portion of overall energy consumption in most households. By minimizing wasted hot water, energy bills are lower and loads on the energy grid are reduced.

Applying off-the-shelf green technology to conventional plumbing systems isn't complicated but presents many opportunities for both water and energy conservation.

Water may seem abundant in many parts of the country, but a growing population coupled with changing climate and rainfall patterns will put an increasingly high price on this finite resource.

the water on the planet is drinkable and much of that is polluted. If you live in a region where rain and groundwater are plentiful, parts of the Pacific Northwest, for example, the idea that there's a water shortage may seem laughable at times. But pretending that supplies of water are inexhaustible is the short view. It is now a problem in some regions of the country and climate change is likely to make that worse in the future, not only in the U.S. but also globally. Some regions are likely to become wetter while others, like the Rocky Mountain West, will become dramatically drier. We no longer have the luxury of taking clean water for granted. Adopting building strategies that save water and energy is simply a sensible reaction to the reality that confronts us.

Heating water accounts for between 15 percent and 30 percent of a household's total energy consumption. In 2001, 107 million households consumed 1.68 quadrillion BTUs' worth of energy to heat water, worth about $21.6 billion.

WASTED WATER

In most households, wasted water adds up to tens of gallons per day, thousands of gallons per year. On a national scale, poor plumbing design and water-guzzling fixtures probably result in 330 billion gallons of wasted water per year. Sound like too much? Do the math, assuming there are 90 million homes each wasting 10 gallons a day, 365 days a year. It adds up to 500,000 Olympic-size swimming pools' worth of water! If each home saved 20 gallons of water each day, in one year 7,300 gallons of water would be saved. Energy costs would be reduced by $151 (natural gas water heating) to $242 (electric water heating).

Distributing Hot Water Efficiently

A lot of energy is used up just getting hot water from one place to another, from a water heater in a mechanical room or basement to the shower where it's ultimately used. Where bathrooms and the kitchen are located in relation to the mechanical room is a good place to start in designing a more efficient plumbing system. When these rooms can be brought closer together, and as close to the water heater as possible, greater efficiencies are possible. It makes the installation of supply and drain lines less expensive because runs are shorter, and it reduces the delivery time of hot water to showers and sinks. In houses with full basements, stacking the plumbing above the water heater makes a lot of sense.

Then there is the distribution system itself, the network of supply lines that carries water around the house. In a conventional trunk and branch system, ¾-in. copper or plastic lines are the main "trunks" and ½-in. "branch" lines distribute water to individual fixtures. These systems, however, do not optimize water flow and as a result lead to unnecessary heat loss in hot water lines. The longer the pipe, and the larger its diameter, the slower the velocity of water moving through the line and the greater the energy loss. Low flow rates (less than 1 gal. per minute) waste more energy than high flow rates (greater than 4 gal. per minute) because water in the lines has more time to shed heat. A lack of insulation around hot water lines, plus the use of sharp 90-degree bends to turn corners, means even more heat loss and waste.

The ideal plumbing configuration uses the smallest volume (shortest possible length and smallest possible diameter) line from the source of hot water to the fixture.

PEX piping over copper

Copper was once the gold standard in residential plumbing. You'll still find copper waste lines in some older houses, but PVC has gradually taken over that role even as copper has remained a first choice among many plumbers on the water supply side. But that's changing. In addition to its high cost, copper can also be attacked by acidic water to the point where it will spring leaks. It does have the advantage of being completely recyclable—so much so that rising commodity prices have made it profitable for thieves to remove entire plumbing systems from seasonal houses when owners aren't around.

Pipe made from cross-linked polyethylene (PEX) has a number of advantages and

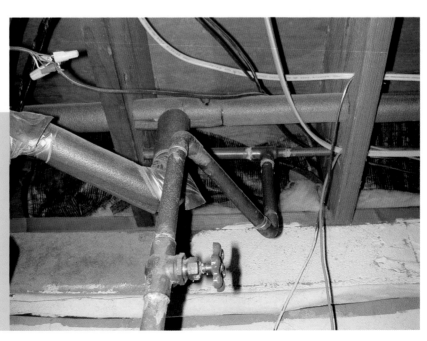

Copper pipe is not only expensive but it can develop pinhole leaks when water is acidic. In addition, a plumber has to solder in a fitting whenever the pipe changes direction, a time-consuming process that adds to construction costs.

Tubing made from cross-linked polyethylene *(PEX) is a greener alternative to copper and PVC tubing. It's faster and cheaper to install because it can bend around corners without an extra fitting and the plastic is highly durable.*

PEX tubing *lends itself to home-run systems, which route water to individual fixtures from a common manifold. One disadvantage with this approach is the increased difficulty of adding an on-demand hot-water circulation system.*

is beginning to take copper's place. Its flexibility allows it to turn corners so supply lines don't have to be interrupted with elbows that are time-consuming to solder in and increase the potential for leaks. PEX is not affected by acidic water as copper is, and it can be used for both hot and cold water supply systems. Because it's easier to install, a laborer rather than a plumber can do the work. That makes it popular among production builders because it reduces construction costs. Because of all these advantages, PEX is a good choice in a green house.

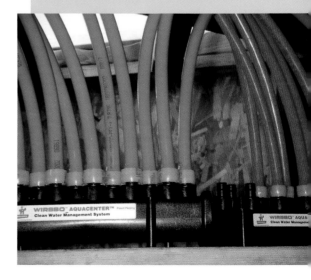

The unique properties of PEX tubing allow it to be configured in a number of different plumbing system designs, including the typical trunk and branch system. It is often installed in home-run configurations in which water is routed to a central manifold and then to individual fixtures. A manifold allows all water shut-offs to be located in a single convenient location.

Water Heaters

Tank-type water heaters are commodity appliances; most run on either electricity or gas. Within both categories, the length of the warranty is a good benchmark for overall quality. Water heaters can last longer than the warranty period, but once you hit that mark it's time to start watching for leaks. In this context, it's better to buy the heater with the longer warranty. Although this doesn't make much apparent sense to someone who plans to be in a house for a short amount of time, there's a lot of embodied energy in producing a water heater. It's wasteful to buy appliances that wear out prematurely.

From an energy standpoint, tank water heaters are rated based on their energy factor (EF). This is a measure of the unit's overall energy efficiency based on the amount of hot water produced over a typical day. The EF takes into account:

- how efficiently the source of energy is converted into hot water

- how much energy is lost from the tank per hour (the standby loss)

- cycling losses as water circulates through the water tank and/or inlet and outlet pipes

The higher the EF, the more efficient the heater. Look for a model with an EF of at least

Tank-style water heaters don't have to be energy hogs. Make sure the tank is appropriately sized for the household and ask for a California builder's model, which has a thick layer of insulation to reduce standby heat losses.

0.60. Electric water heaters generally have higher EF ratings than gas-fired water heaters, but it still costs more to heat the water with electricity than it does with gas.

The energy factor is only one consideration in purchasing a water heater. Sizing the heater to the load is also important. Not only do water heaters work better when they are sized properly, but the more they are used the longer they last. When water tends to sit in the tank without being circulated, standby losses are higher and the tank is more likely to corrode.

No matter what kind of water heater you end up installing, lower the set temperature to 120°F to save energy.

LIFECYCLE COSTS

In determining the best deal for an appliance, consider its initial cost, how much energy it will use annually, its overall efficiency, and how long the appliance is likely to last. These "lifecycle costs" vary considerably when it comes to hot water heaters, ranging from a low of $1,900 for an indirect water heater connected to a high-efficiency gas or oil boiler all the way to $5,680 for a conventional electric storage tank, according to the American Council for an Energy-Efficient Economy. Also near the bottom of the lifecycle cost list are high-efficiency, on-demand gas heaters ($2,370), and high-efficiency gas storage tanks ($2,566).

A gas-fired water heater will cost thousands of dollars less to operate over its lifetime than an electric water heater. But the level of insulation around the tank is also key. A little known option is to buy a California builder model water heater; these water heaters are made by all large manufacturers and available in both gas and electric models. Because California's energy code is among the most stringent in the country, major manufacturers make a water heater with R-15 insulation rather than the typical R-6 insulation just for that market. It may take an additional week or two for your installer to get one, but it will be only slightly more expensive and it will have a higher EF.

RIGHT-SIZING THE HOT WATER HEATER

Overly large water heaters aren't as efficient or long-lasting as correctly sized appliances. How big is that? It depends on what kind of fuel the water heater uses. According to the American Society of Heating, Refrigeration and Air-Conditioning Engineers (ASHRAE), a three-bedroom home with 2 or 2.5 bathrooms should have a 40-gallon gas-heated tank, a 50-gallon electric tank, or a 30-gallon oil-fired tank. If you use a tank-type indirect heater, it should have a 60-gallon capacity.

On-demand heaters

On-demand or tankless water heaters run only when someone turns on a hot water tap. When water starts flowing through the heater, an electric or gas-fired element is activated and water is heated as it flows through the device. When the tap is shut off, so is the heater. One obvious advantage is that there are no standby losses, which in a tank-type heater can account for as much as 15 percent of the total water-heating bill. Assuming the heater is sized correctly, you won't run out of hot water, and a tankless heater can be mounted on a wall or ceiling to free up more floor space.

On-demand heaters run on gas or electricity. Of the two, gas is more economical. Electric tankless heaters draw a lot of current and may require an expensive upgrade to the main panel.

One disadvantage of tankless heaters in general is that they can be three or four times as expensive as a tank heater. If you install the California version of a tank heater, standby losses are sharply reduced, making the benefits of a tankless heater that much less dramatic. Moreover, there's an argument to be made that having unlimited hot water encourages people to take longer showers, thereby reducing energy savings they might have gained.

Indirect heaters

Indirect heaters, sometimes called sidecar heaters, look like conventional tank heaters but the water is heated by a loop from a gas- or oil-fired boiler. One advantage is obvious—you don't have a separate heating element just for the water. Instead, the device uses hot water the boiler is already producing for a hydronic heating system, at least during the winter. Indirect heaters also have the lowest lifecycle costs of any type of heater because they last longer (30 years compared to an average of 13 for some types of tank heaters). They have annual energy costs that rival those for high-efficiency on-demand gas heaters, but they cost much less. The down side is that the boiler runs all summer and is oversized for just domestic hot water purposes so it uses more energy than necessary.

Tankless water heaters begin working as soon as they sense water flow. Without a tank, these models eliminate standby heat loss.

Indirect water heaters that are connected to a gas- or oil-fired boiler and heat domestic water with a heat exchanger have some of the lowest lifecycle costs.

One way to take advantage of tankless heaters is to use them for both domestic hot water and space heating. This can be particularly effective if you are building an addition that requires additional heat, say, a new master bedroom suite. Because of its compact size, a tankless heater can be placed near the bathroom, reducing the length of plumbing runs, and used to heat the space as well as provide hot water.

Eliminating the Wait for Hot Water

In our got-to-have-it-now culture, waiting for hot water is an inconvenience that many people just aren't willing to accept. And standing by the shower while hot water arrives from a distant water heater is more than an inconvenience—it wastes a lot of water and energy. There are several options to beat this delay:

- Circulation systems that keep hot water ready in the line so it's there when you need it.
- Systems that use a timer and thermostat to control when hot water is circulated.
- On-demand systems that pipe hot water to the bathroom quickly just before it's needed.

Among them, constant circulation systems are the least advantageous from an energy standpoint. Yes, hot water is always present, but you'll pay a high price for this convenience. Hot water lines become an extension of the hot water tank, meaning the system is going to show even greater standby losses than a tank alone. Because waterlines are rarely insulated, they are constantly losing heat to the crawlspace, basement, or chilly joist cavities. Even when the pipes are insulated, a circulation pump is running almost constantly causing a parasitic electrical use. Time and temperature

systems are an improvement, but they do not reduce energy costs.

For that, you'll need an on-demand system. A good old American ingenuity solution is the Metlund® pump. It is an on-demand hot water circulation system activated just before hot water is actually needed. When the system is turned on, a small pump pushes hot water to the point of use faster than it would if the water had to pass through a constricting faucet

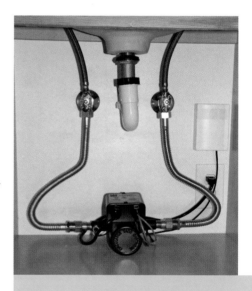

An on-demand water circulation system gets hot water to a distant bathroom quickly just before it's needed. Unused water is re-circulated instead of going down the drain, eliminating most of the wait and all of the waste.

WAITING FOR WATER

According to Gary Klein, an energy specialist with the California Energy Commission, our houses are bigger and more wasteful than they were a generation ago. Since 1970, the median U.S. house grew from 1,600 sq. ft. to 2,400 sq. ft. and the distance to the farthest fixture increased from 30 ft. to 80 ft. The number of hot water fixtures grew from 6 to 12. The result? Larger pipe area, reductions in water velocity, lower flow rates at individual fixtures, and increased distances all add up to waiting 18 times longer for hot water today than we used to. That's progress?

or shower head, thus reducing heat loss and waiting time. In new construction, a dedicated return line carries the unused water back to the water heater, eliminating water waste. In an existing system, a valve and pump located between hot and cold water lines under the sink allows the cold water line to be used as a return.

Because the pump is activated only when hot water is actually needed, there are no

ON-DEMAND WATER CIRCULATION

An on-demand system, like those designed by Metlund, pipes hot water to a shower or sink only when it's called for, returning the water that's still warming up to the hot water tank instead of allowing it to go down the drain. At the heart of the system is a pump that can be activated in one of several ways. With the hot water supply primed, water is available at the tap almost instantly. In new construction, a dedicated return line recirculates water. In a retrofit, the cold water line is used as the return with the help of a special valve.

Dedicated Return Line

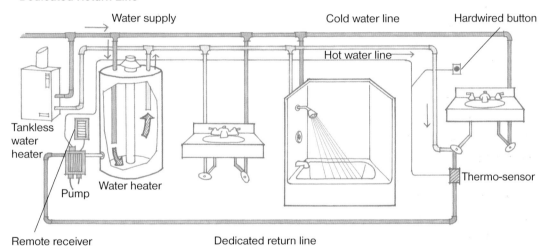

Cold Water Return Line

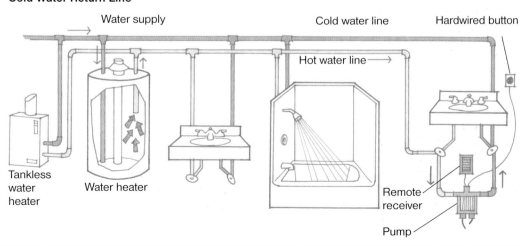

standby losses in the line. This system is not readily adaptable to a manifold plumbing design. But in a trunk and branch system where installation is straightforward and not very expensive, an on-demand system saves both energy and water and it makes a good investment.

Insulate All Hot Water Pipes

A misconception among builders is that pipes don't need to be insulated because they run inside the envelope of the house. What makes this reasoning faulty is that unless a great job of insulation and air sealing has been done, pipes generally run in areas where heat loss is greatest. An uninsulated crawl space is in infinite heat sink because hot water lines continually radiate heat to the ground. There is often significant air infiltration in joist cavities because band joists are notoriously hard to insulate, and that's exactly where hot water lines often run.

At a minimum, insulation should be installed on both hot and cold water pipes for 6 ft. from the water heater to reduce convection of hot water up into the house. Hot water pipes should really be insulated the entire length of the run. If pipes run in insulated exterior walls (which should never be the case in cold climates), pipe insulation can be eliminated in the wall cavity. In hot climates, if cold water lines are too close to the exterior wall, they can cause condensation that will in turn lead to mold. It is just good policy and good insurance to insulate pipes.

What pipes are made from also has a bearing on how much heat they will lose. Water running through PEX pipe shows a greater temperature drop at a given flow rate than does copper piping of the same nominal diameter. This is because the PEX has a larger surface

Waterlines often run through chilly basements and crawlspaces before they deliver water to bathrooms and kitchens. Insulating all hot water supplies is a low-tech way of reducing energy losses. Insulating cold-water lines eliminates condensation.

DOWN THE DRAIN

Drain-water heat recovery (DHR) systems use heat from hot water waste lines to preheat cold water via a heat exchanger. There are several types, both with and without storage tanks, which save preheated water for later use.

These devices cost at least several hundred dollars, plus installation, and more than one may be needed to recover the heat from all the drains in a house. One study conducted by the Energy Research Centre of the Netherlands found that the efficiency of the heat exchange ranged from 51 percent to 63 percent. Higher efficiencies were found in "balanced" systems that piped preheated water to both the hot water heater and the cold side of a shower valve at the same time. The same study found that energy needed for domestic hot water could be reduced by about 40 percent by using balanced DHR.

Energy savings, however, vary considerably because of the many ways that DHR can be incorporated into a plumbing system and because of the different types of systems on the market. Before investing in one of these systems, ask to see documentation that backs up energy-saving claims.

DRAIN WATER HEAT RECOVERY

In a conventional plumbing system, hot water from showers, dishwashers, and washing machines goes down the drain after it's used, taking with it most of the energy required to get it hot in the first place. Through a heat exchanger, a drain water–heat recovery system captures some of that heat and uses it to preheat incoming cold water. Systems can be configured in one of several ways, and energy savings can be significant.

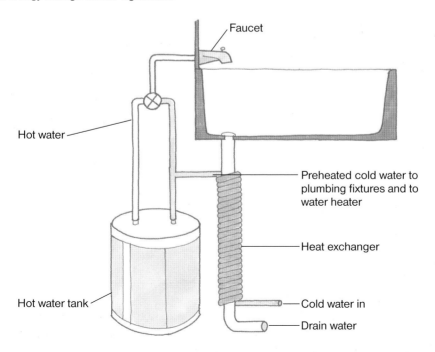

Faucet

Hot water

Hot water tank

Preheated cold water to plumbing fixtures and to water heater

Heat exchanger

Cold water in

Drain water

area and larger inside diameter. The surface area seems to radiate more heat per length of pipe, and the larger inside diameter slows down water flow rate, which increases heat loss. Insulating the piping minimizes this difference. The bottom line is to insulate the entire hot water pipe run with at least R-3 insulation.

Drain water heat recovery systems are another way to squeeze more out of the energy dollars that go into making hot water (see the sidebar and drawing on p. 165).

Saving Water by Reducing Flow

Installing flow reducers on existing faucets and shower heads is an easy way to conserve water. Flow rates for kitchen faucets should be less than 2 gallons per minute; bathroom faucets should produce no more than 1.5 gpm. Government regulation limits the flow on new shower heads to a maximum of 2.5 gpm.

Aerators can reduce water flow at a faucet to between 1 gpm and 2 gpm and cut water use by half. Some older aerators on faucets may be less efficient. To check how yours does, do a simple experiment: a watch with a second hand and a quart container are all you'll need.

Reducing the flow of water, however, makes the system less efficient because a lower volume of water means longer waiting time for hot water and more energy losses en route, which results in more wasted water. The solution is to combine flow-reduction devices with an on-demand water circulation system.

Low-volume showerheads, those using 2.5 gpm or less, can save an estimated 38 gal. of water per day in a typical household when compared to showers with older shower heads. Some flow-reducing showerheads also include a filter, typically charcoal, that extracts chlorine and other heavy molecules from the water. Chlorine is absorbed six times more effectively by the skin than through our digestive systems so the filters are a real benefit for chemically sensitive people and those with dry skin.

High-efficiency toilets

The average U.S. household uses 350 gal. of water per day, not counting any outside activities like washing the car or watering the lawn. Toilets are the single largest consumer of water, on average 27 percent of the total. For the last dozen years, federal energy regulations have required that toilets use no more than 1.6 gal. of water per flush (gpf), so if you're building a new house that's the most the fixture can use (this has nothing to do with the millions of old toilets still in use that consume as much as 6 gpf).

If 1.6 gpf is the new benchmark, it's possible to do much better. High-efficiency toilets reduce water use by at least 20 percent, to 1.28 gpf (4.8 liters). A 1.28-gpf toilet will save a typical family 4,000 gal. of water per year. Pressure-assist toilets compress air in a specialized container inside the water tank as the tank refills after flushing. During flushing, the compressed air results in a high-velocity flush. Some of these toilets use as little as 1 gpf.

Dual-flush toilets are the best of both worlds. Like a standard U.S. toilet, one mode uses 1.6 gpf, but there's an additional option for using half that much water, which can add up to a savings of 1,600 gal. of water a year with average household use.

Composting toilets are not everyone's cup of tea, but if you want to reduce the amount of water you use here's one way of doing it. A number of types are available com-

Federal regulations limit water consumption in toilets to 1.6 gal. per flush, although there are models on the market that use even less.

Pressure-assist toilets using as little as 1 gal. per flush can save thousands of gallons of water per year.

mercially, from small, self-contained units to large-capacity models with composting chambers installed below the floor. They all work on similar principles, turning waste into a small volume of compost over a period of months. Some have fans, heaters, and electronic controls to speed the process.

Plumbing for Gray Water

Gray water is the waste from sinks, showers, dishwashers, and other appliances—everything except toilets (black water). Instead of going straight down the drain, it can be used for irrigation outside or to flush toilets. Plumbing systems that incorporate some way of capturing gray water offer another means of using less water, but the rub is that most cities and counties currently do not have codes in place that allow them. Even so, if you're building a home from the ground up, it makes sense to preplumb for such a system in anticipation of a time when building codes get up to speed.

Concerns over reusing gray water are two-fold. First, some building officials fear that gray water and black water might mix, raising the potential for disease. Second, even though gray water doesn't contain human waste it still contains bacteria that can multiply when the

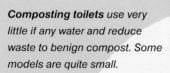

Unlike a conventional toilet, a dual-flush model has a low-volume as well as standard flush mode, reducing unnecessary water consumption for liquid waste.

Composting toilets use very little if any water and reduce waste to benign compost. Some models are quite small.

PREPLUMB FOR GRAY WATER

Reusing water from kitchen and shower drains for irrigation is one way of saving substantial amounts of water. The practice is not allowed by most plumbing codes—at least for the time being. But for new houses in regions where water shortages are a way of life, it may make sense to preplumb the house with a gray water system while plumbing is completely accessible. Conversion costs later would be much higher if modifications were feasible at all.

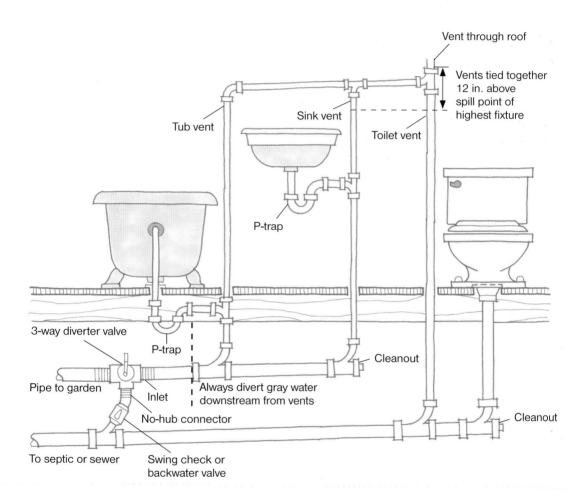

water is stored. That, too, is a possible cause of disease. Gray water should only be used for non-edible plants outdoors.

Appliances That Save

If the system for heating and distributing water holds potential for saving energy and water, so does the selection of appliances for washing clothes and dishes.

Washing clothes uses almost as much water as flushing the toilet: on average, 22 percent of indoor residential water use goes into the washing machine. Conventional washing machines use roughly 40 gal. of water per load, but high-efficiency models can cut that almost in half, to about 23 gal. per load. Front-loading machines are typically more efficient than top-loading models, although there are several top-loaders that are close in water and energy conservation.

When it comes to dishwashers, always choose an Energy Star model. Most major manufacturers now have both energy- and water-saving models. Look for water saving controls on the front of the machine.

Water conservation can be a hard sell in regions where supplies of clean groundwater are plentiful, but overabundance is not likely to be the norm in the future. Climatic changes and increases in demand will put more of a strain on this resource as time goes by, making it more important to build in water-saving

Front-loading washers use about half as much water as standard top-loaders and have more efficient spin cycles to reduce the amount of time clothes have to spend in a dryer.

Energy Star dishwashers *use less energy than conventional models. Look for one with controls that allow water use to be reduced.*

- Design circulation loops with small-volume branch lines.

- Buy a high-efficiency water heater with a low lifecycle cost. Size it correctly.

- To reduce waste, use an on-demand circulation system that primes the hot water line when hot water is needed. Avoid systems that circulate hot water continuously.

- In a trunk and branch system, make branch lines no larger than 1/2- in. dia. and no more than 10 ft. long.

- Insulate hot water lines.

- Reduce the number of restrictions in hot water supply lines, which decrease the effective length of the run. Lines that include sweeping turns rather than sharp 90-degree bends have less internal turbulence and better flow.

- Installing PEX tubing instead of copper or PVC saves time and money during construction and reduces the potential for leaks.

- Buy water-saving appliances and fixtures.

- Set the water heater thermostat at 120°F.

For 5,000 years, Chinese farmers set composting toilets by the side of well-traveled roads in hopes of enticing travelers to stop and use the facilities. They composted the waste and used it as fertilizer for their gardens.

features now. Moreover, no one should have a hard time understanding that on the hot water side, conservation also means a sizable savings in gas and electric bills. Upgrades to make a conventional system green are not technically challenging and not especially expensive. Just smarter.

9

Heating, Ventilation, and Air-Conditioning

The advent of air-conditioning allowed architects and builders to take climatology out of the mix and begin turning out standard house designs that could be built anywhere. Las Vegas would never have become the fastest-growing city in the country if it weren't for air-conditioning, nor would Florida have seen the same explosive growth. Heating and cooling equipment has given us the luxury of building what we want, where we want, without worrying much about local conditions. And all of that is about to come to a screeching halt.

Heating and cooling equipment consumes a lot of energy, and in the coming era of rising costs and unpredictable supplies we're going to need a different way of looking at the interrelated systems we lump together under

THE GREEN FACTOR

Energy conservation, indoor air quality, and comfort are among the core green building issues encompassed by heating, air-conditioning, and ventilation design. These interrelated systems can be complex, expensive to install, and costly to operate, but green building also offers many opportunities to simplify and save:

- HVAC is more than a few pieces of mechanical equipment. It's a system designed as part of the house.

- An HVAC system works best when it takes local climate and building design into account. Many other design decisions—from solar orientation to how much insulation is used—directly affect HVAC design.

- In a green-built home, heating and cooling equipment can be smaller, less costly, and less complicated. Good design decisions elsewhere make HVAC equipment a backup, not the main event.

- Ventilation often gets lost in the shuffle, but it's vital for high indoor air quality. No matter what the heating or cooling conditions might be, some kind of mechanical ventilation is essential.

Heating, ventilating, and air-conditioning systems are installed after many energy conservation steps have already been completed. HVAC equipment should be designed specifically to meet reduced loads, never designed by convention.

Passive solar design reduces heating loads substantially and reduces the need for expensive heating and cooling equipment. This sunspace helps warm a zero-energy house.

the heading of HVAC. Only with designs that are specific to local conditions will houses remain affordable to build and operate. HVAC design is at the end of a long process of reducing energy loads throughout the house. By the time we need to size the HVAC system, the orientation of the house, its passive solar contribution, envelope insulation, and windows should have reduced the load to levels far below current energy code standards. The result should be as small an HVAC system as possible.

This can be a challenge for a mechanical contractor who is accustomed to sizing systems using ballpark estimates: "Three bedrooms, a den, and a playroom," he might say. "This feels like five tons of air-conditioning to

me." Your design, however, may have reduced the load to two tons. To match your design, he will have to perform heat-loss calculations and size a system that's just large enough. The ultimate objective of this process is to get the right-sized system. Systems that are too large use more energy than necessary and don't function as well.

Designing a System

Central to this premise of thinking small are the many passive solar features built into a green house. HVAC design follows other fundamental building steps that can collectively reduce the size of the heating and cooling system by 30 percent to 50 percent. Solar orientation, insulation, window placement and design, even vegetation on the building site all directly affect heating and cooling loads. Designing a system based on real demand, not conventional practice, is essential.

Keeping the size and complexity of mechanical systems under control has the twin benefits of reducing construction costs and reducing long-term operating costs. Keep in mind, however, that while the heating and cooling demand will depend on local climate, the need for ventilation is universal. Health and comfort depend on adequate air circulation no matter what the heating and cooling requirements might turn out to be.

Regardless of what kind of heating system goes into the house—and there are a number to choose from—the HVAC contractor should perform heat loss calculations using Manual J from the American Society of Heating, Refrigeration and Air-conditioning Engineers (ASHRAE). Seat-of-the-pants design based on a contractor's hunches or experience isn't good enough, no matter what the contractor tells you. Too many well-planned

HIGH-EFFICIENCY HVAC

A well-designed HVAC system is no larger than it needs to be to meet the reduced heating and cooling requirements of a green home. Green systems share a number of attributes.

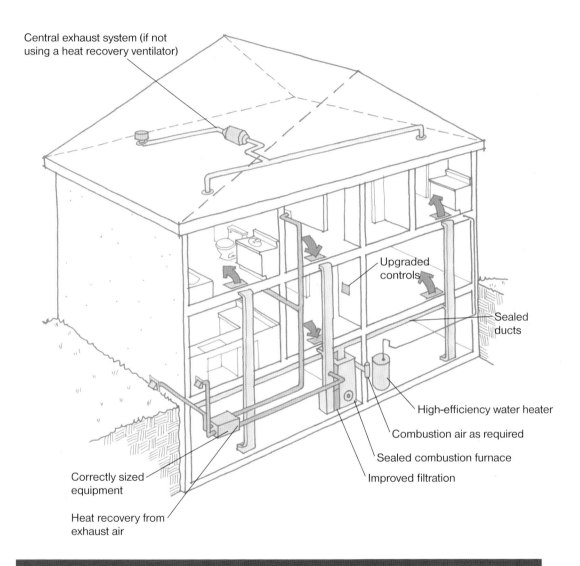

Central exhaust system (if not using a heat recovery ventilator)

Upgraded controls

Sealed ducts

High-efficiency water heater

Combustion air as required

Sealed combustion furnace

Improved filtration

Correctly sized equipment

Heat recovery from exhaust air

passive solar homes have been sabotaged by bad HVAC design. Some of the blame also falls with architects who just leave it to the HVAC contractor to figure out. HVAC systems are called *systems* because they have to be designed as part of the house, not figured out on the fly.

Forced-Air Systems

Forced-air is the most common HVAC system in the U.S., in part because it's one of the least expensive to install. Hot or cold air is moved around the house in a system of ducts, making it relatively simple to add humidification or air-conditioning to a basic heating plant. It can be fitted with high-efficiency air filters to enhance

Forced-air systems are among the most common heating systems in the country. They are easily adapted to air-conditioning and air filtration equipment.

The most common type of disposable filter used in forced-air heating and cooling systems is made from fiberglass. These filters were initially developed to keep coal dust out of blower motors. Old habits may die hard, but other types of filters on the market remove air contaminants more efficiently. Why not use them?

indoor air quality. As long as the system is designed and installed correctly, it works efficiently.

There are some drawbacks. Forced-air systems can create pressure imbalances in the house, contributing to uncontrolled air infiltration and the possibility of back-drafting from fuel-burning equipment such as furnaces and water heaters. Air pressure causes a variety of problems that then have to be addressed by other trades. Ideally, the house stays air pressure neutral or slightly positive. This is hard to achieve when you are moving air through return ducts. And forced-air systems can be noisy.

A variety of devices can be used to condition the air the system circulates—gas, oil, and electric resistance heaters, heat pumps, even wood-burning appliances. We'll get to those, but let's start with the ductwork itself, the backbone of a forced-air system no matter what kind of heating and cooling equipment you choose to install. One key issue is where the ducts run. By the time the installers show up, the house has often been framed and there may be very few options for where ducts can be located. They may be relegated to an attic, crawlspace, or basement where they will encounter very cold or very hot conditions—hardly

MAKING AIR FEEL COMFORTABLE

People are healthier when relative humidity is between 25 percent and 60 percent, and one of the benefits of a forced-air system is that it allows the introduction of moisture into the air. This is almost a necessity in many Southwest locations and a benefit in heating climates during the winter when relative humidity inside can plunge. In houses with radiant heat, portable humidifiers are very efficient for room-by-room humidification.

In the Southeast and mid-Atlantic regions, the opposite is necessary—there's often too much moisture in the air. Air-conditioning is very effective at reducing humidity if it is sized appropriately. That means the AC system should run constantly. If it cycles on and off frequently, it's a sure sign the system is oversized and it will be relatively inefficient in reducing humidity.

Insulated ductwork running through conditioned space both reduces heating and cooling loads and conserves energy.

DUCT TROUBLE SPOTS

Ducts that circulate hot and cold air around the house are susceptible to a variety of problems when poorly designed and installed. A chief cause of concern is leaks that can cause fuel-burning appliances to back-draft because of negative air pressure inside the house. Leaky ducts can also allow warm, moist air to escape into unconditioned spaces, a problem that can lead to the growth of mold.

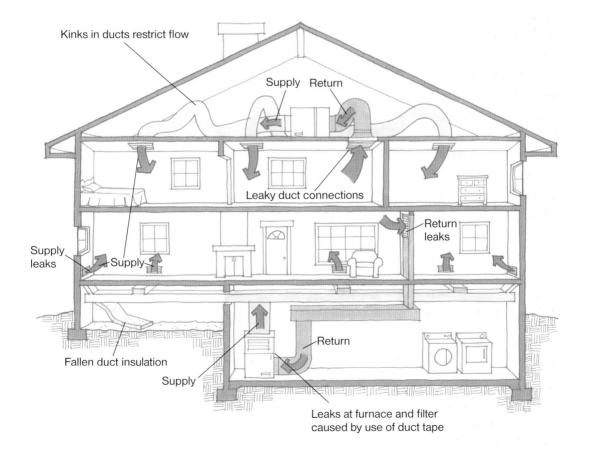

Kinks in ducts restrict flow

Supply Return

Leaky duct connections

Return leaks

Supply leaks

Supply

Fallen duct insulation

Supply

Return

Leaks at furnace and filter caused by use of duct tape

KEEP DUCTS INSIDE

Routing ducts inside the building envelope is preferable to running them through unconditioned attics and crawlspaces. Finding a place to put them can be tough, but one solution is building a dropped ceiling.

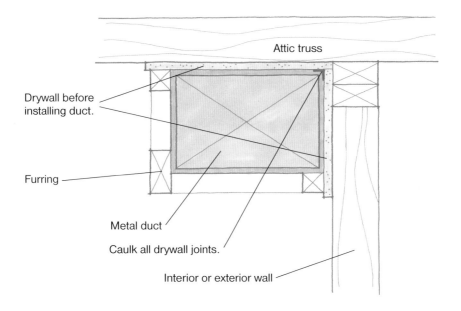

the key to system efficiency. This can be avoided by designing chases so that ducts are within the conditioned space of the house.

There are three main choices for the ductwork: sheet metal, flex duct, and high-velocity duct.

Sheet-metal ducts

Sheet-metal ductwork should be designed according to ASHRAE Manual D, a procedure that seems followed all too rarely these days. Manual D is an essential planning tool that determines pressure requirements for each register in the house and determines how duct-size reductions affect airflow in and out of rooms. In the old days, heat was distributed to supply registers in the lower part of the room and returned through a vent higher in the room, which mixed air thoroughly and made for even, comfortable heating. In an effort to cut costs, returns are often eliminated in individual rooms these days in favor of a central return in, say, a stairwell. Doors are undercut to allow air out of rooms, meaning the return flow of air is now at floor level. This leads to air stratification, which is both uncomfortable and energy inefficient.

In another cost-cutting measure, joist bays are sometimes "panned" by lining them with sheet metal for use as either supply or return ducts. These are a major source of air leaks, and the practice should never be allowed. Ducts should run continuously from furnace to register and all junctions should be sealed with mastic, never duct tape. Metal tape

Sheet-metal ducts are a good green choice. They are less likely to sag than flexible duct, don't contribute any fibers or contaminants to indoor air, and are made from a recyclable material.

No matter what the label says, duct tape isn't a good choice for ducts because it has a tendency to dry out and fall off. Seal ducts with mastic or metal tape.

is a second-best approach but it's harder to use. Low VOC mastic is by far the easiest way to get a good seal and goes quickly once you become accustomed to it. It doesn't need to be pretty, just make a good seal.

Never do this: Lining a joist bay with sheet metal to form a heating and cooling duct is likely to lead to air leaks.

We can't emphasize enough that poorly sealed ductwork can cause indoor air quality problems. When the return duct is leaky it pulls air into the duct from the house. This causes

Tests by building scientists and the Home Energy Rating System found carbon monoxide at dangerous levels in 30 percent of new homes tested in California and Colorado because of poorly sealed ducts.

negative pressure in the house. If it is leaky enough, it will cause back-drafting from gas-fired appliances such as water heaters and

furnaces, increasing the risk of dangerous levels of carbon monoxide inside the house.

Flex ducts

Flex ductwork has become the favorite of production home builders because it's inexpensive and easy to install. Insulated with fiberglass to R-4 or R-6, it makes a continuous run from the furnace/air conditioner to the register. But it only works well when it's hung in a relatively straight line, and that's not often the case. In addition, its spiral reinforcement creates turbulence inside the duct, which requires greater pressure to move air. When it's installed so it sags or is coiled up, flex duct requires even higher air pressure and generally leaves occupants feeling uncomfortable because there isn't enough pressure at the register.

Flex duct is a popular and inexpensive choice although its internal wire reinforcement increases air turbulence and reduces flow. It should be installed without sags and dips.

Here's a good example of how ducts should **not** be installed. The 180° bend in the line will reduce efficiency.

One type of duct to avoid altogether is flexible duct lined with fiberglass. Fibers can escape into the air that homeowners breathe.

High-velocity ducts

Invented by a Canadian company for retrofits, high-velocity pipe is small-diameter (3-in. to 4-in.) flexible pipe that runs from the air handler to registers. It's designed for easy installation and usually runs through conditioned space. This new but burgeoning industry has made great strides in sound-proofing both the pipes and the outlets. Air inside these ducts moves at much faster rates than in conventional systems. That helps conditioned air mix more thoroughly in the room and provides consistent temperatures. It requires a compatible air handler, but it's ideal for getting conditioned air into tight spaces and is especially well adapted to retrofits.

Overall, properly installed and sealed sheet-metal ducts are probably the best choice. They don't sag like flex duct, and their smooth walls do not interfere with airflow as dramatically. And at the end of its service life, the ductwork can be recycled or reused.

Radiant Systems

Air is not the only medium that can be used to distribute heat around the house. The other option is water. Many older houses are still warmed by heavy cast-iron radiators, but hydronic systems today generally rely on either baseboard radiators or a network of plastic tubing installed in the floor. Radiant systems are fundamentally different from forced-air, relying on radiant energy rather than convection. Radiant energy warms *people* in a room rather than the *air*.

Radiant systems have a number of advantages, as well as a few shortcomings. On the plus side, they are easy to assemble and divide

into separate zones, don't alter air pressure in the house, don't make much noise, and can be modified as needs change. The thermal mass of the water in the pipes continues to radiate heat long after the thermostat has turned the boiler off. They are, however, not as responsive as forced-air systems. It takes time for fixtures to warm up, and water damage is a threat if pipes leak. Radiant systems heat, but they are not easily used for cooling; nor can they be used to add humidity to a dry house.

Radiant-floor heat

Unlike baseboard heat, radiant-floor systems never get in the way. You never have to worry about where the furniture goes, and when a system is designed correctly you'll never hear the heat cycle on and off. Water running

Radiant-floor systems that use cross-linked polyethylene tubing to distribute hot water have some advantages over forced-air systems, but the cost is typically much higher and it's not practical to add air-conditioning.

CASE STUDY

Water for a radiant-floor heating system is typically heated by a boiler, but passive solar design and energy-saving building techniques may allow the use of a conventional water heater, a much less expensive option. Here, a high-density OSB board laminated with aluminum heat transfer plates is installed over a SIP floor.

KEEPING HEAT SIMPLE

When I decided to build an office for myself I had several goals in mind. First was the challenge of building it myself (it had been 10 years since I did that kind of work). Second, I wanted the office to feature a constellation of green products and processes that would reflect my green consulting business. Third, it was to be as close to a zero-energy structure as possible while keeping construction costs to less than $100 per sq. ft.

Using structural insulated panels for the floor, walls, and roof helped me put into practice several principles I teach: eliminate the wall cavity, reduce infiltration to less than 0.1 air change per hour, avoid forced-air systems, and build to at least 50 percent above the local building code (for me, that's Boulder, Col.).

Using SIPs meant the building went from foundation to under roof in four days (more about that in the chapter on framing, see pp. 102–103). Windows are "tuned" for passive solar gain with low solar heat gain on east and west walls and high-transmissive glass on the south. When the sun comes up the heat goes off.

I put radiant hot water tubing in the floor and I now heat the entire 1,000-sq.-ft. building with a conventional high-efficiency domestic water heater. It keeps the office at 68° when the outside temperature is five below zero. The super insulation keeps the inside temperature at 85° in summer when it is 105° outside.

When people ask me how much does green building cost, I answer this way: It cost me half of what conventional construction would have cost and I'm twice as comfortable.

—DJ

through the tubing—typically cross-linked polyethylene, or PEX—is set at a lower temperature
than it would be for baseboard heat, which
may mean some energy efficiencies, and your
feet will be warm in winter. That's a plus when
you step onto the tile floor in the bathroom first
thing in the morning.

Radiant-floor heat makes sense in houses with high ceilings because it doesn't waste
energy heating upper-level air that would benefit no one. And when the tubing is installed
in a concrete or other high-mass floor, there
are parallel benefits to be had as passive solar
thermal mass.

On the down side, radiant-floor heat is
very slow to respond. With water running in
the 120°F to 130°F range, it takes hours for
room temperatures to come up. That means
the system runs best at a more or less constant
temperature. But the biggest drawback to
radiant-floor systems is their high cost, which is
far more than a comparable forced-air system.
When the house is well insulated and designed
to take advantage of available solar gain, a
radiant-floor system represents a lot of money
that could have been spent elsewhere. Says
Marc Rosenbaum, a professional engineer
from New Hampshire, "It just doesn't make
sense to put in a ten-thousand-dollar heating
system to provide a hundred dollars' worth of
heat per year."

Sometimes, however, a radiant-floor
system can be run by a conventional hot-water
heater instead of an expensive boiler. For that,
you'll need a well-insulated house that takes full
advantage of its potential for solar gain.

Radiant baseboard

Baseboard and radiant-floor systems are
similar in one respect—they both distribute
heat evenly throughout the room. But because

Radiant baseboard heating units need much
hotter water than radiant-floor systems but they
also are more responsive. One disadvantage is
that the radiators can get in the way.

the water is hotter—180°F—baseboard radiators come up to temperature more quickly so
they're more responsive. Baseboard heat is
quiet, easy to install, and can be expanded if
the need arises. It costs less than radiant-floor
heat. This kind of system is a good choice for a
well-designed home because it's not too much
system for a small demand, and it can be put in
areas that need only supplemental heat.

On the down side, you'll have to plan
rooms around baseboard radiators. Although
most manufacturers say that it's safe to put
furniture right up against the radiators, it's not a
good idea to block too much of the heat that's
being radiated.

Heating Appliances

Whether the distribution system relies on air
or water, something has to produce the heat.
There are lots of options, both in how the heating plants work and what kind of fuel they use.
One of the most important considerations is

how efficiently the device uses fuel. Once the equipment is installed it becomes an ongoing operating cost, year after year, so this decision has important long-term considerations.

High-efficiency gas

Among the most attractive options are high-efficiency gas-fired furnaces that operate at efficiencies of 90 percent or more—meaning that only 10 percent or less of the heat potential in the fuel is wasted. As the price of fuel continues to increase, the 78 percent-efficient units used by production builders are going to look increasingly obsolete.

Many of these high-efficiency units can be vented directly through a wall (direct venting) instead of into a conventional flue. This means a considerable savings in construction costs. Sealed-combustion units use a double-walled vent that draws outside air through an outer jacket and exhausts combustion gases through the core, ensuring that there is no possibility of back-drafting. The exhaust vent insulates building materials from heat, and it means the furnace is not competing with the occupants of the house for air.

Millions of families, many of them in the Northeast, use heating oil instead of gas. Manufacturers have developed more efficient designs for these burners, including units that can be vented directly through a sidewall instead of a chimney. The Canadian Office of Energy Efficiency says these "mid-efficiency" furnaces have seasonal efficiencies of up to 89 percent and use up to one-third less oil than conventional furnaces to produce the same amount of heat. Condensing furnaces, another option, are designed to extract some of the latent heat in flue gases with an extra heat exchanger. Because flue gases are so cool, they can be vented into a plastic pipe but Canadian

High-efficiency gas-fired furnaces waste very little heat potential and are among the most attractive heating options. Look for an efficiency of 90 percent or higher.

A direct-vent gas furnace doesn't need a separate chimney, and because it uses outside air for combustion it isn't going to back-draft carbon monoxide into the house.

Electric space heaters should be reserved for occasional or spot use. They are inexpensive to install but very costly to operate.

researchers found inherent problems with the technology and suggested that the mid-efficiency furnaces were probably a better bet.

Electric space heating

Electric resistance heating should be a solution of last resort. It is the most expensive to run even though it is 100 percent efficient. That said, if you are in a mild climate and have done all the envelope conservation and solar design discussed in this book, it might be an option for backup heat when all you need is a little boost now and again.

Electric heaters are cheap to install and can be turned on only when you're actually using a room. Radiant panels mounted on a wall or ceiling in the bathroom, for instance, make the room cozy when you step out of the shower, but they don't have to operate for very long.

Wood-burning stoves are charming, but not all of them are very efficient. New designs, like this one from Vermont Castings, reduce emissions significantly.

Or they can be put on a simple timer. This kind of spot heating is what makes these devices good. Discretion is the key.

Wood-fired space heaters

In rural areas where firewood is plentiful, a woodstove or wood-fired furnace or boiler might make sense. Government regulations limit the amount of particulates that woodstoves can emit, and those equipped with catalytic converters are nothing like the parlor stoves of old. Even so, wood-burning appliances are not permitted everywhere and on a per-BTU basis contribute the most carbon dioxide to the atmosphere.

For the hale and hearty, burning wood can be an adventure, at least for a while. A small, clean-burning woodstove might be perfect for supplemental heat. But it's far from carefree. Cutting down trees is dangerous work and it requires some expensive equipment. Even if you buy the wood, it may need

FIREWOOD OR FUEL OIL?

In New England, where firewood is plentiful, many homeowners have been persuaded by rising energy prices to depend less on home heating oil and more on their trusty woodstoves. Prices for wood have risen accordingly.

But even at $200 and up for a cord of dry firewood, it's still cheaper than the energy equivalent in heating oil. In terms of energy content, a cord of dry hardwood is roughly equivalent to 140 gallons of fuel oil. At prevailing 2007 prices, the oil would cost about $330.

While wood is still cheaper on a per-BTU basis, wood-burning stoves and furnaces are not as efficient as their oil-burning equivalents.

splitting. And it will have to be stacked, moved, stacked again, and finally loaded into the stove or furnace. The stove or furnace must be regularly emptied of ash. Moreover, firewood is not necessarily cheap. Wood hasn't been immune from the price increases that have affected other fuels.

A more recent variant is the pellet-burning stove, which burns compressed wood pellets sold by the sack. These stoves are equipped with augers that carry the pellets to the combustion chamber automatically, and they produce less ash than conventional woodstoves so they need cleaning less frequently. Like woodstoves, however, they can't be left to operate on their own for extended periods and they don't work when the power goes out.

Geothermal Systems

Just as passive solar systems use free energy from the sun for heat, a ground-source or geothermal system uses the uniform temperature of the earth to heat and cool. No matter what it's doing outside, the temperature in the earth is a constant 55°F at some depth below ground. A heat pump takes advantage of that constant temperature by circulating water through an underground system of tubing and running the liquid through a heat exchanger that contains a sealed refrigerant loop. By reversing the direction of the refrigerant, the system can work as a heat source or as an air conditioner. Another attractive feature:

Ground-source geothermal systems capture energy from ponds, vertical wells, or the earth. They use less energy than conventional systems but they are more expensive to install.

GEOTHERMAL SYSTEMS

Ground-source heat pumps rely on underground tubing to extract latent heat from either water or earth. A water-ethanol mix circulates through tubing in a pond, horizontal trenches, or vertical shafts and then passes through a heat pump. A heat pump can work as either a cooling or heating device, depending on which way refrigerant flows internally.

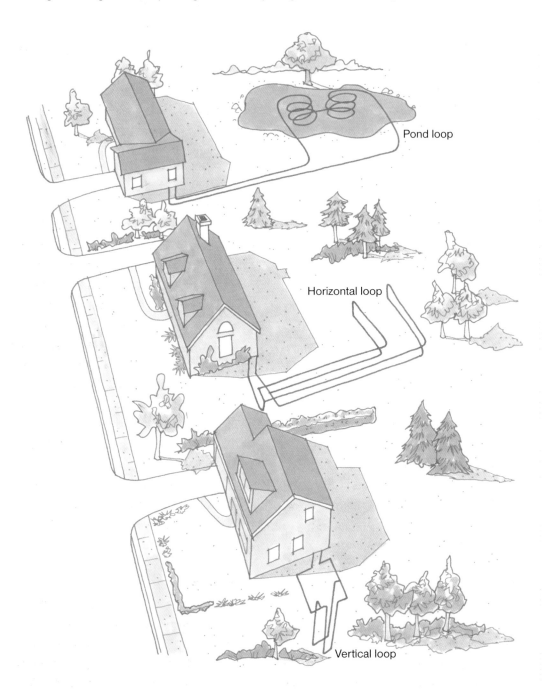

Pond loop

Horizontal loop

Vertical loop

Geothermal systems can be used with either forced-air or radiant distribution systems.

Underground pipes can be deployed in one of several ways, either in one or more vertical holes, in trenches, or in a loop that runs through a nearby ground water table, a pond, or a lake. Specifics vary, depending on the requirements of the house, how much (or how little) land is available for the piping, and the climate where the system is being installed.

Geothermal systems are pricey, but one very attractive thing about them is that they use substantially less energy than conventional systems. Although it does take a small amount of electricity to run the pumps and compressor, system requirements may be low enough for a photovoltaic panel. And because it does not use any fossil fuels, a system like this is non-polluting with essentially no impact on either people or the environment.

"Open-loop" systems are the cheapest to install. These draw on a source of water—from a well, for example—that is circulated through the heat exchanger and then dumped. When the well doesn't produce enough extra water (something on the order of $1\frac{1}{2}$ gal. per minute for each ton of heating and cooling), an installer can switch to one of three closed-loop designs: horizontal, vertical, or a pond loop (see the drawing on the facing page). Space is certainly a consideration. Horizontal installations can require hundreds of feet of trenches, and not everyone has that kind of room in the backyard. If not, the vertical system makes more sense, although drilling costs can make this a very expensive option.

Among the variables in designing a system like this is the type of soil on the site. Soil with a low thermal capacity means more pipes to run. Higher thermal capacity means a shorter loop. In general, soil with more moisture in it makes for a better transfer of heat. Expansive soils are not a good candidate because they can contract away from the pipes, thus reducing the heat transfer tremendously. Another consideration is the antifreeze that's used in closed-loop systems to prevent the water from freezing. Either a type of glycol or alcohol can be used. Both are relatively non-corrosive, but glycol tends to be expensive and toxic to pets.

Overall, a ground-source heat pump is the most eco-friendly heating and cooling system available. But these systems have the same problem as radiant-floor heat: they are very expensive to install.

Air-source heat pumps

Air-source heat pumps also use a closed refrigerant loop and a compressor, but in this case the device extracts heat from the air rather than a water supply or the ground itself. Air-source heat pumps can also operate as air-conditioners. For this reason, they're popular in climates where both heating and cooling are needed. From a sustainable building vantage point, their main drawback is that when air temperatures get too low to allow the system to operate, the system automatically kicks on electric resistance heating elements to take up the slack.

If this is the kind of equipment you install, look for one with a government Energy Star rating, which is about 20 percent more efficient than standard models.

Ventilation

Ventilation, the V-word in HVAC, is too often the missing link in design. We may think of heating and cooling first, but in some respects ventilation is the most important part of the system. Unless fresh air is introduced and polluted air discharged, even a well-heated room won't

mind ourselves that this is a *minimum* requirement. A better rule of thumb would be a ventilation rate of 15 cu. ft. per minute (CFM) per occupant. This boosts the rate of air changes per hour to between 0.5 and 0.6.

Ventilation can be in the form of exhaust, supply, or balanced systems. Keep in mind that there should be continuous ventilation for each room or, at a minimum, the capability to deliver continuous ventilation. In addition, exhaust fans should be provided in both the kitchen and bathroom. Larger exhausting appliances may require their own make-up air.

There also is the issue of air filtration, an important component of high indoor air quality. Filters run the gamut, from inexpensive fiberglass filters to those of HEPA quality. Filtration capacity is rated in MIRVs. The higher the number, the smaller the particulates it pulls out of the air stream. A filter in the range of 7 to 12 is appropriate for most houses. If someone in the house suffers from allergies or asthma, a higher MIRV rating may be called for.

This off-the-grid house uses floor registers to move passive solar heat to the second floor by convection.

Air filters are available that filter out 95 percent of the particles in the air that are 1 micron (a millionth of a meter) or larger.

be comfortable for long. Stale air will drive people out.

Ventilating a house can be accomplished on a spot basis with a kitchen or bathroom fan, or with a heat recovery ventilator (HRV) designed to circulate fresh outdoor air through the house while getting rid of stale air. ASHRAE standards suggest a minimum of 0.35 air changes per hour (ACH), which means that all of the air in the house would be changed roughly every three hours. But we have to re-

Three approaches to fresh air

A simple exhaust system is what most homes have: fans in the bathroom and kitchen suck stale or polluted air out of the house. This is not a very sophisticated ventilation system but it is better than nothing. As long as the fans are used regularly, at least grease, unburned hydrocarbons, and cooking odors can be eliminated in the kitchen, and very damp air exhausted from bathrooms.

A **whole-house fan** can be a valuable ally during the summer. Opening windows at night and turning on the fan allows hot air to be flushed out and replaced with cooler air.

A **ventilation hood over the range** should be standard. Along with a bathroom fan, a fan in the kitchen is a first line of defense in ridding the house of moisture and air contaminants.

Fans should be big enough to handle the job. That means a minimum capacity of 50 cu. ft. even in the smallest of bathrooms. Larger bathrooms need larger capacity fans—figure on 1 cfm for every square foot of floor space in bathrooms up to 100 sq. ft. Large spalike bathrooms will need more. Noise can be a problem and can discourage people from using fans. Manufacturers, however, offer a number of fans that are essentially inaudible. Look for a model with a low "sone" rating. The industry describes 1 sone as the amount of noise a quiet refrigerator makes in a quiet room. Some bath fans have sone ratings as low as 0.3. Cheap fans may be rated at 4 sones or higher.

When bathroom fans are supplying most of the ventilation, they should be upgraded with timing switches or humidity-sensing switches that can power the unit on whenever it senses there's too much moisture in the air. A more elaborate approach is to install a remote exhaust fan in the attic and octopus-like ducts to rooms around the house. A ducted central exhaust fan can serve as either a whole-house ventilation system or as a spot fan. Wired to a 24-hour clock timer, the fan can be programmed to provide fresh air at regular intervals or used on a spot basis with an override switch. Operating at low speeds is enough to meet both spot and whole-house needs. In that case, no extra controls are needed.

The problem with exhaust-only systems is that make-up air can come from just about anywhere—through leaky windows, under the front door, or wherever else it finds an avenue. In a tight house, it increases the chance of back-drafting.

Supply systems, commonly found in forced-air systems, include a fan that draws in outside air and circulates it via heating and air-conditioning ducts. A supply system will pressurize the home slightly. This is good, given that a positive pressure in the home protects it from back-drafting.

A balanced system is better. It creates neutral pressure by exhausting the same amount of air that it draws in. These systems usually supply air to common living spaces and exhaust the air out of the bathroom or kitchen.

Heat recovery ventilators

Taking so much trouble to get the house warm and then turning on fans to suck the heat out of the house may not make a lot of sense. Having healthy air inside the house does carry an energy price tag. A way of mitigating the damage is with a heat recovery ventilator (or HRV), which can recover between 60 percent and 85 percent of the heat from exhaust air. One good use for this re-purposed energy is to heat water for domestic use with a ventilating heat-pump water heater.

Energy collected in a ventilating heat-pump water heater is enough to provide all the hot water for a family of four when it operates for eight hours per day.

Cooling

Cooling requirements, just like the demand for heat, are lower in a well-insulated house. Still, in many parts of the country, buyers demand cooling systems. When it's steamy outside, central air-conditioning is an attractive marketing feature, and it has the added benefit of dehumidify-

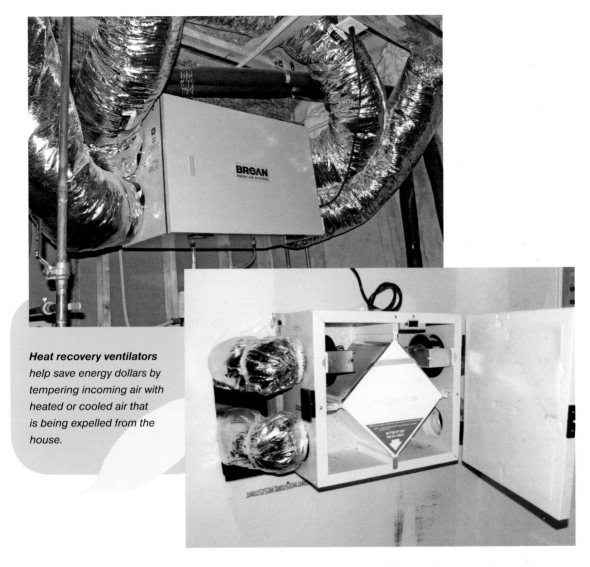

Heat recovery ventilators
help save energy dollars by
tempering incoming air with
heated or cooled air that
is being expelled from the
house.

ing indoor air. Most residential air-conditioning equipment uses a compressor cycle in which a refrigerant is alternately compressed and expanded. Direct expansion (DX) air-conditioning used for conventional forced-air systems pushes a lot of cold air quickly, but the compressor is an energy hog.

If natural ventilation or some of the alternatives to conventional air-conditioning aren't enough, the best that can be done is to search for a system with as high a Seasonal Energy Efficiency Ratio (SEER) as possible. Government regulations require air conditioners manufactured after 2005 to have a minimum SEER of 13, but window units are exempted so efficiencies there tend to be lower. A type of air-conditioning system known as a split system can have a SEER rating of 18 or higher, but these systems are more expensive.

High SEER ratings make a very big difference in energy consumption. Moving from an efficiency rating of 9 to 13 drops energy use by about 30 percent. Still, energy consumption is often significant and it's one reason to look at the alternatives.

Swamp coolers

Swamp coolers, or evaporative coolers, consist of a fan and padding that's wetted with water, all housed in a box that's mounted outside. Incoming air is cooled as water on the pads evaporates. While these coolers can offer real relief in dry climates, they are not as effective in areas that experience high humidity because water doesn't evaporate as readily.

Swamp coolers don't use much energy, or water, and they're easy to install and maintain. In very dry climates, the added moisture makes the house more comfortable. But watch out for mold if there's too much humidity in the air. They work best when they're mounted on the top of the house so they can take advantage of inversion—cold air naturally wants to sink.

Radiant cooling

Water, not air, is the medium in a radiant cooling system. It works something like radiant-floor heating, only in reverse. Radiant cooling systems are not common, and in fact are not currently listed in model building codes. They require precise design and installation, but they can save up to 80 percent of the energy needed by fans in a more conventional air-conditioning system and they are easy to zone

Swamp coolers are low-tech and effective in parts of the country with dry conditions, but they're not a good choice in areas of high humidity.

for different parts of the house. In humid climates, some means of removing humidity and pollen may also be necessary. So while operating costs may be lower, installation can be costly. This option is best for very dry climates where the risk of condensation is low.

Night flushing

A low-tech way of cooling down the house is with a fan that flushes the house with cool night air. It's a perfect complement to passive solar homes with high thermal mass, when,

NIGHT FLUSHING

In parts of the country where air-conditioning is needed only a few weeks per year, a low-tech option is a whole-house fan that draws cool air inside at night. Leave windows open while the fan runs, then close them in the morning to keep cool air inside. The house should remain comfortable in all but the hottest weather.

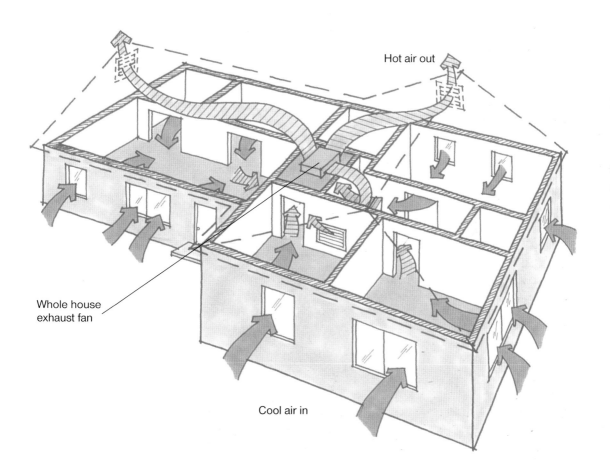

Hot air out

Whole house
exhaust fan

Cool air in

of course, it actually gets cool enough at night to be effective. The fan pulling air through the house can be controlled with a thermostat so it doesn't get too chilly inside. This system may even be enough to take the place of conventional air-conditioning in a climate where high heat is a problem only a few weeks out of the year. Closing the windows in the morning when the house has cooled off thoroughly will keep the inside comfortable for many hours.

Electrical

One of the great luxuries in our lives is the ready availability of electricity, and the whole point of designing an electrical system in a green house is to use less of it while still providing all of the services and aesthetics we expect. One-third of the world's population still has no access to electricity, yet we treat it so casually that we continue to buy lightbulbs that produce more heat than light and load up on electronic gizmos that use power even when they're turned off.

As described more thoroughly in chapter 2, it takes a lot of work and energy to get all those electrons to our doorstep. Electrical generation consumes enormous amounts of fossil fuels, contributing directly to the rise in greenhouse gases, and along with our appetite for ever greater amounts of power comes uncertainty about the future. Do we build new nuclear plants to meet the demand of growing populations? Do we continue to build coal-fired power plants and increase levels of atmospheric carbon dioxide? Will the costs for generating power from solar and wind come down fast enough to make a transition to renewable sources a realistic alternative?

As the world grapples with these imponderables, conservation is for the moment the most economical way to ensure there will be adequate supplies of electricity in the future.

THE GREEN FACTOR

A green strategy for designing a residential electrical system can be summed up in three words: Use less power. Even without investing in photovoltaic panels or wind generators, a green house can use less energy than a conventional home. Points to consider:

• Because so much of the electricity we use is produced in plants that burn fossil fuels, lowering consumption reduces greenhouse gas emissions.

• Lower consumption means lower operating costs.

• Making the most of natural light to reduce reliance on electric lights not only saves money but also makes a house more cheerful and more comfortable.

• Consumers have more choices than ever when it comes to lighting and appliances that are more energy efficient and in some cases more durable than standard designs.

"Phantom loads:" According to the U.S. Department of Energy, 75 percent of the electricity used to power home electronics in the average home is consumed while the products are turned off.

Today, heating, cooling, and lighting consume 67 percent of all the electricity that's generated. There's plenty of room for improvement.

Americans love electronic gizmos. According to the government's Energy Star program, on average each home has two televisions, a VCR, a DVD player, and three phones. If all of these devices were replaced with Energy Star models, it would cut greenhouse gas emissions by 25 billion pounds.

High-efficiency residential lighting and appliances along with designs that increase our use of natural light can significantly cut residential energy use. A happy parallel to lower electrical consumption in a green home is lower operating costs.

This off-the-grid house uses photovoltaic panels to produce all the electricity it needs. Grid-tied systems are more realistic for most homeowners.

What Drives Demand?

The nation's electricity is delivered over a grid of power transmission lines that allow utilities to move power where and when it's needed. What drives the size and number of power plants in this vastly complex system are the peak load requirements that utilities must meet. For some, peak demand is in summer and for others it's in winter, but in each case a utility must be able to meet the highest demand for electricity. Think Phoenix on a late summer afternoon. When it's 116°F outside, people can't live without air-conditioning and by law Arizona Public Service has to provide it.

At night, demand is typically a fraction of what it is during the day and utilities can charge rock-bottom prices (1 cent/KWH) because their enormous generators must be kept running anyway. This figures into green building in two ways: our job as builders is to reduce the need for electricity and to time our needs to avoid periods of peak demand for utilities. Generating power with photovoltaic (PV) panels is one way to do that because peak PV production happens to coincide with peak loads for utilities in summer. Between 2:00 and 5:00 in the afternoon, PV panels are generating at optimum levels and that helps utilities "shave" the peak load. In winter, passive solar systems help reduce the amount of fuel required on the coldest of days.

Unless we succeed with reducing demand with these and other strategies, we may get a new coal-fired or nuclear power plant right in our own backyard.

Lighting

The standard for interior residential lighting is the incandescent bulb, a marvel at the time of Thomas Edison but in reality a heating appliance that gives off light as a by-product. One reason we like incandescent bulbs is the warm light they cast, the result of the tungsten filament that glows white hot when current passes through it. But the bulbs are so wasteful of energy that a number of efforts are under way worldwide to ban them (Australia has already adopted a plan to phase them out completely by 2010). A variety of alternatives use less power and last longer.

Compact fluorescents

Compact fluorescents, or CFLs, aren't necessarily new, they have just taken a long time to get into people's homes. Initially, they used the same gases found inside older fluorescent

Incandescent lightbulbs produce more heat than light, needlessly wasting energy when better options are readily available.

Compact fluorescent lights are widely available, even in dimmable versions. They last longer than incandescents and use less energy.

tubes but the cold, blue-white light they gave off was off-putting to most people. Today, CFLs give off light in many colors (called color temperatures) so they can look more like the familiar incandescent bulbs with a warmer light.

CFLs have a number of advantages over incandescent bulbs: they use 75 percent less energy, last six times longer, generate less heat, and reduce energy costs associated with cooling. Each bulb will save $30 or more in energy costs over its lifetime when compared to standard bulbs. Dimmable versions are now becoming available. One downside from a green standpoint is that the bulbs contain small amounts of mercury, which means they have to be recycled. Because they last so long, that could be a decade or two away but mercury is toxic and we don't want it in landfills. Each bulb contains about 4mg of mercury, not a lot when you consider that the largest source of mercury in the air comes from burning fossil fuel, such as coal (the most common fuel used to make electricity in the U.S.).

CFLs are no longer a specialty item so it's possible to shop for deals. Even the "big guys" are getting into the retail game. Wal-Mart^{SM} has committed itself to selling 100 million CFLs as a way to reduce our dependence on electricity. Reaching that goal would require that only one out of every three Americans buy a single CFL.

Light-emitting diodes

Even more efficient than CFLs are light-emitting diodes, or LEDs, which are now available for a variety of household applications. They use 90 percent less energy than equivalent incandescent bulbs—even less than CFLs—but last as long as 100,000 hours before failing and do not contain any mercury or other hazardous materials. They have been used

for years in commercial and industrial lighting, exit signs, and stoplights. It is only in the last couple of years that we have started importing LED fixtures from Asia and Europe. As with so many energy-efficient technologies, LEDs have been in widespread use in Europe for years and American manufacturers now have unique and attractive fixtures specifically designed for LEDs. They are, however, more expensive than even a compact fluorescent and not as widely available. Like so many green product introductions, residential LED bulbs and fixtures will get less expensive as demand rises.

Light-emitting diodes, which are even more efficient than compact fluorescents, are now finding their way into the marketplace. They can run as long as 100,000 hours.

Lighting Design

A lighting plan for a green house, like every other topic covered in this book, is really about intelligent design—that is, design that accommodates the people who live in the house. Start by figuring out what they really need, not what would be part of a conventional plan that's supposed to fit every house. When are different parts of the house used? What kind of light is best for the tasks that will be performed there? How long will light be needed, and at what times of the day?

If the house has been well designed, natural light will be the first choice for daytime use. Careful placement of windows (south being the best choice) can make any room more inviting. Using high windows or fixed-glass panels over operable windows allows light to penetrate deep into the house (south-facing clerestories have the added benefit of helping with heating costs). From a functional standpoint, window placement too often seems haphazard or intended merely to satisfy the local building code. But if windows are thought about more broadly, they can take the place of electric lighting in many rooms. Using natural light to the fullest advantage not only saves energy but also makes us feel better and work more efficiently. The ultimate goal is to place windows such that every room in the house is daylighted and no lighting energy is needed until the sun goes down.

Once natural light has been factored into daytime living patterns we can start looking at how the house will be used at night, room by room. The worst kind of night lighting is a ceiling fixture in the center of the room—it may meet code but it's not especially inviting. Ambient lighting that washes walls or ceiling with softer light is more comfortable. Table lamps are always an improvement over ceiling lights.

Windows are an important part of a lighting plan and should be considered before specifying electrically operated fixtures. Clerestory windows can help throw light deep into the core of the house.

Task lighting does a more effective job of lighting just the area you need for preparing food or paying bills. If you're not sure how to go about a lighting plan, it might be worth investing in a lighting designer early in the design process.

Lighting where you need it

Adjusting the level of light to match the need saves energy and makes a room more comfortable. Dimmers really do save energy, and being able to adjust the light level to the situation can make a huge difference in how light feels. A light over the kitchen table, for instance, can be turned all the way up when the kids are doing their homework and turned down to a soft glow when they're in bed for the night.

A good lighting plan includes different kinds of light—ambient lighting for generally getting around and task lights where work is performed.

Lighting controls, including dimmers and motion sensors, help reduce wasted electricity.

Bathrooms may need bright lights for applying makeup but only dim light late at night.

Many rooms, in fact, benefit from a mix of different light sources that are used at different times. In the kitchen, for instance, bright under-cabinet lights help for food prep while recessed ceiling lights on dimmers provide general ambient light and spot lighting over the sink is helpful for cleanup. Lights can be used separately or altogether depending on the need. In other rooms, desk and table lamps reduce the need for bright ambient lighting.

If the garage has a ceiling full of fluorescent fixtures, using several switches instead of one makes it possible to get just the light you need—lighting up just one corner for a work bench or the whole garage for working on the car. Taking a cue from commercial buildings and using occupancy sensors or timers to turn lights off when they're not really needed also can cut energy consumption.

Outdoor lighting

From Christmas lights to outdoor landscape lighting, there are plenty of ways to green up the outdoor lightscape. The days of using a dozen 100-watt floodlights outside should be over. CFLs for exterior uses are widely available, and low-voltage systems help reduce energy consumption. Motion sensors can turn on lights as cars approach the house or as people walk toward the door. Low-voltage lighting uses a fraction of the energy of conventional landscape lighting.

Solar outdoor lighting can save money both on installation and on the electric bill. It is as simple as planting a self-contained fixture in the ground and waiting for the sun to charge an internal battery. Although batteries and bulbs will have to be changed occasionally, solar cells last indefinitely. Be aware, however, that you get what you pay for with these fixtures. Cheap plastic models will self-destruct after a couple of years of service, and their bulbs have very short lives. It's worth paying more for higher quality fixtures.

Energy-Efficient Appliances

Whether building a new home or upgrading existing appliances, choosing Energy Star models will save substantial amounts of energy. This joint program of the U.S. Department of Energy and the Environmental Protection Agency sets strict guidelines for energy use so that rated models use 10 percent to 50 percent less

In 2005, the Energy Star program helped American consumers save enough energy to cut greenhouse gas emissions equivalent to the output of 23 million cars and trim $12 billion from utility bills.

Outdoor lighting should be more thoughtful than installing a bank of incandescent floods and spots. Low-voltage and CFL bulbs make more sense.

Solar outdoor lighting fixtures can be an attractive way to save money. Stay away from bargain brands.

When shopping for appliances, look for the Energy Star label, which ensures lower energy consumption than conventional models. Front-loading washers are typically more efficient than top-loaders.

power than standard models. Using Energy Star appliances saves an average household $80 a year in energy bills.

The rapid development of new technology in appliances has made older models obsolete. Energy standards are updated regularly and while the Energy Star label is always the place to start, manufacturers from around the world are eyeing the U.S. market and introducing models that are even more efficient.

High efficiency comes with a higher price tag, but in some instances saving water can be as important as lowering energy bills. A new dishwasher or washing machine that uses substantially less water than a standard model can be a real blessing in areas where water is becoming increasingly scarce.

Electronic devices are a common source of energy "leaks" that are easy to overlook. Some of the most common are the little red lights on TVs, computer equipment, stereos, and other products that have an instant-on function. Because everyone hates to wait for anything, manufacturers have built in circuits

that stay on all the time so the devices power up very quickly. These produce what are called phantom loads because devices can still draw power even when we think we've turned them off. The worse culprits are security systems, cable TV boxes, VCRs, and televisions. The best solution is to use power strips that actually turn off the power to the device.

Electric Heating

Electrical resistance heating should be used sparingly. These heating elements are inexpensive to install but expensive to operate. An electric heater might make sense in a super energy-efficient home where only limited spot heating is needed or in a bathroom just to take the chill out of the air after a shower. There are specialized heating units for just those purposes. Radiant heating units made by Enerjoy, for example, are designed to provide spot heating. They can be mounted on the ceiling in rooms that need a little extra boost and are particularly effective next to a tub or shower. Radiant units heat people, not the air, so you feel the heat instantly. Another tried-and-true approach is an infrared bulb in a ceiling fixture. These should be on a timer so they aren't on any longer than necessary. Both work on the same principle.

Electrical space heaters can be useful in rooms rarely used, like guest bedrooms. On the few nights that they are inhabited, an electric space heater can fill in. Otherwise, the room can remain unheated.

Solar and Wind

Solar electric panels, called photovoltaics, are covered in depth in chapter 13. But in general, PV solar makes sense only if you have reduced electrical loads throughout the house. Solar is still very expensive electricity and to use it for

an old, outmoded refrigerator, for example, is a waste of your investment.

But it still might make sense to prewire the house for solar so that panels can be added in the future. This can be as simple as running 1-in. metal conduit from the attic to the basement—easy to do when the walls are opened up but expensive and complicated after the fact. If there's a solar installer in the area, ask for a consultation on how big the system might be and what type of wire needs to be run for the easiest installation in the future. It's an inexpensive upgrade that can save the homeowner money and trouble later (solar installers are good with roofs and wires but not so great at finishing drywall).

Wind generation

What could be greener than a wind generator in the backyard? Not much, providing your backyard gets enough steady wind to make one worth the high cost. As a rule of thumb,

the American Wind Energy Association says the economics of buying one begin to make sense when the average wind speed is at least 10 mph and utility power costs at least 10 cents a kilowatt hour.

Residential wind generators are typically tied into the grid so that when there's not enough wind (below the turbine's cut-in speed of between 7 mph and 10 mph), all the power comes from the utility. As the wind picks up, more of the power comes from the turbine and less from the utility. Storage batteries are not usually part of the system.

In the right spot, a backyard turbine can cut power bills to next to nothing. But they are pricey. Depending on average wind speeds, the AWEA says, you'd need a turbine rated at between 5 kilowatts and 15 kilowatts to make a significant contribution to the 9,400 kilowatt-hours of electricity that American homes use on average. Even a 1 kW wind generator costs well over $10,000.

- Before deciding where electrical lighting should go, make windows part of the overall lighting plan.

- Skip incandescent lightbulbs in favor of alternatives that use less power: compact fluorescent lamps or light-emitting diodes.

- Choose Energy Star appliances.

- Install dimmer switches, timers, or motion-sensing switches on electric lights.

- Plug electronic devices with standby features into a power strip that can be switched off when the devices are not in use.

- Go for lighting plans that match the light source with the anticipated use of the space—task lighting instead of glaring overhead lights, for example, or lights that can be adjusted depending on how they're used.

- Use electrical resistance heating only for heating small spaces on a spot basis, in rooms used only occasionally, or as a backup in a super energy-efficient home.

- When considering solar power, make sure it won't be used to power inefficient, outdated appliances. When solar is beyond the budget, consider roughing in conduit to the roof so panels can be installed later.

Buy green power

If these technologies are outside the scope of your job or your budget, there is still a great investment you can make. Utilities in many parts of the country now have the ability to sell you green power called *green tags.* What that means is that for an additional charge per month you can buy electrons that were produced somewhere in the country by wind, hydro, solar, or biomass. This money is then invested in more renewable energy production. It is a way for everyone to have a small investment in the country's energy future. What's best is when your local utility is the one building the wind farms. That way you can go visit your electricity source. Wind farms are beautiful and represent a great hedge against future increases in utility costs.

Reducing our consumption of electricity has benefits on many levels. There is the immediate benefit of lower power bills, of course, but the big picture is even more compelling. Seemingly minor changes in habit—buying CFLs rather than incandescents, for instance, or making sure that our computers and stereos are really "off" when we're not using them—have huge implications when they are widely adopted. Lower power demand means not forcing utilities to build new generating plants, which has a consequent impact on air and water quality. The cumulative effect of conservation is far-reaching, and all without much of an effort on our parts and with no compromise in creature comforts or convenience. That's hard to beat.

Insulation

Next to orienting the house on the site, choosing the quantity and type of insulation are the two most important decisions that affect the comfort and energy efficiency of a house. It is the most important phase of implementing the principles of building science discussed in chapter 2. Like the foundation and framing, insulation is a fundamental component, incorporated into the shell of the building during construction. With the possible exception of attic insulation, it's tough and expensive to alter the insulation package once the house is built. It pays to make the right choices at the start.

Insulation defines the thermal barrier of the house: This is the pathway for heat loss (or, we hope, for heat containment). We typically

THE GREEN FACTOR

Insulation is the key to energy conservation, a cornerstone of green building. Poorly insulated houses waste energy, and most heating and cooling equipment runs on fossil fuels, which are not sustainable over the long haul. Well-insulated houses not only save energy, thus lowering operating costs, but also keep people more comfortable. Key considerations in choosing the type and amount of insulation:

- While comparing R-values is one way of choosing one type of insulation over another, these numbers can be misleading when site conditions and construction techniques are not factored in.

- Insulation is a basic building component that's difficult to alter after the fact. Although houses can be retrofitted to add more insulation, the process is expensive and often difficult.

- Recommended R-values from such sources as the U.S. Department of Energy's model energy code should be viewed as bare minimums, not maximums.

- Well-insulated, well-sealed houses need effective ventilation.

Insulation is the key to comfort and energy savings and can have a significant effect on the health of the building. In general, more is better: treat code recommendations as minimums.

focus on the R-value of insulation: that is, its inherent resistance to the flow of heat through the building envelope. These numbers can be somewhat deceptive and although R-value is a key consideration, it's not the only one. How effectively insulation blocks the flow of air, and moisture, through wall and ceiling cavities is another. In this regard, some types of insulation perform better than others.

Not very long ago, builders insulated houses almost by rote. The job usually meant unfurling rolls of fiberglass batting and stuffing them into wall and ceiling cavities. Fiberglass batts are still the most widely used type of insulation in the U.S. Inexpensive and available just about anywhere, fiberglass batts are seemingly easy to install. And there's the rub. This insulation is effective only when installers are fussy about the details. And, unfortunately, most of the time they aren't. There are many other

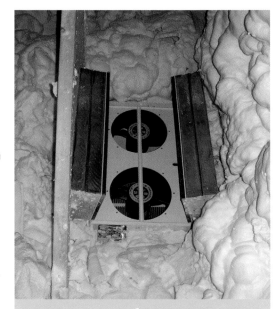

Insulation that acts as an air barrier as well as a thermal barrier, like spray-in foam, makes mechanical ventilation a virtual necessity. Without it, inside air becomes stagnant and unhealthy.

YOU CAN'T ALWAYS GET WHAT YOU WANT

One of the potential frustrations of building is discovering that materials readily available in some parts of the country are difficult or impossible to find where you live. That can be the case with insulation.

A few years ago, my wife and I built a house in southern Maine. The walls were framed with 2x6s. Our builder normally used fiberglass batts, but we wanted something that would be more effective at stopping air leaks.

In the roof, we opted for high-density urethane foam. It cost substantially more than fiberglass would have, but we knew it would do an excellent job. There wasn't enough money in the budget to foam the entire house, so we asked for damp-spray cellulose in the walls. While its nominal R-value wasn't dramatically different from fiberglass, we thought it would do a better job of blocking potential air leaks and we

liked the idea that it consists mostly of recycled newsprint. But our builder had never used it, and none of us could find an installer in the area.

In the end we settled for fiberglass batts in the wall. Our builder, a careful guy with a sharp eye, called the installer back twice to get the job done correctly and I'm convinced there were still gaps that we just didn't see. In one howling winter storm after we'd moved in, we actually heard the wind whistling through the cover plate of a receptacle in the master bedroom.

Later, I learned there was a cellulose installer 25 miles away. If we'd looked harder, we might have found him. New technology and building techniques can be slow to filter into rural areas where building traditions are strong— you have to look.

—SG

WHERE TO INSULATE

Insulation forms a thermal barrier that keeps conditioned spaces comfortable. While recommended insulation levels vary depending on the climate, ceilings should typically have more insulation than walls. No part of the thermal barrier should be skipped.

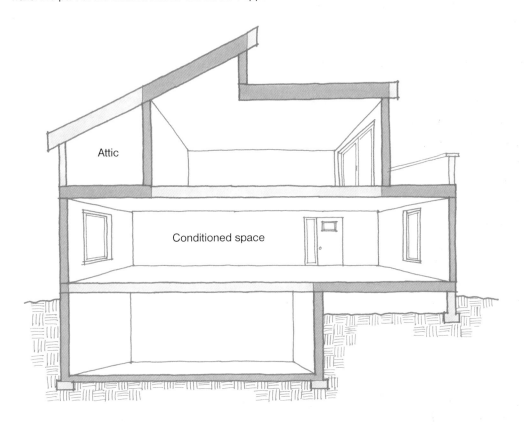

choices and although alternatives can be hard to find in some local markets, they are well worth exploring.

A corollary to insulation is ventilation. A thick layer of insulation that keeps the house snug also traps moisture, dust, and other irritants inside, especially in houses that are buttoned up for months at a time during cold weather. An increase in energy efficiency and air tightness with insulation makes a compelling case for whole-house ventilation to keep occupants healthy (see chapter 14 for more on this topic).

Old Assumptions Don't Work

As recently as the mid-1990s, oil seemed plentiful and supplies of natural gas were abundant—enough, we thought, to serve as a bridge toward a solar and hydrogen energy economy sometime in the future. Those factors were enough to keep insulation bumping along its familiar path.

Code officials and many energy consultants calculated optimal insulation thickness according to payback. Payback was based on the average rate increases in energy costs over 30 years, roughly 6.5 percent per year.

By 2002, the rules of the energy game were changing, altering the assumptions about future energy costs and, as a result, the relative value of insulation. Terrorist attacks on U.S. soil in 2001 and violent political upheavals in the Middle East and elsewhere changed our thinking about energy security. Natural gas simply stopped flowing in some U.S. wells, and we became a natural gas importer. Prices for natural gas and home heating fuel doubled and in some markets tripled. This has changed the economic equation for determining insulation payback.

Given what's happened in the last couple of years, what will the price of energy be in another 5, 10, or 15 years? If a house is built to last a half-century or more, what kind of unpleasant energy realities will its occupants have to deal with then? What kind of energy will they use? No one, of course, knows the answers to those questions. But even without a crystal ball it's obvious that the more insulation installed in our houses now the better off we will be.

We'll discuss zero-energy homes in the chapter on solar energy, but sustainable building starts with reducing the heating and cooling loads of the home as much as possible.

And many of the insulation guidelines we've been using for years just don't cut it anymore. Instead of looking on these recommendations as optional targets, we need to view them as bare minimums. If model energy codes recommend R-19 walls, for example, we may really need R-24 or even R-30. In no case should a house be insulated to lower standards, even if that means giving up something we'd like to have—fancy countertops, pricey flooring, even square footage. In general, a house should be designed with insulation that performs 50 percent better than code.

Form Follows Function

Because different types of insulation have different insulating values (R-values), what you choose determines how the house is framed and detailed on the outside. For example, if you are a stick builder, an R-30 wall requires 2x8 studs or two staggered walls of 2x4s. That starts to get challenging and expensive. Alternately, the house can be framed with 2x6s and wrapped with 2 in. of rigid extruded polystyrene, which makes framing easier, but siding and trim harder to detail. Or you could use structural insulated panels (or SIPs). An

HOW MUCH IS TOO MUCH?

Building scientists are big fans of insulation—lots of insulation. Expectations have gradually risen when it comes to how much insulation should be installed in roofs, walls, and floors. As an indication of how far we've come, R-11 fiberglass batts were once the norm in exterior walls and even in roofs—and not just in areas that enjoy mild climates. It can be surprising to open up a wall or roof in snow country and find skimpy amounts of batt insulation that was poorly installed in the first place.

There is a point of diminishing returns for investing in ever thicker layers of insulation—that is, the practical value and financial savings from thicker insulation are eventually outweighed by higher costs. But aiming for a 50 percent improvement over what building and energy codes require is a reasonable compromise and will pay handsome dividends in comfort and performance over the years to come as energy prices rise. So, for example, if codes call for an R-19 wall, aim for something closer to R-28.

HOW MUCH INSULATION DO YOU NEED?

Recommendations from the U.S. Department of Energy cover six climate zones around the country. Insulation levels should never be less, but builders should consider more insulation for improved energy savings. In Zone 1, for example, it's a good idea to insulate walls to R-27 instead of the recommended R-18.

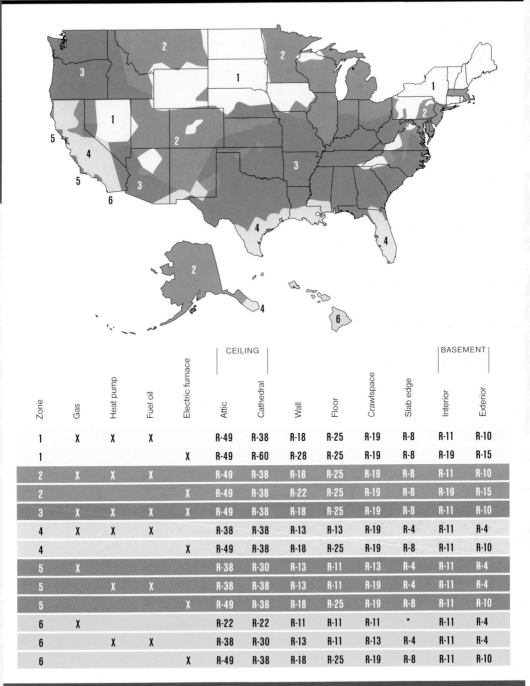

Zone	Gas	Heat pump	Fuel oil	Electric furnace	CEILING		Wall	Floor	Crawlspace	Slab edge	BASEMENT	
					Attic	Cathedral					Interior	Exterior
1	X	X	X		R-49	R-38	R-18	R-25	R-19	R-8	R-11	R-10
1				X	R-49	R-60	R-28	R-25	R-19	R-8	R-19	R-15
2	X	X	X		R-49	R-38	R-18	R-25	R-19	R-8	R-11	R-10
2				X	R-49	R-38	R-22	R-25	R-19	R-8	R-19	R-15
3	X	X	X	X	R-49	R-38	R-18	R-25	R-19	R-8	R-11	R-10
4	X	X	X		R-38	R-38	R-13	R-13	R-19	R-4	R-11	R-4
4				X	R-49	R-38	R-18	R-25	R-19	R-8	R-11	R-10
5	X				R-38	R-30	R-13	R-11	R-13	R-4	R-11	R-4
5		X	X		R-38	R-38	R-13	R-11	R-19	R-4	R-11	R-4
5				X	R-49	R-38	R-18	R-25	R-19	R-8	R-11	R-10
6	X				R-22	R-22	R-11	R-11	R-11	*	R-11	R-4
6		X	X		R-38	R-30	R-13	R-11	R-13	R-4	R-11	R-4
6				X	R-49	R-38	R-18	R-25	R-19	R-8	R-11	R-10

*No slab edge insulation recommended.
Source: U.S. Department of Energy

8-in.-thick panel isn't much more expensive than a 6-in. panel, so it's possible to bump insulating values up significantly without complicating window and door trim, siding, and other exterior finishes because OSB makes up the exterior surface. This kind of juggling is often required to make the best overall choices. Your exact route will probably take a variety of factors into account:

- the appropriate level of insulation for the region where you build
- your experience with alternative building practices
- the availability of different kinds of insulation
- how much experience your insulation contractor has
- the design of the house
- local cost comparisons for different types of insulation

Another complication deals with how R-values are measured. Typically, that's done in a lab or an otherwise controlled setting. But the values are somewhat misleading—some-

thing like the EPA's rating for vehicle mileage. In an ideal, constant-temperature world, with no sun and no wind and assuming the insulation has been installed diligently, this is how a given type of insulation might work. That, of course, is far from the case.

Nominal R-values for an entire wall assembly can decline dramatically when building components interrupt the insulation. This is where it all gets interesting. Wood, for example, has a lower R-value than the insulation used to fill wall cavities. A typical wood-framed wall loses an average of 15 percent of its nominal R-value because of framing that acts as a thermal bridge between indoors and outdoors. So what was designed as an R-19 2x6 wall actually performs at about R-16. That's before you account for doors and windows, which also lower whole-wall R-values. The same wall, if it were framed with steel studs, loses about 50 percent of its nominal R-value before adding doors and windows because steel is such an effective conductor of heat through the building envelope.

What's the point? Certainly not to get lost in a thicket of statistical information and lab reports. But the variables suggest that it's

Structural insulated panels have several advantages: the elimination of wall and ceiling cavities that can trap water vapor and the absence of thermal bridging that lowers the efficiency of insulation in conventional stick-framed construction.

R-VALUES OF COMMON TYPES OF INSULATION

Insulating values differ widely among various kinds of insulation. But be careful: R-values by themselves aren't the whole story. Some types of insulation are better air barriers than others, while doors, windows, and the framing itself all lower thermal performance.

Insulation type	R-value per inch of thickness
Fiberglass blanket or batt	2.9 to 3.8
High-performance fiberglass blanket or batt	3.7 to 4.3
Loose-fill fiberglass	2.3 to 2.7
Loose-fill rock wool	2.7 to 3.0
Batt rock wool	3.2 to 4.2
Loose-fill cellulose	3.4 to 3.7
Perlite or vermiculite	2.4 to 3.7
Expanded polystyrene board	3.6 to 4
Extruded polystyrene board	4.5 to 5
Polyisocyanurate board, unfaced	5.6 to 6.3
Polyisocyanurate board, foil-faced	7
Spray polyurethane foam	5.6 to 6.3
Polyurethane (skin faced)	7.1

not enough to take the R-value stamped on the insulation's packaging at face value. There are too many variables. What we really need is an appreciation for dynamic R-values that take into account a variety of other factors. A good place to start is a calculator available at the website of the Oak Ridge National Laboratory (www.ornl.gov) that predicts actual R-values in built walls and roofs and allows you to see how performance improves when altering various building components.

Making Sense of Insulation Choices

When it comes to choosing insulation, builders and homeowners who want a sustainably built house have two competing issues to consider.

One is how well a given type of insulation performs—that is, its R-value. Also take into account its resistance to the movement of air and moisture and its durability. All of that relates to energy conservation and building durability. Beyond that is the question of how well the insulation meets the general tests of sustainable building: whether it can be made from recycled material, the amount of energy it takes to produce, and whether it contains additives harmful to people who live in the house or the environment in general. That's where it gets complicated.

Because resource conservation is an important underlying principle of green building, it makes sense to consider how much recycled content a particular kind of insulation contains.

RECYCLED CONTENT

One of many considerations in weighing one type of insulation against another is the amount of recycled content it contains. The more the merrier, and just about every type of insulation on the market contains some recycled material, thus reducing waste and manufacturing costs.

Some material is inherently more difficult to recycle than others—not all types of recycled glass, for example, are suitable for all new fiber-glass insulation. But across the board, recycling now keeps hundreds of millions of pounds of waste out of landfills.

In terms of percentages alone, slag wool, cotton, and cellulose lead the pack by using 75 percent or more recycled material in newly manufactured insulation, according to a report by *Environmental Building News.*

Using recycled materials in manufacturing reduces waste that must be landfilled, lowers the amount of virgin materials that must be used, and should save energy because producers don't have to start from scratch each time they make something—all good things. Incorporating recycled materials into new products is more than showing corporate goodwill or responsibility: It's inherently easier with some types of insulation than it is with others. For example, cellulose has high recycled content because the raw materials are easy to get and easy to process. Manufacturers of other types of insulation may have trouble getting as much recycled material that's suitable for use in new products.

That is one of many considerations. In the end, no single type of insulation does everything perfectly. There are tradeoffs with all of them, either in terms of their thermal performance, cost and availability, how many chemical additives they contain, and whether they can be recycled at the end of their useful life. In general, however, what's most important is performance, creating an effective thermal barrier that saves money and resources over the life of the building.

Fiberglass batts

For a variety of reasons, fiberglass batts get used more often than any other type of insulation in U.S. homes. They are available at virtually any building supplier in a variety of thicknesses and densities, both faced and unfaced, and sized for both 16-in. and 24-in. on-center framing. The devil is in the details. Batts have to fit the stud cavity perfectly if they are going

If fiberglass batts are the insulation of choice, make sure they are formaldehyde-free.

Fiberglass batt insulation can be effective, but it is susceptible to air leaks if batts don't fit perfectly. Even minor gaps at the top of a wall cavity seriously degrade performance.

to be effective, and they must be cut and fitted carefully around pipes, ducts, wires, and electric boxes.

Fiberglass installation glitches that seem insignificant have a surprisingly big impact on how well batt insulation works. The California Energy Commission found that a 4 percent void—that's only a $1/2$-in. gap at the top of a stud bay—reduces efficiency by up to 50 percent. When it is compressed, fiberglass loses some of its insulating potential—a good reason not to pack an R-19 batt made for a 2x6 wall into a 2x4 stud bay. It must be installed with the correct loft as well as the right fit.

For these reasons, installing batt insulation calls for a methodical attention to detail, not blazing speed. And that may not happen when the job is left to a subcontractor who can't wait to get out the door and on to the next job. Few fiberglass installers take the time to do it right.

A PROBLEM WITH RECESSED LIGHTS

Recessed lights are a common source of trouble in an insulated ceiling. Batt insulation compressed over the top of the light loses some of its efficiency and blocks the flow of air beneath the roof deck.

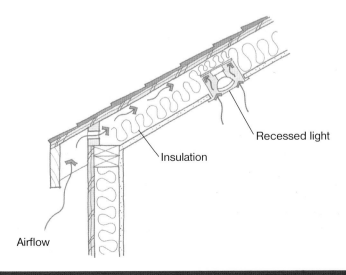

Recessed light

Insulation

Airflow

Although the International Agency for Research on Cancer does not consider glass fibers a carcinogen, manufacturers in the U.S. are required to put cancer warning labels on

---

Fiberglass batt insulation comes in three flavors—foil-faced, kraft-faced, and unfaced. Foil facings are the least permeable to water vapor but may trap moisture if not detailed correctly. Kraft paper is more permeable, blocking some moisture vapor but allowing some drying as well. Unfaced batts are not designed to block water vapor and on exterior walls are used in very cold climates with a separate polyethylene vapor retarder.

---

packages of fiberglass insulation. At the least it is a skin and lung irritant during installation. Moreover, there is still debate over the effects of formaldehyde, used as a binder in some brands of fiberglass batt insulation. European standards for permissible levels of formaldehyde are 10 times lower than those in the U.S. Here, rules are based on the OSHA standard setting exposure levels that a 35-year-old worker should be allowed to encounter over an 8-hour workday, or 100 parts per billion (ppb). Today's batts meet that standard.

In Denmark, the standard of 10 ppb is based on the permissible exposure of an 18-month-old child roughly 18 in. from the source of formaldehyde over a 24-hour span. You can imagine why the standard is so much lower. California has a proposed standard of 27 ppb for the *entire home* one week after construction is finished. On that basis, fiberglass batts that contain formaldehyde don't

meet the proposed standard in California or regulations in Europe. There are batts on the market that don't use formaldehyde, but in general the industry is fighting tighter restrictions on formaldehyde because it is a cheaper binder than the alternatives.

Given the difficulty of effective installation, lingering health concerns involving glass fibers, and the presence of formaldehyde binders in some brands of batt fiberglass, it makes sense to explore other available alternatives. There are better choices. If fiberglass is the only practical choice, it must be installed very carefully, ideally in conjunction with a layer of rigid foam on the outside of the building.

Non-fiberglass batts

Batt insulation also is made from mineral wool—produced from certain types of rock or blast-furnace slag—as well as two natural fibers, cotton and wool. Rock and slag wool, more common for residential use outside the U.S., are said to be comparable in cost to fiberglass, but may be substantially more in some markets. With a higher density than fiberglass, it has a higher R-value (up to 4.2 per inch, according to one manufacturer) and it's better at deadening sound. It's also highly resistant to fire, and it doesn't lose its insulating value when it gets wet.

Slag wool uses a great deal of recycled material. Thermafiber Inc., a producer in Wabash, Ind., claims that post-industrial recycled content in its batts is greater than 80 percent. Batts are available in thicknesses up to 6 in. and in 16-in. and 24-in. widths, and they come both faced and unfaced.

Mineral wool is common in commercial, industrial, and marine applications, but we don't hear much about it for use in houses. Economics probably plays a major role. Producers view commercial construction as a

Mineral wool, a category that includes rock wool and slag wool, is more common in commercial construction than residential construction and as a result may be somewhat harder to find through regular residential suppliers. But it is available with R-values greater than 4 per inch, and slag wool has high recycled content.

its UltraTouch® cotton batt insulation is made from 85 percent post-industrial denim waste. Batts are reassuringly soft and can be handled without itching. They are made without chemical irritants, have minimal embodied energy, and are 100 percent recyclable. Like mineral wool, however, cotton batts come in more limited thicknesses than fiberglass and they are not produced in a faced version. They are made for a friction fit in 2x4 and 2x6 walls with R-values ranging from R-13 to R-21.

What could be more reassuring than wrapping your house in wool, more or less like pulling on a thick sweater made of a completely natural and sustainable material? That's what much bigger market, so that's where they are focused. Mineral wool batts are not available in as many thicknesses or lengths as fiberglass, and because mineral wool is likely to cost somewhat more than fiberglass, it's not the first product budget-minded builders are going to ask for. Costs also explain why blown-in mineral wool may be hard to find. Thermafiber®, for instance, stopped selling blown-in insulation altogether simply because it couldn't compete with cellulose.

Even so, slag wool and rock wool have several decided advantages over fiberglass batt insulation. If they're available in your market, they are worth considering.

Wool and cotton batts

Both cotton and wool batts are niche products, available from select manufacturers and at a higher cost than other options. But they are attractive on other levels. Bonded Logic Inc. says

Cotton batt insulation, made mostly from post-industrial denim waste, won't make your skin itch and it's completely recyclable. In addition, cotton insulation has a low embodied energy and roughly the same insulating value as fiberglass.

Wool batt insulation, like cotton, is a completely natural product that won't cause any irritation during handling. It's hard to find in the U.S. but can be ordered directly through some foreign manufacturers. Expect to pay a premium.

manufacturers of wool insulation are banking on. Manufacturers in New Zealand and Europe say their batt and loose-fill wool have been treated with boron compounds against rodents, insects, and mold; contain no chemical irritants; and need no precautions for installation. The insulation is fire-resistant and self-extinguishing; and it's completely biodegradable. It's also hydroscopic, meaning it's capable of absorbing a substantial amount of moisture and then drying out without damage.

Wool has a very strong feel-good component, but high cost and low availability are two big drawbacks. Finding a retailer who carries wool insulation can be difficult if not impossible (you may be able to order directly from the manufacturer). Moreover, the National Association of Home Builders Research Center says wool insulation has not been thoroughly tested, at least not in the United States. Given those conditions, it's not a very practical choice even if it is appealing in the abstract.

Loose-Fill Insulation

Loose-fill insulation has taken many forms over the years. In the 1950s, vermiculite and rock wool dominated the market for wall cavities and ceiling installations. Blown fiberglass subsequently became the insulation of choice, especially in attics where it's easy to apply. Cellulose, which is mostly recycled newsprint, has been around for a long time but only in the last decade has it taken market share from fiberglass. A persistent myth about cellulose is that because it's made from newsprint it must be flammable. Actually, it's treated with borates to make it fire-resistant. It chars but it doesn't burn.

Before borates became the treatment of choice for cellulose, manufacturers used ammonium sulfate. When dry, the compound has no odor but if the insulation gets wet or the walls are closed up too soon after the damp-spray cellulose is applied, the smell can linger. This additive is something to avoid.

Whether it's fiberglass or cellulose, loose-fill flows around wires and pipes, electric boxes, and other obstructions, filling wall and ceiling cavities. In this respect, it is less susceptible than batts to air leaks and therefore should be a better thermal performer. Cellulose and fiberglass are competitive in cost but cellulose has a higher insulating potential: R-3.7 versus R-2.8.

Both cellulose and fiberglass are especially effective in an attic where they can be applied in as thick a layer as the homeowner wants to pay for, boosting the all important insulating value at the top of the house for relatively little money. When loose-fill is blown into

There's quite a range in the amount of energy it takes to manufacture different types of insulation. Cellulose, for instance, needs less energy to produce than expanded polystyrene, mineral wool less than fiberglass. It's one point to consider, but use numbers cautiously. There is no global standard for how to measure "embodied energy" and exactly which parts of manufacturing and transportation should be included.

Cellulose combined with a binder and sprayed into wall cavities fills even small voids effectively, sharply reducing the amount of air movement and with it the risk of condensation inside walls and ceilings.

Chemical additives in cellulose insulation make the recycled newsprint fire-resistant. Exposed to the flame from a propane torch, it chars but will not burn.

the attic, the key is to make sure it's applied in a uniformly thick layer and at the density recommended by the manufacturer. Marking battens and standing them up at intervals across the attic joists, or marking the bottoms of rafters, can ensure the insulation is going in evenly. Make sure to protect soffit vents with baffles so the flow of air into the attic is not blocked.

In addition to loose-fill applications, cellulose and fiberglass can also be sprayed into wall and ceiling cavities when mixed with a binder. This is a best-of-both-worlds installation. The spray is a latex liquid mixed with the insulation at the nozzle. The binder creates a matrix that reduces airflow through the insulation and helps it stick to the sides and back of the cavity. It flows around all the pipes and wires in the wall, filling the voids left behind in a sloppy batt installation. The ultimate benefit is that it greatly reduces the "cavity factor" that causes so many building science nightmares. By reducing airflow, this type of insulation also reduces the potential for damaging water vapor to get into walls and ceilings while greatly reducing air infiltration.

Sprayed cellulose and fiberglass can either be installed with a fiberglass mesh to hold the insulation in place or sprayed and "mowed." Cellulose is often sprayed to overfill the cavity and then flattened so it is flush with the studs so drywall can be installed.

Neither loose-fill fiberglass nor cellulose contains formaldehyde. Cellulose is typically treated with a borate compound. Moreover, cellulose meets all three criteria for being green: it improves energy efficiency, has low toxicity, and is made with recycled content. Probably for those reasons, it is the top choice of most building scientists and should be near the top of the list for homeowners weighing their options.

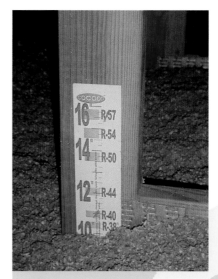

Blown fiberglass and cellulose *piled high in open attics make an effective thermal barrier at the top of the house. Marking rafters or trusses is a good way to ensure you get the right depth.*

Spray-In Insulation

Spray-in foams have very good R-values—up to 6.5 per inch—and do an exceptionally good job of air sealing. They are also among the most expensive residential insulation options—a classic case of spending more up front for increased comfort and energy efficiency long into the future. Foams are typically urethane-based, but a new type of urethane is made from soybean shells. Blowing agents, which fluff up the ingredients as they are applied, vary but ozone-destroying compounds that were used in the past have gradually been weeded out. Some are foamed with water.

Air sealing is particularly important in the wall between an attached garage and the house so unburned hydrocarbons and other indoor air contaminants are not allowed to filter into the house. If air pressure inside the house is negative, pollutants will be pulled into the

__Metal channels__ attached to the inside of a conventionally framed wall allow a thicker layer of spray-in foam without increasing the depth of framing members. The practice also reduces thermal bridging.

__When the foam is scraped back__ to the metal channel, the flattened wall is ready for an interior finish.

house every time the door is opened. This is most likely in northern climates because a car might be started in the garage and allowed to warm up. If the driver goes back and forth into the house, the pollutants follow. All too often the garage is attached to the kitchen where the kids are. Spray foam insulation is the best product to stop air movement through walls.

Spray foams are available in both low-density, open-cell and high-density, closed-cell varieties that are applied with specialized spray equipment. Foam expands on contact (open-cell foams increase 100-fold in volume, high-density foams about one-third that much), so they're both excellent at sealing even tiny gaps. They're especially effective around band joists, an area that's tough to insulate properly with more conventional products. Some production builders use low-expanding urethane foam to seal exterior surfaces and joints then follow up with fiberglass to keep costs down.

Some green builders object to the fact that most spray-in foams are made with petro-chemicals. That may be true, but fossil fuels

One difference between high- and low-density foams is the degree to which they allow water vapor to pass through. Low-density foams are more vapor permeable than high-density foams, but they both form extremely effective air barriers.

used in this way offer a big payback for many years—much more, say, than burning up a tank of gas in the family SUV to run some errands. It's oil well spent. Foam is highly effective both as an air barrier and as a thermal barrier. The worst you can say about spray foams is that they're typically more expensive than the alternatives.

Cementitious foam

A variation on spray-in foam is a product called air-krete®, which is made from air, water, and cement. With an R-value of 3.9 per inch, the foam has the consistency of shaving cream when initially foamed but hardens into a non-shrinking mass. According to the company, this insulation contains no hazardous materials or formaldehyde and is noncombustible.

From a green standpoint, air-krete is a very attractive product. Like spray-in polyurethane foams, it's very good at filling voids and providing an effective air seal. But it does not contain any petrochemicals or ozone-depleting blowing agents. While the company says it is steadily expanding its ranks of installers, it's not available equally in all parts of the country, at least not yet.

Rigid Foam

Rigid foam insulation is an increasingly important building material. Historically, extruded polystyrene (XPS) has been used to insulate foundations below grade. Rigid foam insulation applied to the outside of a framed wall can help to keep the dew point (the temperature at which water vapor condenses into liquid) outside wall cavities. That keeps wall cavities drier and reduces the risk of mold and decay. Applying a layer of rigid

foam on the exterior of a house framed with light-gauge steel is essential in making the thermal barrier effective. Without it, walls can lose 50 percent of their nominal insulating value.

Using foam this way improves the overall R-value of the walls, reduces air infiltration, and reduces the thermal bridging effect of the framing material. Polyisocyanurate (R-6 to 7.5 per inch) is now being applied by some builders over roof sheathing to isolate the attic (and the ductwork running through it) and reduce heat build-up in summer (for more on ductwork, see chapter 9). This type of rigid foam has OSB adhered to one side as a nail base for felt paper and shingles. It is great for a retrofit project while re-roofing a house and can even be added to an existing ceiling during a retrofit.

There are three main types: expanded polystyrene (EPS) for low-moisture environ-

Rigid foam insulation applied to the outside of a building reduces thermal bridging and air infiltration while moving the dew point inward to reduce the risk of condensation inside wall cavities.

ADDING RIGID FOAM INSULATION

Rigid foam insulation applied on the outside of a house reduces thermal bridging, the tendency for framing members to leak heat through the building envelope. Another advantage is that the foam helps to move the dew point outward, reducing the risk that water vapor will condense on cool surfaces inside the wall cavity. Rigid foam is essential in houses framed with light-gauge steel.

OUTSIDE CORNER DETAIL

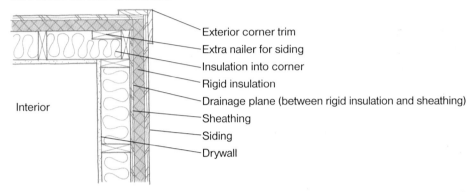

Interior

Exterior corner trim
Extra nailer for siding
Insulation into corner
Rigid insulation
Drainage plane (between rigid insulation and sheathing)
Sheathing
Siding
Drywall

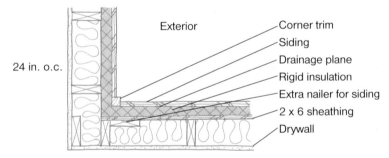

Exterior

24 in. o.c.

Corner trim
Siding
Drainage plane
Rigid insulation
Extra nailer for siding
2 x 6 sheathing
Drywall

INSIDE CORNER DETAIL

ments; closed-cell extruded polystyrene (XPS), which can be used in moist conditions; and polyisocyanurate for use in walls and roof sheathing. EPS uses steam or pentane to expand the foam pellets into a sheet product. XPS often uses a hydrochlorofluorocarbon (HCFC), a compound consisting of hydrogen, chlorine, fluorine, and carbon. Although 90 percent better than earlier-generation CFCs, which cause ozone holes in the atmosphere, HCFCs still emit 10 percent of the gases that combine with stratospheric ozone, undermining the atmosphere's ability to absorb ultraviolet light and consequently leading to high rates of skin cancer.

The same is true with polyiso boards. The highest insulating value (R-7.5) is in boards that use HCFCs. These boards are often covered with an aluminum skin that reduces the off-gassing of the blowing agent but they still off-gas over time, which reduces the R-value. Newer types of polyiso board are manufactured with a proprietary non-HCFC blowing agent and are more benign. This reduces the R-value to 6 per inch.

INSULATION RETROFIT

It's amazing how one can stay oblivious to the obvious. For the 15 years I've owned my 1972 vintage house, every winter brought dramatic icicles to the eaves outside the dining room. They made fine Christmas decorations but the winter of 2006–07 was a doozie in Colorado and the icicles got the better of us. An ice dam formed behind them and started a waterfall down the inside wall. I knew what needed to happen.

I hired my friend Rick Lewis to come in and investigate what was causing all of the heat loss. We took off the drywall adjacent to the beams above the waterfall. Wind whistled through leaks in the wall, and the 1972 insulation had been installed so haphazardly that I could see the sheathing. R-0 in that spot.

Rick also probed the ceiling and what seemed like a well-built cathedral ceiling had barely an R-11 insulation job. Time for a heavy-duty retrofit. I got the idea from my roofer. When I replaced my roof I installed 2-in. polyiso rigid foam insulation with OSB laminated to the top before I re-roofed. The material is much like half of a SIP. This gave me an additional R-15 on the cathedral ceiling of my living room.

I figured that I could use the product upside down in the dining room and get the additional insulation I needed without taking off the roofing. The idea worked perfectly. The panels were cut to fit between the beams. The exterior wall was stripped back to studs, caulked at the sheathing, and foamed at the spaces that created the infiltration. Then we re-insulated with no-added-formaldehyde, encapsulated batts from Johns Manville, and within a couple of days we were warmer than we had ever been. The rigid foam was installed with the OSB down, covered with drywall and painted. The dining room is cozy and prettier than ever.

—DJ

Sloppy installation of the insulation ensured significant heat.

New fiberglass batts in place, properly installed.

Polyiso board is installed in the ceiling, adding an additional R-15.

Careful detailing and caulking provide for a tight, air-sealed project.

- Treat insulation recommendations from the Department of Energy as minimums. Aim for insulation levels that are 50 percent better.

- Use insulation that completely fills wall and ceiling cavities and reduces or eliminates air leaks—structural insulated panels, spray-in foam, or spray-in cellulose or fiberglass are the best products for this.

- Avoid fiberglass batt insulation that contains formaldehyde and cellulose that contains ammonium sulfate.

- Avoid fiberglass batts if possible; if they must be used, make sure the installer knows what he's doing. Supplement batts with a layer of rigid foam insulation on the exterior of the building.

- Do not use light-gauge steel framing on exterior walls without a layer of exterior insulation to counteract thermal bridging.

- When calculating the desired thermal performance of a wall or ceiling, don't forget to include the effects of doors, windows, and other materials that penetrate the building envelope. In general, real performance will be lower than the nominal R-value of the insulation you're using. Plan accordingly.

- Don't confuse a thermal barrier with an air barrier. One retards the flow of heat, the other prevents air infiltration and the migration of water vapor into wall and ceiling cavities. Both are important.

Radiant Barriers

Radiant barriers are used in the attic to reduce heat gain from the sun. They're primarily used in regions with high cooling loads. There are several types, including sheathing with a radiant barrier bonded to one side or aluminized Mylar® that is rolled out and stapled to the tops

of the rafters or roof trusses. Another product type looks like bubble wrap with aluminized Mylar on one surface.

In all cases, the reduction of radiant heat gain can be significant and helps reduce the temperature in attics (which can climb to 160°F on hot days). This is particularly important if ductwork is running through the attic.

With so many insulation choices, it's easy to get lost in the details. Look at what's available in your market and weigh the pros and cons of each. When you have a choice, avoid insulation with obvious drawbacks (fiberglass batts that contain formaldehyde, for instance) and make sure it's installed properly. But the bottom line is to invest in enough insulation. Don't settle for energy code minimums when an effective thermal barrier is so fundamental to good green building.

A radiant barrier beneath the roof deck lowers attic temperatures during the summer, thereby reducing cooling loads in the house. This type of insulation comes in several forms, including sheathing with a layer of aluminized Mylar bonded to one side.

Siding and Decking

Siding, or cladding as it is called in the world of architecture, is primarily an aesthetic element that covers the structure of the house. From the point of view of sustainable building, siding makes three important contributions: it makes the building more weather resistant, less likely to burn down, and more durable. Typically, though, these functional attributes take a back seat to what siding does to the look of a house, what real estate agents call "curb appeal." Outside decks are in something of the same category—not a functional necessity but definitely valued by home buyers.

People often assume that siding is the primary weather barrier on the house. It isn't. That task falls to the drainage plane beneath the siding in much the same way that shingles

THE GREEN FACTOR

Siding is the first line of weather defense and makes an important aesthetic contribution to the architectural character of a house. In areas where fire danger is high, siding can reduce the risk of loss. Some things to consider:

• Poorly installed siding, or the wrong choice of material, increases the likelihood of early replacement—a source of unnecessary waste and expense. Some materials last for many years with a minimum of care.

• An essential element of siding is the drainage plane behind it, the weather barrier that keeps water from penetrating the building and causing mold and decay.

• Top grades of wood siding and decking are durable as well as beautiful but declining stocks of old-growth trees have made it more difficult to find and more expensive.

• Recent innovations, such as fiber-cement siding and wood/plastic composite decking, are excellent replacements for natural products that offer a number of advantages, including low maintenance and the use of recycled material.

Siding may appear to be the most important weather barrier on a house, but that task actually falls to a drainage plane installed over the sheathing which diverts water away from the house. Eventually, all siding leaks.

cover and protect the primary weatherproofing barrier on the roof—the building paper or membrane covering the sheathing.

That's not to say there aren't important considerations to take into account when choosing siding. Modern manufacturing techniques have blurred the distinctions between natural and man-made products—fiber cement siding, for example, can look almost exactly like wood clapboarding, and some types of vinyl look so much like wood shingles, even from a few feet away, that you have to reach out and touch them to know. This has made it easier to choose siding that appeals to our aesthetic traditions even as we look for durability and performance. Although there are tradeoffs with some siding choices, having more options is a good thing in an age when the mostly wood products we've grown accustomed to are getting harder to find and more expensive.

Drainage Planes

All cladding leaks. Eventually it will fail, and moisture will find an avenue inside to the

sheathing and, eventually, to the structural elements below. The secret to longevity is giving moisture a way of draining down and away from the building. In grandpa's day, buildings were wrapped with asphalt-impregnated felt paper, just like the roof. As production building became the norm and houses were built as rapidly as possible, for as little money as possible, shortcuts were taken. Too often in recent years, the housewrap or drainage plane has been eliminated and siding installed directly over building sheathing of OSB or plywood. These houses start to fail after just a few years. Problems have prompted the insurance industry to cease paying for mold and moisture damage to improperly constructed homes. Two major insurance companies already have stopped underwriting homes in California and Texas due to the proliferation of mold problems, or they are excluding mold claims on existing policies.

A drainage plane is an intentional design element to ensure that any moisture that gets behind the siding has a way to evaporate or drain down the wall and away from the build-

Housewrap, manufactured under several trade names, is designed to let water vapor through while preventing the passage of bulk moisture. It should be layered correctly (top course over lower course) so it sheds water.

Corrugations in the house-wrap ensure that there is positive drainage for any water that intrudes behind the siding.

ing. Combinations of materials can achieve this goal cost-effectively. First among them is housewrap. Several manufacturers have products that shed water yet still allow water vapor to escape—Tyvek® and Typar® are two well-known brands. Think of it as Gortex™ for your house. If you are using an Exterior Insulation and Finishing System (EIFS) or stucco, there are specialized housewraps designed for this application. Don't use standard housewraps.

Another approach is to use felt paper and cover it with a product that allows water to pass through and drain to the bottom of the cavity. There are several such products on the market, including Home Slicker,® a ¼-in.-thick matrix applied beneath siding, DuPont's Tyvek Drain-

A WARNING ABOUT HOUSEWRAP

Housewraps such as Tyvek and Typar have largely displaced old-fashioned tarpaper as the weather barrier between sheathing and siding. These products allow water vapor to pass through while preventing liquid water from getting in where it can cause structural damage. Manufacturers claim that housewraps can be used beneath any type of siding.

Joseph Lstiburek, a well-known building scientist, isn't so sure. He argues that contaminants called "surfactants" that leach out of certain types of wood affect the water repellency of housewraps, and to a lesser extent building papers, and eventually allow the passage of water. Once water gets in, peeling paint and decay can follow.

Lstiburek suggests isolating the wood from direct contact with housewrap, by either back-priming trim and clapboards, using a commercial product that keeps siding away from direct contact with the building, or making a rain screen with an air space between the siding and the sheathing. According to Lstiburek, you should be equally cautious about applying stucco directly to any plastic-based housewrap, which may encourage the capillary flow of water.

Recent developments in housewrap include specialized products that provide a way for water to drain away from the building.

wrap,® and a product called Rainscreen.® All of them are designed to eliminate trapped water behind the siding.

A third method is to nail furring strips vertically to the studs over the housewrap and attach the cladding to them. This creates an air space between the housewrap and the cladding, guaranteeing that moisture will drain to the bottom of the wall. In all cases. there must be a way for the water to get out and away from the house.

Integrity of the housewrap, however, is key. If it's damaged during construction, it must be replaced or repaired before the siding is installed. Rips, inadvertent knife cuts, and holes from rough handling render housewrap useless. Seams should be overlapped before they are taped (top course over the lower course) so that weather tightness is not wholly dependent on tape that may fail down the road.

Housewrap can do an excellent job of protecting sheathing, but not if it's torn or damaged. It should be layered so water drains down, and joints should be overlapped not just taped.

MAKING A RAIN SCREEN

Creating an air gap beneath the back of the siding helps protect the house from water that's driven through the siding or drawn in through capillary action. It also promotes drying and helps reduce the risk of mold and decay. If the siding is painted, the paint film will last much longer.

The method described here and shown in the drawings on pp. 232–233, used by builder Mark Averill Snyder to cure a chronic paint-peeling problem, combines Grace Ice & Water Shield, a self-sticking bituminous membrane, tar paper, and ⅜ in. by 2 in. plywood furring strips. The membrane (applied to the bottom of the wall) and the tar paper make up the drainage plane. Furring strips nailed to the house, directly over the studs, support the siding.

To promote ventilation and give water a way to drain out of the wall, Snyder used Cor-A-Vent, a roof vent product, and insect screening at the bottom of the wall plus an ingenious vent at the top of the wall that's hidden by a trim board. The result? Fully protected sheathing and a much longer life for paint.

Layers of material keep water away from the house behind this rain screen. Tar paper covers the top edge of flashing over door and window casings, which in turn are lapped over tar paper that protects furring strips along the side casing.

BUILDING A RAIN SCREEN

A rain screen is an exterior detail that creates an air gap between the back of the siding and the sheathing to prevent siding from being waterlogged. Furring strips nailed over a layer of #15 tarpaper make a nail base for the siding. At the bottom of the wall, a vent promotes air circulation. Ice & Water Shield provides another layer of protection.

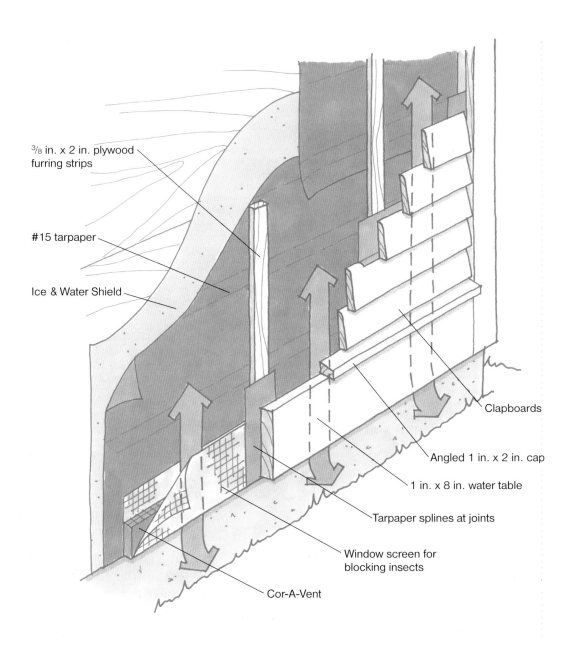

³/₈ in. x 2 in. plywood furring strips

#15 tarpaper

Ice & Water Shield

Clapboards

Angled 1 in. x 2 in. cap

1 in. x 8 in. water table

Tarpaper splines at joints

Window screen for blocking insects

Cor-A-Vent

VENTING A RAIN SCREEN WALL

At the top of the wall, rabbeted 1x4 trim provides a way for air to circulate, allowing the back of the siding to dry out. A rain screen makes paint last longer and helps to discourage mold and rot.

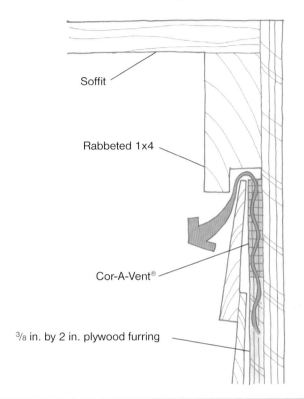

Soffit

Rabbeted 1x4

Cor-A-Vent®

3/8 in. by 2 in. plywood furring

Siding Materials

There are several benchmarks for deciding whether a particular kind of siding is green. Because siding is a relatively expensive part of the house, durability is one of the most important qualifiers. The object should be to find a material that not only helps to protect the house but also does its job over the long haul. Installing good materials at the outset means they won't have to be replaced (at considerable cost) prematurely and won't contribute needlessly to the local landfill.

If siding fails because it's not suitable to a specific climate or simply not up to the task, it can't really be considered green. Exterior Insulation and Finish Systems (EIFS) is a good example of a material that isn't suited to some climates. Certain early types of composite wood siding also had a history of failure that led to some very disappointed (and bankrupt) builders and homeowners as well as class-action lawsuits.

The second key benchmark is the source of the material. For example, if you're using wood siding, consider whether the material is certified by the Forest Stewardship Council rather than produced from unspecified sources. Finally, safety is a factor in the suitability of some materials. Cement siding is particularly appropriate in fire-prone climates, for example, where wood siding is not.

Wood siding

Wood siding goes back to the days of the Pilgrims. With vast stretches of virgin forest to cut, it was by far the most accessible material at the time. It literally grew in the backyard, and it could be turned into building materials with very few tools (and an awful lot of sweat). Wood was appealing architecturally, and houses clad in wood became a building standard that would rule for the next 200 years.

Before insulation became common, the biggest maintenance issue with wood siding was keeping it painted. With nothing in the wall cavities to trap moisture, water that leaked in could evaporate and get out the same way it got in. Although long-term exposure to water could rot the siding, it was fairly easy to replace damaged boards once in a while. When we started to insulate houses in the mid-20th century, however, everything changed. Trapped water had fewer ways to get out of the house and that created ideal conditions for mold and rot to become epidemic. Today, any kind of softwood siding with the exception of cedar and redwood should be considered prone to decay. It's one of the least-effective ways to side a home.

Shingles and shakes

Cedar shingles create a nostalgic look that's still popular in New England and the upper Midwest. (Can you imagine a genuine Cape Cod cottage clad in anything but shingles?) Previously, cedar was a natural choice because of its availability and inherent rot resistance. With the exception of a few regions where it remains popular in new construction, however, most cedar siding installed these days replaces worn or damaged shingles. Because it's so labor intensive to install, this cladding is unaffordable for many people building new homes.

Moreover, from a green perspective two issues make it unattractive.

First, is the availability of trees. We have cut most of the old-growth cedar in the lower 48 and replaced natural forests with tree plantations. The last of the great cedar trees are in western Canada, and they are being clear-cut at an alarming rate. Second, cedar is really just tinder waiting for a match. In parts of the country where forest fires are prevalent, houses sided or roofed in cedar are sitting ducks for fire. And fire safety is a very green issue.

There are several species of cedar used to manufacture shingles—western red, Atlantic and northern white, and Alaskan yellow—and a growing number of companies offer FSC-

Cedar shingles are a traditional siding in some parts of the country, but they are labor intensive to install as well as expensive. If that's the siding of choice, shingles should be made from FSC-certified wood.

certified cedar. At a minimum, shingles should have no knots or defects below the weather line. Better yet are the top grades made from clear lumber and "rebutted and re-squared" (sold as R&Rs), which substantially speeds up installation and reduces waste. They are indeed beautiful and the best grades of shingles made from heartwood will prove extremely durable. Assuming you can find FSC-certified shingles in the species you want, their high cost and the need for skilled labor to install them remain two serious drawbacks.

The heartwood of cedar and redwood *is naturally resistant to insects and rot, but declining supplies of big trees can make top grades an expensive choice. Cedar and redwood should both be FSC certified.*

Redwood and cedar planks

Like cedar shingles, cedar siding is naturally resistant to rot. Redwood of old has even better resistance to termites and rot. Forestry issues, however, now overshadow the use of both species.

Redwood is still used on the West Coast on the assumption that it is the species in general, not the cut of wood, that is rot resistant. In fact, only the heartwood has those characteristics. If you've used redwood in the last decade, you've probably noticed that most of the boards show a mix of white and red wood. White wood is sap wood from the exterior of the tree, only heartwood is red. Younger redwood trees grown in plantations are harvested before the heartwood can develop fully, and sap wood will rot just like pine. It has little or no natural insect resistance.

Plywood siding can suffer with extended exposure to the weather, but it makes an excellent nail base for a retrofit in which insulation and new siding are added.

T-111 ROT REPAIR

My house, built in 1972, had T-111 installed directly over plywood sheathing without a layer of felt paper to act as a drainage plane. When I insulated the exterior during an energy update and renovation, I found many places where water had leaked through the siding and sheathing and caused rot at the bottom of studs and bottom plates. I had to replace the rot before I could continue installing the insulation and add fiber cement siding.

The process included removing all the ¾-in. window and door trim. This allowed me to foam the gaps between the framing and trimmers (a cause for great infiltration and discomfort). I then replaced the trim with brick mold. Its thicker profile allowed for 1 in. of foam and the cement siding.

I installed 15-lb. felt paper over the entire exterior. The 1-in. closed-cell XPS then went over the felt. Closed-cell foam is better as a secondary moisture barrier. I used pre-primed 1x4 corner boards so I could caulk the butt joints of the siding. Then I installed 1x6 corner boards over the lap siding for decorative effect and to cover the 1x4s.

This combination of foam and hard siding had an unexpected effect of producing an amazing acoustic barrier. Neighborhood dogs ceased to be a problem.

—DJ

On top of that, unless either cedar or redwood purchased today is FSC certified the source is questionable. Some of the largest redwood operations in California have acquired land in leveraged buyouts from family land holdings. They are cutting the last of the old stands, and when the big trees are gone, they will be gone forever. Buying FSC siding is the only way to know that the wood you are using has been sustainably forested. If you've seen a cathedral-like redwood forest, like Muir woods in Marin County, Calif., and been lucky enough to peer up at 1,000-year-old trees, you can feel the heartbreak in what we have lost.

Architectural plywood

Fewer homes today are built with plywood siding. Texture-111 was common in the '70s and '80s. Today, those homes look pretty tired and dated. With extended exposure to the weather, plywood tends to warp and delaminate. T-111 can serve as a perfect base for rigid foam on the exterior of the house during a retrofit. Used in this fashion, the surface is protected from decay. But as a choice for new construction, plywood ranks low on the desirability list.

Stucco

Conventional stucco, which is a cement-based mixture applied in two or three coats, is a durable finish that does not require a great deal of maintenance. Stucco siding has an average warranty life of 15 years, although when it is installed properly it can last 50 years or more. By nature, stucco is a green product that's preferred by natural building proponents because it is made only with lime, silica sand, and white cement. It can be installed directly over concrete block or stone, wood-sheathed walls, or special XPS foam for exterior insulation. When used in straw-bale construction (see p. 9), stucco requires a special lime-rich mixture so it can wick water to the outside.

Stucco, though expensive, makes an excellent siding choice. When properly applied it is extremely durable and requires very little maintenance.

As with any siding material, a stucco finish should include a drainage plane under the insulation (a double layer of D paper is recommended) or between the stucco and concrete block.

Like cement siding (see p. 240), stucco is an effective fire-resistant barrier when used over wood-frame construction. If there is a downside, it is that stucco is very labor intensive, and should be installed by professionals for a clean, smooth finish. Because of that, it may be the most expensive siding option of all. In parts of the country where plasterers are scarce, stucco is probably not a reasonable option even though it's a good green choice.

Synthetic stucco

Exterior Insulation and Finish Systems (EIFS) is also called synthetic stucco. This multilayer system, developed in Europe and introduced to the U.S. 30 years ago, can resemble traditional masonry stucco finishes. According to an industry trade group, EIFS is used on nearly 30 percent of commercial building exteriors.

Both drainable and barrier systems are available. Drainable EIFS, when installed perfectly, provides an insulating exterior finish without the worries of water damage associated with barrier EIFS. Those problems resulted in class-action lawsuits several years ago resulting from water damage.

Barrier EIFS resists water penetration, but it does not allow any water that gets behind the surface to drain out of the wall. If water does get behind the exterior, it is something like sealing damp wood inside a plastic bag; some houses with this type of cladding started to rot in as little as three years. Water seeped in through fine cracks, often a result of faulty installation and poorly detailed flashing. Not only was mold and decay a problem but fiberglass insulation inside the wall cavity became soaked, making it ineffective and aiding decay of structural framing. Drainable systems are not as susceptible to this problem because they provide a way for water to exit the wall.

The benefit of an EIFS exterior is the additional layer of foam insulation on the outside

Exterior insulation and finish systems, or EIFS, can look just like traditional stucco. But unless the layers making up the cladding are carefully detailed, water can be trapped inside and damage sheathing and framing.

EIFS WALL SYSTEM

Exterior Insulation and Finish Systems combine synthetic stucco with insulation. They should be detailed so any water that penetrates the outer layer can drain down and away from the building. Barrier systems can trap water if there are any faults with flashing or cracks in the surface, raising the likelihood of mold and rot.

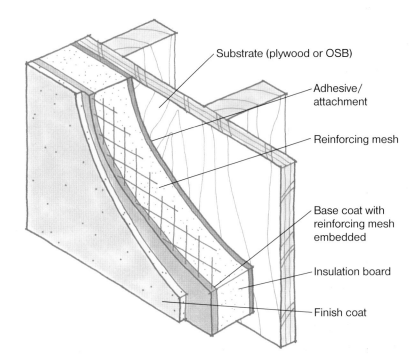

Substrate (plywood or OSB)

Adhesive/attachment

Reinforcing mesh

Base coat with reinforcing mesh embedded

Insulation board

Finish coat

of the house, which both reduces the thermal bridging of studs and other framing members and reduces drafts (up to 55 percent when compared to conventional wood-framed or brick buildings, according to the industry).

Drainable systems incorporate sheets of extruded (XPS) or expanded polystyrene (EPS). A plastic or glass fiber mesh is attached with special fasteners to create a drainage plane. Alternatively, a grooved foam board allows drainage. The mesh covers building paper or housewrap, over the sheathing of OSB or plywood. A cement/polymer base coat covers the insulation board and provides a base for embedding the fiberglass mesh. Then a flexible, acrylic-modified finish coat is applied over the

base coat. Application of a special sealant and flashing is also required to provide watertight seals and to divert water from critical junctions between EIFS and building components.

The principal green benefit with EIFS is the exterior layer of insulation. But expert installation and very careful detailing are essential. It's more expensive than some other siding choices but less than traditional stucco. Overall, it ranks as a second-tier choice.

Brick

Brick is a symbol of quality construction and durability, both attributes of green building. It's most often used as a façade over wood framing, but it requires virtually no maintenance

It takes a lot of energy to make brick, but
*it is an extremely durable cladding available
in many textures and colors. Because of high
transportation costs, it should be ordered
from a local kiln if one is available.*

and should protect a house from weather damage for many years.

Because brick is basically baked mud, it's a natural building material. It's also fire resistant and typically keeps most siding problems at bay. Brick, however, should come from local kilns. There is already more embodied energy in brick than most other types of siding (kilns use a lot of energy and bricks are fired for a considerable amount of time), and shipping it long distances only makes the difference more dramatic.

Providing it is sourced locally, brick is an attractive green product. It's available in many patterns and colors.

Cement siding

Fire is a major concern in many parts of the country, particularly the West, making fiber-cement siding a very attractive option. Wildfires often get into a house through soffits in roof overhangs. Attic ventilation acts as an accelerant, and flames attack rafters and any other exposed wood in the attic and roof. Fire actually burns down into the living space. By using cement siding, either in clapboard style or in panels, flames are slowed as they try to climb up the siding. Cement soffits, regardless of siding type, are a great way to inhibit the spread of flame.

Another advantage of cement siding is paint retention. It holds paint two to three times longer than wood, sharply reducing the need for exterior maintenance. In sum, increased safety, durability, and reduced maintenance are three green benefits. To top it off, cement siding is often the least expensive siding option available.

Installation is one potential drawback. It takes a contractor who knows which tools to use and how to manipulate this brittle product. Fiber cement siding cuts differently than wood: Although you can use a circular saw, you have to use a diamond blade because the material is so abrasive. Conventional steel or carbide blades dull in no time—you'll go through a box of them in just one house. Another option is to use specially designed shears to cut the material, eliminating the clouds of dust created with a circular saw. It takes time, however, to learn how to get accurate cuts. A guide and a square can help tremendously.

Fiber cement has many green attributes and comes in panel form as well as planks that are applied horizontally. While it's a little finicky to install, fiber cement holds paint well; is very durable; and resists fire, rot, and insects.

Vinyl siding

Polyvinyl chloride (PVC) has become a con-tentious topic in the green building world for several reasons. Despite the durability and low cost of vinyl siding, many green proponents think that using so much PVC on a house just can't be green. PVC is reviled by many health and environmental activists who cite its toxic manufacturing by-products and additives, its pervasiveness in the environment, and the fact that post-consumer PVC is extremely difficult to recycle.

Low cost, low maintenance, and durability helped to make vinyl siding a very popular choice, not only on production homes but custom houses as well. However, it does have some unfortunate environmental tradeoffs that make it a second-tier choice.

A key issue lies in the manufacturing of vinyl chloride monomer (from which POLY-vinyl chloride is made). Dioxin, a by-product, is a persistent environmental toxin that is not biode-gradable. If a vinyl-sided house burns, dioxin is released into the atmosphere. Exactly the same thing happens when PVC gets into a municipal waste stream and goes to an incinerator or is burned in a backyard refuse barrel. Studies have also linked exposure to vinyl chloride and PVC additives to cancer and other diseases. These and other concerns have prompted calls for a complete phase-out of PVC.

If there is an upside, it's that vinyl siding is relatively inexpensive, durable, and effec-tive, especially in very wet climates. It reduces maintenance because it doesn't have to be painted, just washed off once in a while, and it typically lasts a long time. For those reasons, vinyl siding is widely used.

Siding, of course, is only one of many building products made from PVC. Whether it should be used on the exterior of a house is a question typical of the dilemmas that home-owners and builders face in green building as they try to balance competing interests. In this case, it's durability and economy versus the threat of toxicity in the environment and the potential for disease among those who are involved in its manufacture. For some homeowners and builders, low cost and low maintenance may be deciding factors. But there are too many types of siding on the mar-ket that don't come so heavily burdened with health and pollution concerns to make this a first choice.

Decking

Outdoor decks and porches create another liv-ing zone for many houses, something between inside and out, and they are frequently part of house plans in all parts of the country. From a green-building perspective, there are two principal considerations: attaching the deck to the house in such a way that it does not lead to water leaks and structural damage and, second, choosing the material for the deck boards and the underlying structure.

Installing a ledger

House and deck are connected by a ledger, the framing member attached to the house to support one end of the floor joists on the deck (see the drawing on p. 244). Ledgers have a troublesome reputation, not only because they can fail catastrophically when installed improperly, but also because they're often detailed to encourage mold and decay.

Many a carpenter has made a week's pay by pulling apart a rotten wall where a ledger had been nailed or bolted to the house without thought to the potential for leaks. Water running down the outside wall of the house seeps behind the ledger and becomes trapped. In time, mold and decay attack the sheathing and eventually the structural framing of the house. Decay can be extensive.

Ledgers should be lagged or through-bolted to the rim joist or studs of the house after the drainage plane has been installed. That means the building felt or housewrap goes on the house first, then the ledger. This provides one line of defense against leaks. The second comes in the form of flashing formed over the top of the ledger and extended up the sidewall of the house at least 4 in. The top edge of the flashing should be tucked beneath the housewrap to prevent any water infiltration. Siding is installed after that.

Peel-and-stick flashing, like Ice & Water Shield made by Grace Building Products, can be used to protect this problem prone area.

It can be applied over the ledger and up the wall of the house, then protected from sunlight with a piece of metal or vinyl flashing. Relying on the membrane alone is to bank only on the

Self-adhering membranes can be used to seal ledger flashing to the house, but it is a better practice to tuck the top of the flashing beneath the housewrap or tar paper covering the sheathing.

adhesive and not overlapping layers of material, to create the seal. That said, an important benefit of this material is that it's self-sealing around nails or other fasteners.

Some builders go an extra step to protect the house and deck framing. In addition to careful flashing over the ledger, they advocate the use of stand-offs between the house and ledger. These consist of blocks or spacers that create an air space of $\frac{1}{2}$ in. or so between the house and the ledger so that any moisture able to find its way in has a place to drain. If you use this approach, make sure the spaces are made from solid, pressure-treated material.

On some houses, and often in multi-family buildings, floor joists are extended through the wall of the building to become joists for the deck. This "through the wall" approach begs for water intrusion around the joists, and it should never be used in new construction.

In some instances, the ledger shouldn't be connected to the house at all. On log houses, for example, it's difficult to flash the ledger-house connection correctly. Or there may not be a structural member in the house wall that can pick up the loads exerted by a deck ledger. In cases like these, making a free-standing deck eliminates any potential for leaks

ATTACHING A DECK LEDGER

A ledger is a vital structural connection between an exterior deck and the house. It should never be installed before housewrap or tarpaper, and the junction between ledger and house should be protected by flashing. Improperly installed ledgers are a common source of rot in sheathing and framing members—often an expensive problem to correct and potentially dangerous for occupants of the house.

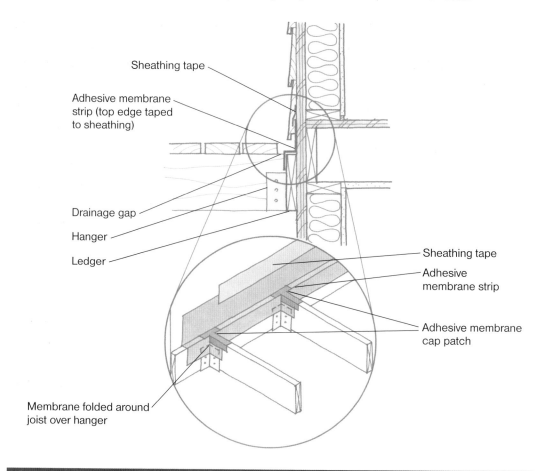

Sheathing tape

Adhesive membrane strip (top edge taped to sheathing)

Drainage gap

Hanger

Ledger

Membrane folded around joist over hanger

Sheathing tape

Adhesive membrane strip

Adhesive membrane cap patch

and solves a potential structural problem at the same time.

Decking materials

Redwood and cedar were once the decking materials of choice. Besides being beautiful, both species are naturally resistant to insects and are relatively mold and rot resistant. Decades of service could be expected. Today, redwood and cedar are not as abundant; both have been harvested with abandon along the Pacific Northwest coast. Clear-heart redwood is particularly difficult to find because it comes from old-growth trees.

As supplies of these trees have gradually declined and suitable stock has become increasingly expensive, other materials have taken their place. A variety of other wood species—including Ipé, Meranti, and Cambara—are now widely available. Vinyl, wood-plastic composites, and pressure-treated softwoods are other potential choices.

Treated lumber

For decades, southern yellow pine and several species of western softwoods pressure-treated with chromated copper arsenate (CCA) were the standards for outdoor decking. Long-standing health concerns over arsenic (an active component of rat poison) and chromium eventually prompted the withdrawal of CCA-treated lumber from most residential applications at the end of 2003. Chemical treatments that took CCA's place are less toxic to people and the environment, although not completely benign. Treated lumber can't be discarded in ordinary municipal waste, it should not be burned, and it requires some care in handling.

Lumber treated with chromated copper arsenate (CCA) was pulled from the residential market at the end of 2003 because of continuing concerns over its toxicity. One tablespoon of ash left from burned CCA lumber is enough to kill a cow.

In addition, treated lumber is not the most aesthetically durable decking material. Southern yellow pine can warp, split, and check with exposure to weather, creating an unsightly if still functional deck. It should be treated regularly with some kind of water repellent or preservative. So in addition to its chemical-related drawbacks, treated lumber needs more regular care and is not as hardy as some other decking choices. It is, however, relatively inexpensive.

In time, organic compounds are likely to take the place of the metal-rich chemical treatments now in use. Chemical companies that produce wood treatments are working on new types of preservatives, but their widespread availability is probably still some way off. Creating an effective non-metallic treatment for wood that's in contact with the ground has proved a challenge.

Redwood and cedar

Some homeowners will demand redwood or cedar despite the expense. If that's the case, use only FSC-certified wood that comes from sustainable sources. There are increasing supplies of both from certified forests from California

Pine (shown here), fir, and hemlock treated with chemical preservatives should prove durable, and they are less toxic than the CCA-treated lumber they replaced. While relatively inexpensive, they are less appealing from a green point of view than composites and FSC-certified lumber.

to British Columbia. There is, however, still unregulated forestry in Canada that is destroying precious and fragile ecosystems.

Remember that only the heartwood of these species offers the kind of rot and insect resistance that makes this lumber durable. Sapwood does not offer nearly the same level of protection.

Composite decking

Composite decking has become one of the more prominent poster children of green building. It takes material out of the waste stream (shrink wrap and wood waste) and converts it into a superior building material. The combination of plastic and wood provides multiple benefits. It outlasts conventional wood decking; it is insect and rot resistant; it accepts paints and stains; and it's more comfortable underfoot since it doesn't splinter.

Trex® was the original but it has since been joined by similar products from a number of manufacturers. It's available in different

Cedar (left) and redwood (right) are favorites for natural decking, and they are still a good, although expensive, choice—providing that the lumber is cut from heartwood and that it's FSC certified as coming from sustainable sources. Otherwise, you're better off with another material.

Composite decking that combines recycled plastic and wood fiber is a great product that will outlast many species of wood and needs little maintenance. It's an excellent choice for sustainable building.

colors and textures and while it doesn't look exactly like wood it's fairly close. Decking may come in the form of solid planks, or as hollow-core extrusions and tongue-and-groove planking.

One downside of composites is that they are not stiff enough to be used for structural purposes. That's not a problem for decking itself, but composites can't be used as a replacement for structural framing. Wood composites aren't cheap. But the fact they're made from scrap materials that would otherwise go into landfills, and the lack of any real maintenance, both do much to recommend them.

Plastic decking

Recycled-content plastic decking is available in many styles, configurations, imprints, and colors. The key is that it should be made from recycled content and not all of them are. Several of them are produced from virgin plastic, a decided disadvantage for a green product.

Plastic decking comes in many forms. It needs little maintenance and lasts a long time. But make sure it contains recycled material, not produced from virgin plastics.

Regardless of the source, be sure to follow the manufacturer's installation instructions. All plastic decking expands and shrinks dramatically with fluctuations in outdoor temperatures; the movement can pull screws or nails right out of the decking when it is exposed to hot sunshine in the summer.

PVC decking has many of the advantages of PVC building materials in general: it won't rust or rot, insects won't devour it, and vinyl decking requires no more maintenance than an occasional scrub. It's a relatively expensive option, and it shares the same drawbacks as anything else made from this plastic.

Tropical hardwoods

More wood species than ever are imported for use as decking. Ipé is probably the most common and it has some very attractive characteristics for decking. Dense and hard, Ipé can be left to weather without any chemical treatments as long as you don't mind it turning a silvery gray in color. It's a little tougher to install than softwood decking because it has to be pre-drilled for nails or screws. But it should last a very long time.

Two other candidates are Cambara, resistant to insects and rot, and Meranti, which comes from Malaysia, the Philippines, and Southeast Asia. Meranti is not as rot or insect resistant as Ipé, but the wood is about as strong as red oak.

As market demand increases, different species from Central and South America are steadily being introduced to the U.S. market. Many come from rainforests that are primary

Ipé, a family of South American hardwoods, is so dense it won't float. This also helps explain why Ipé does not readily burn and gets a Class A fire rating, the same as concrete and steel.

FSC LUMBER IS NOT ALWAYS MORE COSTLY

A common complaint about lumber certified by the Forest Stewardship Council is that it costs too much. That's not always true.

I used 1x6 Ipé when I enlarged the deck on my house. The first lumberyard I went to said it carried certified Ipé, but no one was able to provide chain-of-custody documentation that would verify their claims. Without it, I wasn't convinced what they were selling was FSC-certified lumber.

I went to another yard in town. It also carried Ipé, but this time the yard was able to document its FSC certification. I had no qualms about buying the lumber. What's more, the certified lumber was substantially lower in cost than the uncertified lumber I'd been offered initially.

—DJ

Ipé is a South American hardwood *that proves hardy outside even without any chemical treatments. It's extremely dense and hard and has a Class A fire rating. When it's FSC-certified, this is a good choice for decking.*

BEST PRACTICES

- Install a drainage plane beneath the siding to divert water away from the house. This can be housewrap, building paper, or one of several commercial products manufactured for this purpose.

- Consider installing a rain screen beneath the siding that includes an air space between the back of the siding and the housewrap or building paper.

- With the exception of cedar and redwood, avoid all siding made from softwoods.

- If you choose a traditional wood siding, either cedar or redwood shingles or planks, make sure the wood is certified by the Forest Stewardship Council.

- Consider fiber cement siding in either panel form or as lap siding.

- Avoid vinyl siding if you can.

- For deck construction, take pains to detail the deck ledger correctly. Protect the house first with a drainage plane, make sure housewrap and flashing are layered correctly to prevent water from getting behind the ledger, and attach the ledger only to solid framing.

- Give preference to one of the plastic-wood composite decking materials.

- If you choose cedar, redwood, or one of the tropical hardwoods, make sure it is FSC-certified material.

habitats for biodiversity. The key with all of them is to make sure the wood is FSC certified. If you want to be sure, ask the supplier for a copy of chain-of-custody documentation that shows the wood has been sustainably harvested and that it's not being sold as something it isn't. Supplies of FSC-certified tropical woods may be harder to find but they don't have to be more expensive—that depends on the supplier. As consumers become more educated about the difference, availability should increase.

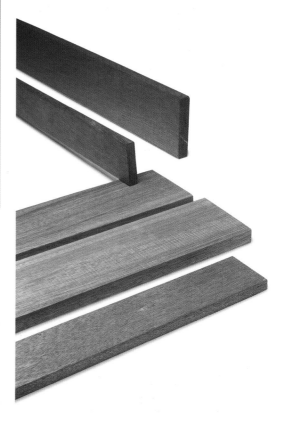

Cambara (top) and Meranti (bottom) are two tropical hardwoods that are increasingly available in U.S. markets. They make good decking choices when purchased through sustainable sources.

Solar Energy

Solar is green. Period. Tapping into the free, and still underexploited, potential of solar energy sums up what sustainable building should be. It's non-polluting, reduces or even eliminates our reliance on fossil fuels, doesn't require a lot of maintenance, and lowers the cost of heating and cooling our homes. One of its few drawbacks is the high cost of getting started. That will change.

In designing a green house, solar energy comes both first and last. First, because it figures into basic design decisions about the house: where it's located on the site, how the building is oriented toward the southern sun, where different rooms are located to take advantage of natural light and solar gain, and the size and placement of windows and ovehangs.

THE GREEN FACTOR

Making use of solar energy is at the heart of sustainable building. Passive solar design covers site and solar orientation, room layout, materials selection, and window type and placement, all of which can substantially reduce heating and cooling costs. Active solar systems—solar hot-water collectors and photovoltaic panels for the generation of electricity—are the other half of the equation.

- Solar panels, which can heat water, a nonfreezing liquid medium, or even air, are available in a number of styles and price ranges. A basic system for producing domestic hot water has a very low cost when installation is rolled into a mortgage—this can quickly represent a net savings in energy costs.

- Photovoltaic panels are still expensive, but with the help of improved technology and government incentives the cost of PV electricity in some areas is competitive with utility-generated power.

- Combining green-building techniques with active solar systems can result in a "zero energy" home, one that produces as much energy as it consumes over the course of a year.

Solar hot-water collectors and photovoltaic panels mean less reliance on utility power. While the initial cost of the equipment is still relatively high, energy independence is an enticing possibility.

All of those considerations are cumulative, reducing the ultimate heating and cooling loads required for comfort. Chapter 3 covers features of passive solar design (see p. 43), and subsequent chapters discuss components integral to the house that set the stage for active solar decisions.

What comes last, after everything else has been decided, are the components of active solar heating and photovoltaics. With careful design and engineering, homes can use virtually no fossil fuel. Zero-energy homes, which are being built across the country, make as much power as they consume over the course of a year (see the case study on pp. 256–257). They are proof that this approach to building is feasible.

In general, the goal is to create a house that consumes at least 50 percent less energy than one built conventionally, with a corresponding reduction in heating and cooling costs. There are a number of strategies that help, none of them on its own very complicated:

- sizing south glass to capture as much solar heat as possible without overheating in swing seasons

- using operable windows to scoop up breezes and expel stale air and arranging windows for cross ventilation

- blocking summer sunlight with roof overhangs, shade trees, or other vegetation

- choosing building materials for their mass and their potential to store solar heat in winter and to keep houses cooler in summer

Passive solar design is a prerequisite for an investment in solar hardware. Houses with south-facing glass, adequate natural ventilation, and reduced heating and cooling loads are natural candidates for solar collectors and photovoltaic panels.

TRACKING THE SUN

A key to designing solar systems is calculating the amount of usable sunlight the site will get, which depends on time of year and latitude. This chart is for 28° north latitude, roughly on a line with Houston, Tex., and Tampa, Fla., and shows the altitude angle of the sun as a function of time of day and season.

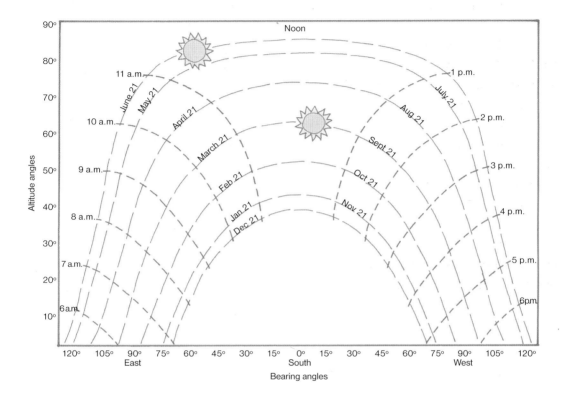

This chapter deals with the variety of active systems that provide heat and electrical energy—solar collectors and photovoltaic systems that can get the home to zero energy. They vary considerably in complexity and cost as well as in their potential for reducing the consumption of fossil fuels. At one end of the scale is something as simple as installing solar panels that preheat water before a conventional water heater kicks in. At the other are elaborate systems that allow homeowners to protect themselves completely from the uncertainties of escalating energy costs.

Solar Hot Water

Solar hot water systems use energy that's free and available. That's what makes them great. Other than the small amount of electricity they consume for pumps and controls, these systems require no power and produce what is in effect free hot water year after year. When combined with a small PV panel they can be totally independent of the grid. A solar water heater is basically a prepaid utility bill. Systems range in cost from $2,000 to $8,000, depending on climate and water needs. While that's not exactly cheap, a solar hot water system will

Integral solar collectors like this SolaHart® are effective in regions where below-freezing temperatures are not a threat. They work on the principle of convection and contain no moving parts.

improve cash flow month after month as long as you live in the house. Water consumption and energy costs vary, of course, but it can all add up to a tax-free return on your investment of up to 25 percent.

If the cost of the system can be rolled into the mortgage, it can amount to only $20 or less per month. All you have to do is save that much in lower hot-water costs and you have a positive cash flow. Tax credits and rebates can make the picture even brighter. Even if the budget doesn't allow the addition of a solar hot water system at the time of construction, it makes sense to rough in some of the plumbing. That makes it easier to install a system later.

There are both active and passive systems. Some incorporate pumps to move liquid through a solar collector, while others rely on the natural movement that comes with convection. Passive systems are generally less expensive but not as efficient as active systems, and both types require some kind of backup source of heat for cloudy days. In addition, all of them require a storage tank. That can be in the form

PREPLUMB FOR SOLAR

Getting a house ready for solar panels in the future isn't difficult. All it involves is running two 1-in. copper lines from the attic beneath a south-facing roof to the area where the water heater will be located. Lines should be fully insulated with the highest R-value foam insulation available.

Whether a solar collector is active or *passive, a storage tank is an integral part of the system.*

of a preheat tank for a conventional water heater, called a two-tank system, or an integrated tank that serves both purposes.

Active closed-loop systems

There are two basic types of closed-loop systems: one for climates that don't experience freezing temperatures and one for cold-weather areas. Where low temperatures are not a concern, a direct circulation system is a good choice. It circulates water through a solar collector and then into the house where it can be used for bathing or washing dishes. In an indirect system, a pump circulates a fluid that won't freeze through solar collectors and then to a heat exchanger where it heats domestic hot water. For regions that get cold weather, this is the system to use.

In a thermosyphon system, the tank is above the collector so hot water from the collector naturally rises into the tank. These

SOLAR HOT WATER SYSTEM

This is a typical solar hot water installation with the collector on the roof and a solar pre-heat storage tank in the basement adjacent to the domestic water heater. The solar tank serves the hot water needs of the house when it is hot enough. When the temperature is too low the conventional water heater bumps up the temperature and distributes water around the house.

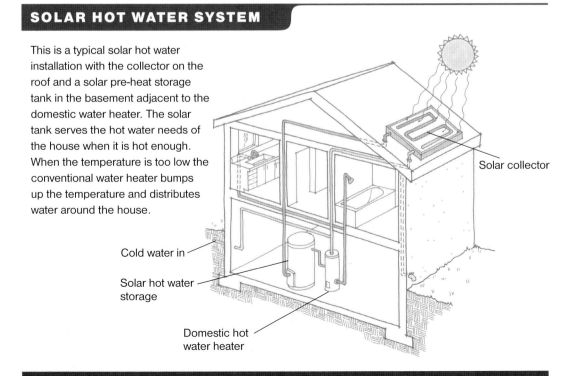

Solar collector

Cold water in

Solar hot water storage

Domestic hot water heater

Roof-mounted photo-voltaic panels are part of the strategy for creating a zero-energy home. When the panels generate more power than the house needs, the excess is sold to the electric utility. PV arrays at this house are set at two different angles to maximize summer and winter sun angles.

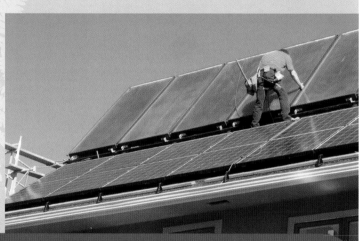

Solar collectors mounted above the photovoltaic array provide hot water, a major energy consumer in a conventionally built house, and feed a radiant-floor heating system as well as a hot tub in the backyard.

HOUSES WITHOUT ENERGY BILLS

Building a "zero-energy" house—one that produces as much energy as it consumes—melds a variety of green strategies. It's not as farfetched as it may sound, and the approach isn't limited to houses with unlimited construction budgets. Eric Doub, president of Ecofutures Building in Boulder, Col., can pull it off in a retrofit of a typical 1970s ranch for as little as $50,000.

Prescribing a generic zero-energy retrofit isn't easy, Doub says, because of variables in location, budget, and the house you're starting with. But even a ranch with plywood siding and only enough insulation to meet the 1970 code can become a "darn near zero energy home" with the application of green-building techniques. Here's how Doub does it:

- Upgrade the shell of the house to provide passive solar heat gain, lower heating bills in winter, and retain cool air during the summer. If it's in the budget, add 1 1/2-in. resilient channel to interior studs to make a thicker, better-insulated wall and add 1-in. rigid foam insulation to the outside of the building.

- Following the principle of "Build Tight, Ventilate Right," make sure indoor moisture and air quality are properly managed through mechanical ventilation, such as a heat recovery ventilator or exhaust fans on programmable timers.

- Install high-quality windows. Doub typically uses fiberglass windows with triple glazing or Heat Mirror glass. Removable insulation for windows at night can be key.

- In the crawlspace, seal vents and install a vapor retarder over exposed earth. Only then design the HVAC system and hot water generation.

- Install evacuated-tube solar collectors for space and water heating. These can be installed vertically and require only a 5-ft.-wide wall.

- Add photovoltaic panels.

In one Ecofutures retrofit, a 1,500-sq.-ft. Colorado home will have 6 evacuated-tube solar collectors of 30 tubes each and 5.4 kW of photovoltaic generating capacity.

Even after using some electricity for the electric modulating boiler to boost the solar-preheated water, the owners will still generate more electricity throughout the year than they use.

Evacuated-tube collectors, which generate heat even on cloudy days, can supply radiant-floor systems or fan coils in the air stream of a fully ducted house. In one of Doub's projects, he is making one ductwork system serve three purposes—evaporative cooling, space heating with fan coils, and fresh air distribution from an energy recovery ventilator

Whatever the sources of heat, all zero-energy homes work on what Doub calls the "charge and coast" principle. On a sunny day, no matter what the outside temperature, a house will "charge up" and then "coast" at 72° to 68° for up to two cold, cloudy days before *any* backup heat kicks in.

Fully loaded: The combination of solar collectors and PV panels spells near energy independence for homeowners at the Net Zero Energy home of Eric Doub of Ecofutures Building in Boulder, Col.

Surplus power turns homeowners into energy suppliers, with checks from the local utility to prove it.

systems are generally more expensive than the batch system, and the contractor has to consider the weight of the storage tank when designing the roof.

Solar Collectors

Collectors are what gather and concentrate solar energy, passing it directly to water that will be used in the house or to a liquid that will transfer heat to water in a heat exchanger. There are three basic types—flat plate collectors, integral collector-storage systems, and evacuated-tube collectors—and the choice depends at least in part on climate.

Flat plate collectors

These are the most commonly used solar collectors for residential water systems. They are designed for specific climates. In warm climates, where temperatures stay above freez-

ing, they can be plastic sheets that roll out over the roof. (Hot Sun Industries makes such a product that's often used to heat pools and spas.) Another type of flat plate collector, better suited to cold climates, consists of an insulated, weatherproof box that houses a copper plate and piping coated with a heat-absorbing black finish called a selective surface. This black coating absorbs the entire solar spectrum. Glass on the top of the collector is of the high solar gain-low iron variety so it lets in as much light and solar energy as possible. When freezing temperatures are a threat, water can be drained from the system at night, or the system can be filled with ethylene glycol (the same stuff used in car radiators) and connected to a heat exchanger.

The collector and storage tank should be sized to meet the needs of the family in summer. For two adults, that amounts to about

Solar collectors can be inconspicuous, like the roll-out plastic sheets on the roof of this house. This type is suitable for warm-weather regions.

Box collectors *house heat-absorbing copper pipes behind high solar-gain glass. In cold weather regions, use antifreeze as the heat transfer medium.*

20 sq. ft. of collectors. For each additional person, add about 8 sq. ft.; if you live in a northern climate, add 12 sq. ft. to 14 sq. ft per person. Storage tanks are typically sized at 1.5 gal. per sq. ft. of collectors.

Integral collector-storage systems

Manufactured since the early 1900s, these systems are still widely used in Australia but are not as common in the U.S. These are some of the simplest collector systems available. In the

Evacuated-tube collectors *are more expensive but also more efficient than flat-plate collectors and can generate hot water even on cloudy days.*

1930s, more than half the houses in Florida had integrated systems (SolaHart is a current manufacturer, see the photo on p. 254). A glazed storage tank mounted on the roof is attached directly to the collectors. Water moves through convection: hot water rises into the tank, and cooler water is displaced into the collector to be reheated. These systems are very efficient and have no moving parts. Hot water can either be fed to a conventional water heater or used directly. They are used only in climates where freezing temperatures are not a concern.

Evacuated-tube collectors

In the U.S., evacuated-tube collector systems are used more frequently in commercial buildings. They incorporate parallel rows of transparent glass tubes that look like clear fluorescent lightbulbs and a central glass tube that contains a working fluid (temperatures generated by these collectors can run over the boiling point of water). Although they are more expensive than flat-plate collectors, evacuated-tube collectors generate heat on cloudy days and can be used for space heating as well as for domestic hot water.

Active Solar Space Heating

Hydronic heating systems, described in chapter 9 (see p. 173), are good candidates for a solar assist. In one configuration, a liquid is pumped through a large array of solar collectors and then into the network of tubing for a radiant-floor system. While this sounds ideal, combining the comfort of a radiant-floor system

Unlike an active system, a less expensive, passive batch solar heater does not use pumps and controls but relies on convection to move water. As water is heated in the collector, it rises to the top of the tank and then falls via gravity to the solar storage tank/backup water heater.

with a nearly free source of hot water, it also requires a large tank (10,000 to 60,000 gal.) to store hot water for cloudy days. A solar collector can also be used in conjunction with a heat exchanger and fan for auxiliary forced-air space heating.

Air systems

We usually think of solar collectors as a type of water heater, but they can also be designed to heat air rather than a liquid. These systems are less common and can come in one of several varieties:

- Flat-plate collectors that heat air, which is then ducted into the house to augment or replace conventional forced-air heat, at least while the sun is shining. Dampers close off the system at night and on warm days.

- Vertical collectors mounted on the south wall of the building. These are not glazed,

using instead a corrugated metal panel to collect heat. These are more often used for commercial buildings like warehouses and factories.

Manufacturers of prefabricated sun spaces like to sell sloped glass for the roof, but this design can produce real overheating problems. Vertical glass is always easier to manage and shade.

- Glass rooms or sunspaces on the south side of the house produce warm air passively. During the day, hot air rises to the top of the room and enters the house through vents. A wall separating the room from the rest of the house is often masonry that serves as thermal mass, which continues to give off heat after the sun goes down on both sides of the wall. If there is sufficient mass, good glazing, and careful design, these rooms can function as green houses year-round. They provide less heat to the house under those conditions, however. Sunspaces can produce too much heat in summer if they aren't shaded and vented properly. Too often people want the best of both worlds; a year-round greenhouse and passive solar heating all winter. You have to make the fundamental decision of how you want the space to work and design for that.

Air heated in a south-facing sunspace can be circulated passively via vents in the top of the wall. In summer, these spaces must be shaded and vented to avoid overheating.

Photovoltaics

Photovoltaics are a space-age technology brought to you by 30 years of R&D on the part of government and private industry. With the exception of the batteries used in some systems, PV systems have no moving parts and should last indefinitely. If batteries are used,

---

Photovoltaic modules covering an area one-third as large as the land now occupied by roads could supply all the electricity consumed in the U.S.

---

they must be replaced every 7 to 10 years, but with improvements in technology, this drawback should become less of an issue in the future. There are two basic system types: grid-tied and independent.

A grid-tied system consists of solar panels and an inverter that converts the direct current produced by the panels into alternating current that can be used in the house or fed back into the utility grid. This system may or may not have a battery backup. If you are going to use a grid-tied system, be sure your local utility has a "net-metering" program. That means it will buy back power at the same price you pay for it. All utilities have to buy back your power, but some buy it back at wholesale prices (1 to 3 cents per kilowatt-hour) but charge you 8 to 14 cents per kilowatt-hour.

An independent system (often referred to as "off the grid") is designed for self-reliant living and provides most or all of the electricity you need. These systems are more common in rural areas where utility connections are very expensive. They always include batteries for nighttime use and for cloudy weather.

For an off-the-grid installation, storage batteries are essential. Grid-tied systems, which use a net-metering system, don't need batteries.

Sizing requirements are very different for off-the-grid and grid-tied systems. A grid-tied PV system is a "feel good" arrangement, not only because the home is demanding less of utility power plants but also because it can provide at least some power when the utility is down. In areas where dirty or intermittent power is common, a small PV array can be a lifesaver. If it can't keep up with demand, utility power can kick in. When you're off the grid, however, you're on your own. Every watt has to come from the PV panels or the batteries.

Cell designs vary

While all PV cells are designed to convert sunlight into electricity, there are several distinct types. Single-crystalline or mono-crystalline cells are grown as silicon crystals then sliced into thin wafers. These are embedded with metal contacts to collect electrons that are released as light hits the crystal.

Poly-crystalline cells are cast ingots of silicon that consist of multiple crystals, which are then sliced into wafers. They are slightly less efficient than mono-crystalline cells. If one cell is shaded, the performance of the entire panel goes down dramatically. Amorphous (thin film) is yet another variation. Here, silicone is deposited on a substrate and applied

According to the U.S. Department of Energy, PV systems installed in the last 20 years produce enough power for 250,000 houses in the U.S. (and 8 million houses in the developing world).

to another surface, such as glass, metal, or plastic. These panels are less expensive to manufacture but have about one-half the output of mono-crystalline cells. One advantage is that if any portion of the panel is shaded, the panel will still produce electricity.

Although new technologies are beginning to emerge, today's photovoltaic panels rely on silicon crystals that generate current in the presence of sunlight.

Individual photovoltaic modules are assembled into panels of a manageable size, typically 20 sq. ft. to 35 sq. ft.

circuits, and it regulates the 60 cycles per second frequency (called hertz) of electricity provided to the AC side. These are typically referred to as sine-wave inverters and the function is important when utility line current is "dirty," meaning it has variable line voltage and frequency. This is often the case in more rural areas. An inverter protects sensitive equipment like computers and other high-tech equipment. The inverter is sized to the panel output and the load requirements of the home.

Whatever their type, PV cells are arranged in modules that create a predictable voltage. Sets of four or more modules are framed together to make a panel, typically 20 sq. ft. to 35 sq. ft. in size to make installation easier. An array is a number of panels that determines the total output of the system defined in kilowatts (a kilowatt is the amount of power it would take to keep ten 100-watt lightbulbs burning).

The cost of PV-produced electricity is measured in "levelized" costs per kilowatt hour, which is the cost of the system over its lifetime divided by the total electrical output. The levelized cost is now about 30 cents per kWh, according to the U.S. Department of Energy, making it cost-effective for houses more than a quarter mile from the nearest utility line.

Inverters

Inverters feed direct current into the system's storage batteries (just like your car) and then convert excess power into alternating current that can be used in the house or fed into the utility grid. Alternating current is better for transporting electricity over long distances, so the closer the inverter is to the solar panels the less line loss there will be.

An inverter is the brain of the system. It has a high surge capacity to protect connected

Mounting a PV system

PV panels are often mounted on the roof, and that can be problematic. The primary job of a roof is to keep water out of the house and any time that barrier is penetrated the risk of a leak is increased. For more than 25 years the convention has been to attach solar panels to "L" brackets that are lagged into roof sheathing, and it doesn't make sense. First, there is the strength of the attachment. Roofs are subject to wind loads and if wind can get under the collectors, it can rip them off the roof. Running a lag into 1/2-in. OSB isn't good enough. For a secure connection, fasteners should be lagged directly into rafters or trusses. Second, every time you run a fastener into the roof you've created a hole and a potential leak. Sealing the connection with caulk is a joke.

So the solution is to use brackets that have a cylindrical post "stand-off" that supports the PV rack. The post is threaded to receive the rack bolts and is flashed with conventional jacks, exactly what's used to flash plumbing vents. That way you know you have strength and a good waterproof seal.

Standoffs attached directly to rafters or roof trusses and then flashed with conventional roof jacks make more secure and weatherproof connections for photovoltaic panels than "L" brackets attached only to roof sheathing.

Integrating panels into a shade structure, such as a trellis, accomplishes two goals—you'll get active solar electricity right along with passive solar shading. Another option is a building-integrated PV array, which consists of a PV array that is incorporated into the roofing material itself. There are variations that look like standing-seam metal roofing, slatelike tiles, and three-tab shingle strips. Building-integrated systems are more expensive than other installation alternatives, but for the aesthetic conscious consumer it's a perfect product.

Finally, there are ground-mounted arrays. This approach allow panels to be placed anywhere on the property with good solar exposure, and it allows the option of using a tracking mechanism so the panels can follow the sun across the sky. Tracking systems improve the output of panels by roughly 40 percent in summer and 25 percent annually.

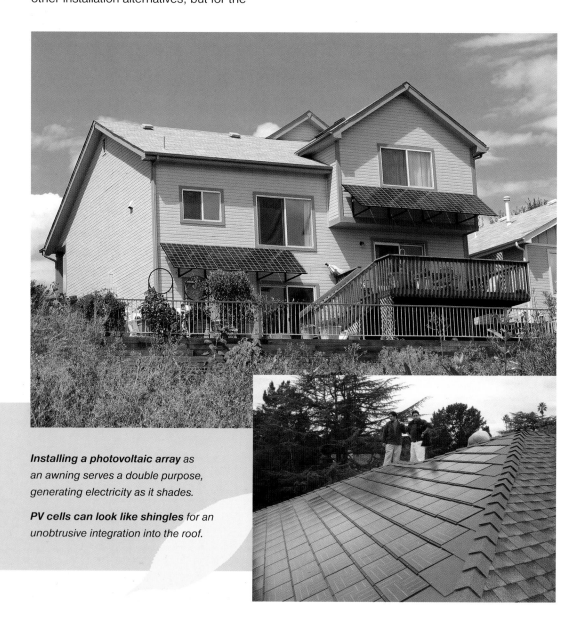

Installing a photovoltaic array as an awning serves a double purpose, generating electricity as it shades.

PV cells can look like shingles for an unobtrusive integration into the roof.

Ground-mounted photovoltaic arrays can be located in an area with good solar exposure and offer the option of adding a tracking mechanism for improved performance.

Sizing a PV system

Photovoltaics are sexy to some homeowners. They like the idea of installing PV panels, and sometimes that happens in the absence of a careful assessment of the electrical loads of the building and the family's lifestyle. Photovoltaics aren't magic. These systems work the same way any electrical system does: the greater the load, the more panels will be required. How much sunlight the house gets during the year (based on climate as well as latitude) are obvious and important variables.

PV systems have dropped dramatically in cost over the last few years, and prices are likely to continue downward as rebates increase and panels become cheaper as well as more efficient. However, at the moment a wholesale replacement of grid power with PV panels is beyond the financial reach of most people. It's more realistic to think of what a modestly sized PV system can do in the way of backing up essential equipment (like a computer) in case of a power outage, supplementing grid power with a net-metering device, or providing power when the utility's grid is just too far away.

Photovoltaic cells can be incorporated into walls and windows, such as this skylight. Some light will be transmitted through the glass even as it produces electricity.

To calculate the electrical load on the system, you'll have to keep in mind that the demand for electricity is likely to change over

---

The U.S. Department of Energy says a residential PV system costs between $8 and $10 per watt, but government incentives and volume purchases can lower that to between $3 and $4 per watt. All but two states in the U.S. have some type of solar or renewable incentive.

---

time. You'll need more generating capacity in the winter because lights run longer and people are inside for greater lengths of time.

The size of the family, or lifestyle habits, can change, as can the variety and amount of equipment a family will be plugging in.

If the system is used as a backup for utility power, it will incorporate batteries. Certain appliances should probably not be wired into the backup system because they draw so much current. They include space heaters, water heaters, clothes dryers, dishwashers, older refrigerators and freezers, and electric ranges. In general, any appliance that uses electricity for resistance heating or cooling will be a heavy draw on the system. Modern refrigerators, however, are much more energy efficient than older models and are often placed on backup circuits.

Phantom electrical loads, discussed in more detail in chapter 10 (see p. 197), are a particular problem with off-the-grid PV

SIZING A PV SYSTEM

So how big does a PV system have to be? It depends entirely on what you want it to do—reduce the amount of utility power you buy, back up vital equipment such as an office computer, or completely replace grid power. In other words, there is no simple answer.

You'll have to start by calculating the amount of power—expressed in watts—that appliances and equipment you want to connect to the system actually use. You should be able to find this information stamped somewhere on the appliance. If the label shows how many amps the appliance draws, multiply that number by the voltage of the circuit (120 volts for most household circuits).

Make a list and start adding it up. You'll discover that electrical consumption varies considerably. A hair dryer, dishwasher, or clothes iron might easily draw 1,200 watts or more while computers, radios, window fans draw much less. Keep in mind that most appliances are not used constantly so they create intermittent electrical

loads. Motors draw more power when they start than they do to run. As you make the list, you'll begin to understand why reducing your need for electricity is so important.

If you plan to use a PV system as a home office back-up, a 1 kilowatt output should be adequate to power a computer, monitor, and printer and some light circuits with room to spare. The same 1 kilowatt system would not be enough to run your clothes dryer even if it were the only thing plugged in. So intended use is key.

Finally, there is the question of how much roof area in square feet you'll need for the PV array. You'll need about 100 sq. ft. of roof area for every 1 kW of generating capacity, more if you plan on using "thin film" photovoltaic panels incorporated into roofing materials.

In all, sizing a PV system isn't simple. To get started, check the government's Energy Efficiency and Renewable Energy program, on the web at www.eere.energy.gov/consumer.

systems because of the high per-watt cost of generating power.

PV system components

Panels that turn sunlight into electricity, inverters that make alternating current out of direct current, and storage batteries are all vital pieces of a PV system. But there's more to it than that.

No matter what type of system you choose it will have to include disconnects. These allow an electrician to work on any part of the system without concern that wires are hot. Disconnect switches are installed between any source of power and the service entrance.

Both the AC and DC sides of any PV system must be grounded, regardless of system voltage. Use a reliable grounding electrode, such as a ground rod.

To protect wiring from overheating and possibly causing a fire, make sure there is an inline circuit breaker between any power source (panels, batteries, inverter) and the utility's grid. These breakers also protect the system.

Metering

Metering serves several purposes. The primary meter is installed between the PV system and the utility. Net metering means you can spin

BUILDING A PV SYSTEM

Photovoltaic modules are only part of the system. Other elements are an inverter, breakers, and in this case a bank of batteries for backup. This system includes ten 100-watt modules, each with a maximum output of 5.2 amps, which feed both DC and AC circuits.

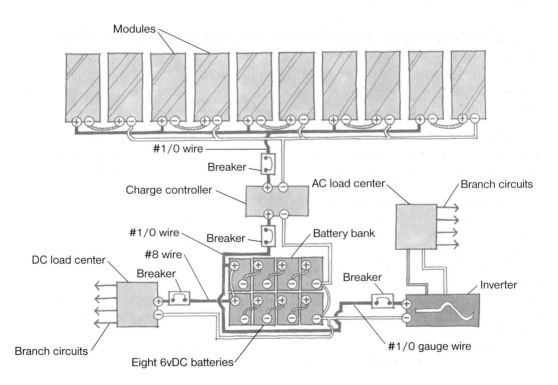

Electrical meters can run backward when PV systems produce more energy than is being used in the house.

energy usage but can't sell electricity back to the utility beyond your zero energy usage level. This is determined by your state public utility commission.

Home energy use meters. Home readouts are vital to understanding and operating a PV system, and the meter should be located in a spot where it's easy to see. At a minimum, a home-use meter should show the electrical output of the array, battery voltage, and any error messages from the inverter. More sophisticated designs show electricity use in real time, and they can have an interesting effect on home life. Homeowners will learn to see differences in electrical consumption at different times of day and in different seasons and in time can use the meter to control consumption.

A Prius car, a gas/electric hybrid, has more comprehensive instruments than a conventional car, showing the driver when the bat-

your electric meter backward when you are producing more power than you are using. Typically you can never be your own utility, meaning you can only zero out your meter

Meters allow homeowners to check the output of photovoltaic panels as well as track consumption. They're a useful aid in conservation and can help identify phantom electrical loads that decrease the system's efficiency.

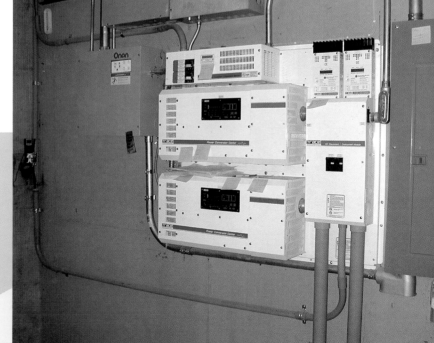

tery is in use, when the gas engine has kicked in, miles per gallon at any given moment, and average vehicle miles per gallon. Prius drivers report that they maximize mileage fuel efficiency by learning how to use the instruments, and advanced PV metering can have the same impact. With a glance at the meter you can tell whether lights and equipment have been left on. You can also identify how large your phantom loads are by turning off everything and seeing how much current is still being drawn. Behavior is the best energy saver of all and it is free.

High-tech but as stately as ever, this colonial with a solar-shingle roof shows that cutting-edge solar technology can be at home with virtually any architectural style.

Utility switch. The utility disconnect is required to shut off any connection to the grid. This switch must be mounted outside the house next to the primary electrical service entrance. The switch protects line workers from the possibility that current from the PV system could back-feed into the grid. The utility keep records of all interconnected PV systems and will either call or send out a lineman to flip off the switch when workers are at work.

Plan for the future

Just like preplumbing for solar hot water systems, it's a good idea to prewire for future PV installation. If homeowners can't afford the high upfront cost of a PV system at the time of construction, a PV system may become more attractive in the future. While it's easy to wire

BEST PRACTICES

- Consider active solar systems (hot water and photovoltaic panels) once all other steps have been taken to minimize energy loads on the house.

- At a minimum, preplumb the house for solar collectors even if a system is not in the cards at the time of construction.

- Install a 1-in. metal conduit from a south-facing roof to the main electrical panel to accommodate future installation of photovoltaic panels.

- When mounting solar panels on the roof, use threaded stand-offs that are fastened into trusses or rafters rather than L-brackets fastened only to roof sheathing. They should be flashed just like a plumbing vent to reduce the risk of leaks.

- For photovoltaic panels, consider a tracking system that follows the movement of the sun, which will increase the electrical output by 25 percent a year.

also declined. Like hot water systems, if the PV system saves more each month than the carrying costs of the loan to install it, you can have a positive cash flow the first month. Newer technologies on the horizon promise to cut the energy payback.

Don't let current costs keep you from exploring the use of solar energy. It is the future. The planet has been powered by solar energy for 4 billion years and only in the last century have we forgotten our roots. With the concentration on global climate change in public discourse, solar will play a larger and larger role in reducing our net carbon production. It is the final step in building a zero-energy home, and with good design it can be done at an affordable price. Learn everything you can and follow the builders who are on the forefront of building market-rate, zero-energy homes.

for PV during construction, it is a bit more complicated once the walls have been sealed. To make the addition of this equipment easier, all you really have to do is run 1-in. metal conduit (not PVC) from the south roof area to the electrical box.

There is everything to like about photovoltaics except the cost, and on this front there has been steady progress in the last 25 years as production and PV technology advanced. According to the U.S. Department of Energy, net metering and state incentives in California have driven the cost of PV-generated electricity to below 11 cents per kilowatt hour, the same as some utility power. Energy payback—the length of time it takes for a PV panel to produce as much power as it took to manufacture it—

Indoor Air Quality

Indoor air quality is the sleeping giant of the homebuilding industry. That's because we know something isn't right about many of the materials we use, but we're not quite sure what that means or what the implications are. Most of us, for example, have probably used construction adhesive that comes with a label warning that the product can cause nerve and liver damage, even cancer. But we use it anyway, year after year. It's like our attitude about smog: If you can't see it from your front porch, why worry about it?

It's not just adhesives, paint, and solvents used to build a house that pose potential health risks. There are many materials that become part of a finished house—paneling, furniture, carpet—that contain toxic compounds threaten-

THE GREEN FACTOR

Maintaining high indoor air quality, an important component of green building, becomes more complex as the number of chemicals used in household furnishings, products, and building materials continues to expand. As houses become tighter, they are more likely to trap chemicals in the air we breathe. In fact, air quality can be much lower inside where we spend almost all of our time than it is outside.

Green-building strategies for improving air quality include appropriate mechanical ventilation and air filtration. It should also include a broader appreciation for the kinds of hazards we may encounter and efforts to eliminate them where possible:

- Contaminants can be either chemical or biological in nature.

- Mold spores, which are impossible to eliminate, can blossom into growing colonies when moisture is not controlled.

- Chemical hazards include the likely culprits—solvents, paints, vehicle exhaust, certain adhesives, pesticides—as well as ordinary households products and building materials that off-gas formaldehyde and other potentially hazardous compounds.

- Radon, a naturally occurring gas, is the second most frequent cause of lung cancer in the U.S. after smoking.

Nontoxic adhesives are readily available and make a greener choice than those containing volatile organic compounds.

ing the health and well-being of the people who live there. Other contaminants, ranging from pet dander to mold and dust mites, may seem more benign because they are natural in their origin. Not so.

Indoor air quality is an important leg of green building not only because there are so many potential airborne threats to health but also because we spend so much time inside in contact with them. We know frighteningly little about many of the chemicals we come in to contact with in our own homes or how we should build to cope with them. Much of what we do know is from our European counterparts. They have been building tight homes for 25 years and were the first to identify indoor air quality as a problem. When homes were very leaky it wasn't an issue—all that free ventilation got rid of toxins in the house. But as homes got tighter and more synthetic chemicals replaced natural products, the impact of poor indoor air quality became more apparent.

As short on answers as we sometimes seem to be, we do know more today than we did a decade ago. Increasingly, the public health community is pointing the finger at homes and schools as the source of health problems, particularly among children. When *Scientific American* reports that of all the

> **The EPA estimates that as many as 15 percent of Americans are allergic to their own homes. According to the *New England Journal of Medicine*, 40 percent of children born today will suffer some form of respiratory disease.**

chemicals regulated by the U.S. Environmental Protection Agency only two are more prevalent outdoors than indoors, it seems we have a problem.

Setting Standards for Exposure

Part of the problem is how we set standards for indoor air quality, and what those standards actually mean in terms of health risks. Take formaldehyde, a common pollutant that is off-gassed by a variety of everyday products. In Denmark, the maximum exposure for formaldehyde for the *entire house* is one-tenth of what

This countertop substrate is wheatboard, a particleboard replacement made from rapidly renewable resources and without the urea-formaldehyde binders that would add contaminants to indoor air.

the EPA allows for a *single product* in the U.S. The Danish standard of 10 parts per billion is based on safe exposure for an 18-month-old child 18 in. from a source (such as carpet). The EPA maximum exposure standard was borrowed from the Occupational Safety and Health Administration (OSHA), which is based on safe exposure for a 35-year-old male in an industrial environment 8 hours per day.

The state of California likens formaldehyde to the canary in the coal mine of home toxins. Like Denmark, the state looks at the entire house one week after construction and runs a test for formaldehyde for five days, allowing 28 ppb. The World Health Organization recommends less than 50 ppb inside houses. The EPA allows 100 ppb *per product*. Add up the particleboard cabinets, countertops, shelving, some paints, some carpets, fiberglass batt insulation, and many other products that off-gas formaldehyde and you're likely to have high levels of this chemical in the air.

If only air-quality problems were limited to formaldehyde. There are currently 75,000 chemicals licensed for use in the U.S. Approximately 15,000 are sold in volumes greater than 10,000 lb. per year. Yet under the Toxic Substances Control Act, the EPA regulates just five chemicals. A patchwork of studies from the federal government indicates that everyone in the country carries more than 100 chemical pollutants, pesticides, and toxic metals in their bodies.

How is a builder to know what to use and what to avoid? Actually, there are a variety of steps that can be taken to lessen our exposure to indoor toxins. We'll get to that, but first let's take a look at some of what we're up against.

Contaminants and Their Impact on Health

Contaminants in our homes fall into two broad categories—biological and chemical. Biological contaminants can either originate indoors or outdoors and are known as bioaerosols. The list includes mold, dust mites, pollen, animal dander, and bacteria. Molds produce particulates in the form of microscopic spores and gases and are responsible for that telltale smell in a moldy basement or closet.

Bioaerosols are extremely small living organisms, or fragments of living things, sus-

Mold is a common cause of low indoor air quality. While mold spores are impossible to eliminate, construction techniques that control moisture should make it difficult for mold colonies to grow.

pended in the air. Dust mites, molds, fungi, spores, pollen, bacteria, viruses, fragments of plant materials, and human and pet dander (skin that has been shed) are some examples. They cannot be seen without a magnifying glass or microscope. These contaminants can cause severe health problems. Some, like viruses and bacteria, cause infections (like a cold or pneumonia). Others cause allergies. Both allergic responses and infections may be serious or even fatal.

A susceptible person suffers an allergic reaction when a substance provokes the formation of antibodies. We call these substances antigens or allergens. Bioaerosols may cause allergic reactions on the skin or in the respiratory tract. Rashes, hay fever, asthma (tightness in the chest, difficulty in breathing), and runny noses are common allergic reactions. Some people develop a severe allergic reaction in the lung, which can destroy lung tissue. This is called hypersensitivity pneumonitis. It is not an infection, but repeated episodes can lead to infections of the lung, such as bacterial

pneumonia. Hypersensitivity pneumonitis can be triggered by exposure to very small amounts of an allergen once a person is sensitive to it. Symptoms can range from tightness in the chest, coughing, and difficulty in breathing to low-grade fever, muscle aches, and headaches.

Mold

Houses are like a Cracker Jack® box—they come with a surprise inside, but in this case the surprise is often mold. Mold spores are everywhere. They can remain inert for decades. All they need is a source of moisture and they can start to grow.

Mold grows on organic material, especially cellulose. The most common location is in the wall cavities of wet areas. This is why our understanding of building science is so important. On occasion the moisture comes from outside sources, leaks in siding and housewrap. Other sources are leaks in plumbing inside the walls. Most often the problem is inadequate air sealing that allows moist air to penetrate into stud cavities, migrating through

In time, mold can attack the structural integrity of sheathing and framing.

A PUNCH LIST FOR MOLD

Building green lessens the risk of mold, but what do you do when mold begins to grow?

- If you find mold or mildew, try to find and eliminate sources of moisture that are feeding the colony, such as a plumbing leak. Reduce relative humidity inside and dry the air with a chemical or mechanical dehumidifier. Drip pans should be emptied daily.

- Open closet doors to allow air to circulate. Use a 40-watt lightbulb to dry and heat air in closets.

- Vent bathrooms and clothes dryers to the outside.

- Trim back trees and shrubs around the house to let in more light and sun.

- Remove debris from your yard, roof, and gutters.

- To clean mold and mildew growth from walls use chlorine bleach, diluted three parts water to one part bleach. Commercial products can also remove mildew and mold. Follow product instructions carefully. Very moldy items should be replaced.

- Change heating and cooling system filters monthly.

- Vacuum air return covers or screens regularly.

- Check air conditioners for mold before each cooling season and have coils cleaned as needed.

- Have ductwork checked for loose insulation, leaks, or signs of condensation where the system enters the house. Insulate ducts on the outside of the ductwork. Keep ductwork clean.

- Use an electronic air cleaner or HEPA filter.

- Make sure that crawlspace vents work and are not blocked. If your cooling ductwork runs through the crawlspace, consider closing crawlspace vents during the summer. Using fans in crawlspaces during the summer when humidity is high may increase the relative humidity in the crawlspace and inside the home. Use fans only when outside humidity is well below 50%.

---

insulation that doesn't stop air movement and condensing on studs or sheathing. If the moisture stays constant, as it typically does with air leaks, the mold will create mycelia or roots that eat into the wood. This is the mold organism. By the time you see evidence of mold, it has already grown into the wood or paper that supports it. Like an iceberg, most of the problem is invisible.

Mold and mildew may also be found in the ductwork of your heating or cooling system. If there are leaks in the ductwork, or places where moisture and outside air get into the system, mold and mildew can grow on accumulated organic material. Sometimes they are found in the coils of an air conditioner or in the connection between the air conditioner and the ductwork. Moisture problems are worse

where ductwork insulation is on the inside as opposed to the outside of the duct. The insulation's porous surface collects dust and moisture. Mold and mildew may also grow on dirty furnace and air-conditioning filters. Plumbing leaks and dampness in attics, basements, and crawlspaces can increase humidity inside your home and promote the growth of agents that will be released as bioaerosols.

Mold colonies produce more spores. They can cause unsightly stains and may release varying levels of toxic chemicals called mycotoxins into the air. Some molds are harmless, some beneficial, and others are deadly. The primary concern is not what type you may have in your home but how to prevent it from growing. From a practical standpoint, that means keeping moisture out of wall and ceiling

Mold growing inside this wall cavity was apparent only when wallpaper was peeled away. Warm, moist air condensing inside wall cavities is one possible cause.

cavities, topics that are discussed in detail in chapters on building science (see p. 23) and siding (see p. 227). Spray mold prevention coatings on the studs before the trades arrive onsite. Coatings will inhibit future mold growth.

The health impacts from mold range from slight allergy-like symptoms that won't go away to serious flu like problems and even long-term disabilities like asthma. Children are affected the most by mold conditions and are most likely to suffer long-term problems from exposure.

Fixing a house after mold has been found is costly and often very difficult. What's more, the discovery of mold may raise other troubling questions. Do you, for example, report it to your insurance company? Today's litigious society has made insurance companies skittish about mold. You may even have a disclaimer in your policy excluding claims related to mold. If

not and you do make a mold claim, your insurer may drop your policy. If that weren't enough, when you sell your house you will be required to disclose any known problems. Many potential buyers won't even look at a house that's had mold problems. Making a house mold-proof by controlling moisture is the best and simplest solution.

Dust mites

If you think the movie *Alien* was scary, just look at a dust mite. Dust mites and their waste are the most common allergens in indoor air. Dust mites eat human and pet skin (dander) as it is shed. And when a person sheds some 7 million cells per minute, there's plenty of chow to go around. Dust mites live in rugs and carpets, sheets, mattresses and pillows, and upholstered furniture. Between 10 percent and 15 percent of the population is allergic to dust mites. Of the people who have other allergies, 40 percent also are allergic to dust mites. They can't be eliminated, but reducing the amount of floor area covered by carpeting can help.

Unlike carpeting, which can trap dust, animal dander, and moisture, the stained concrete floors of this handsome interior won't degrade indoor air quality.

Chemical contaminants

Chemical contaminants include both gases and particulates. They come from many sources, some obvious and some not so obvious. The usual list of suspects would include combustion gases from water heaters and kitchen ranges, pesticides, smoking, and radon. But don't stop there. The list also should include building materials and furniture, carpet, countertops, cleaning products, and personal care products like hairspray.

Volatile organic compounds (VOCs) are chemicals that evaporate easily at room temperature—that's the "volatile" part. "Or-ganic" indicates that the compounds contain carbon, primarily from petrochemicals. VOCs are often detectable by smell, but not always. Either way, they can be harmful. We come into contact with thousands of different kinds of VOCs: solvents like benzene and toluene, formaldehyde, and ethylene glycol to name but

Every year, 700 new chemicals are introduced into the environment but less than 1 percent of them are tested for their impact on human health. Many of these end up in our homes in "new and improved" products.

a few. They are found in a variety of everyday products that give themselves away by odor— mothballs, varnishes, paints, gasoline, and vehicle exhaust—but many others that seem very ordinary: caulk, cosmetics, air fresheners, newspapers, vinyl flooring, carpets, and upholstery fabrics. Exposure can trigger a variety of acute and chronic conditions, from eye irritation, headaches, and nausea to liver damage, nerve damage, and cancer. Most studies to date have been conducted on single chemicals. Less is known about the health effects of combined chemical exposure that is common inside our homes.

We're not going to rid houses of hairspray, kitchen ranges, and chlorine bleach. Nor are we going to stop lighting candles, cooking, or breathing. But that still leaves a number of pollutants that can be monitored more carefully and, in some cases, avoided altogether. Combustion gases, for instance, enter the living space through cracks in the combustion chamber of a furnace, or from back-drafting due to negative air pressure inside the house. Yet carbon monoxide poisoning is preventable via regular furnace inspections, sealing ductwork, or buying sealed-combustion furnaces andwater heaters. Every house should be equipped with carbon monoxide detectors. The best health protection measure is to limit exposure to products and materials that contain VOCs when possible and to choose low-VOC or no-VOC products whenever possible.

Building Products That Off-Gas

It probably wouldn't be possible to catalog every chemical, harmful or not, that we come in contact with through building products and furnishings. But among the most common are formaldehyde, which comes from a widely used adhesive called urea formaldehyde; vinyl chloride; plasticizers called phthalates; and a compound called styrene-butadiene latex that

is found in carpeting. Many are produced in enormous quantities and find their way into a variety of products. We usually like what they can do for the products we use, but we won't like their potential effects on our health.

Formaldehyde

One of the most widely used adhesives in the construction industry, urea formaldehyde is durable and inexpensive. It is very common in wood products made with particleboard such as cabinets, countertops, and shelving. The problem is that formaldehyde is also a potent eye, upper respiratory, and skin irritant. It off-gases from these products for years, leading to a number of potential health problems: wheezing, coughing, sneezing and skin irritation, depression, difficulty in sleeping, rashes, nausea, diarrhea, and chest and abdominal pain. Formaldehyde is known to cause cancer in animals and is a suspected human carcinogen.

A study at Ball State University suggests that low levels of formaldehyde commonly found in U.S. homes are enough to trigger a variety of symptoms in concentrations as low as 0.09 parts per million, a level common in many U.S. homes.

Vinyl chloride

Vinyl chloride, the monomer from which polyvinyl chloride (PVC) is made, is also ubiquitous. Vinyl chloride is thought to be connected to a long list of serious health problems, including cancer and damage to the nervous, circulatory, and immune systems. It is now so widespread that it is found in polar bear fat. Vinyl chloride is not toxic when it is bonded into chains, such as

PVC, but it is present as PVC is manufactured and often in its disposal, particularly when burned. One of the by-products in the manufacture of vinyl chloride is dioxin, a carcinogenic and persistent environmental chemical. (That means it doesn't biodegrade.)

Vinyl chloride monomer is linked to a wide variety of health ailments, the most significant being liver cancer but also including central nervous system disorders and pulmonary abnormalities. It also has been linked to acroosteolysis, a syndrome affecting peripheral nerves in the hands and fingers, characterized by numbness, tingling, excessive sensitivity to cold and pain, and dissolution of the bones. In soft vinyl products some unbonded vinyl chloride molecules are volatile. That's the characteristic smell of a new car, beach balls, and shower curtains. Our nose knows.

Phthalates

Petroleum-based chemicals added to plastics help make the material more useful. PVC additives include plasticizers such as phthalates that make our upholstery comfier and our pipes more flexible. Today, phthalates are one of the top offenders in a group of 70 suspected endocrine-disrupting chemicals (EDCs) that we use in our homes and yards. In January 2006, the European Union placed a ban on six types of phthalate softeners. When we're done with these products, we dump them or burn them in our incinerators, where their runoff filters into our national waterways. Even if you eschew plasticized products in your personal lives, it's impossible to avoid contamination; EDCs are in the bodies of every man, woman, child, and fetus in the U.S.

A study in 2005 was the first to show a connection between phthalate exposure and incomplete genital development. It found that pregnant women with higher urine concentrations of some phthalates were more likely to give birth to sons with "phthalate syndrome"— incomplete male genital development, a disorder previously seen only in lab rats. Environmental exposure to EDCs is the suspected

To keep up with the world's affection for all things plasticized, the U.S. produces a billion pounds of phthalates a year. The additive is used to make plastics more useful and more user-friendly.

cause of declining male testosterone levels over the past two decades, as well as declining male birth rates in industrial areas such as Seveso, Italy, and the Dow Chemical Valley in Sarnia, Ontario.

Research has found that phthalates leach from vinyl flooring and are found in dust in homes and in wash water, raising a particular concern for children who naturally spend time on the floor.

Styrene-butadiene latex

Most of the carpeting sold for residential use includes a solvent-based adhesive and a binder that helps hold carpet fibers to the backing. The "new carpet odor" that people may notice after carpet is installed is usually 4-phenyl-cyclohexene (4-PCH), which is a by-product of the styrene-butadiene latex binder. This chemical has a very low odor threshold, which means it can be in the air at only trace levels and still be detected by the human nose.

Immunotoxicologist and neurotoxicologist Gunnar Heuser has found consistent, objective evidence of injury in patients exposed to

When buying carpet, look for a sticker from the Carpet and Rug Institute certifying that the product meets its standards for low-VOC emissions.

new carpet. He wrote: "A full workup shows abnormalities that are consistent with other types of chemical injury, including [an] abnormal neuropsychiatric exam consistent with what is typically found in head injury patients, altered natural killer cell function, increased TA1 cells of the immune system, autoimmunity [meaning that the body's immune system has mistakenly identified its own tissues or cellular components as foreign and directed antibodies against them] including autoantibodies to thyroid, myelin of the nervous system, and antinuclear antibodies."

A Johns Hopkins University School of Hygiene and Public Health study supported the hypothesis that exposure to butadiene is associated with the risk of leukemia.

The Cure for Dirty Air

Air laden with contaminants isn't a foregone conclusion. The first line of defense is to make the envelope mold proof (for more, see the chapters on building science, roofing, and siding). We can't control mold spores but we can control moisture. By following green-building practices, the house should be protected for its lifetime. Skimping on the details is to invite trouble—nothing else matters if mold makes the occupants sick.

When it comes to other potential contaminants, the strategy is pretty simple: minimize exposure to toxic materials, either by keeping them out of the house altogether or by choosing safer alternatives to building products that contain hazardous compounds.

Isolate the garage

A garage can be a cauldron of unhealthy materials: fuels, solvents, adhesives, and especially carbon monoxide. One of the consequences of negative pressure inside the house is the likelihood that car exhaust will be drawn in from an attached garage. In cold climates, a homeowner might start the car in the garage and leave it there to warm up. With an attached garage, and a leaky door or wall between it and the house, exhaust gases can easily get inside. In the mid-'90s the EPA conducted a test of indoor air quality on a variety of homes in Denver and concluded that car exhaust from attached garages was by far the greatest toxin in interior air. Garage workshops in general are a great source of harmful chemicals. Pesticides, cleaners, polishes and waxes, workshop chemicals, paint and paint strippers—the list of possible contaminants is long indeed.

Two approaches should be used together. First, the wall between the house and the garage must be airtight. The best way to en-

Volatile organic compounds in conventional solvent-based wood stains and finishes lower indoor air quality. Using water-based finishes, or allowing finishes to cure completely before wood products are installed, are healthier choices.

sure that contaminants do not reach the house is to insulate the wall with spray-in foam insulation. Don't forget the wall/ceiling intersection if there is an attic above. If there is another bedroom above the garage, seal the floor joists in a similar fashion. The intent is to isolate the air in the garage from the house. Second, install an attic fan on the opposite side of the garage from the door. The fan should be on a timer to run for 10 or 15 minutes after opening the garage door or the light goes on. That way the exhaust gasses are evacuated away from the house.

Radon mitigation

Radon is the second most frequent cause of lung cancer behind smoking in the U.S. It is a radioactive gas that percolates through rock and soil to find its way into the house. Radon is measured in picocuries/liter (abbreviated as pCi/L), with 4 pCi/L the current maximum level suggested by the EPA before mitigation is recommended. A radon collection system consists of perforated PVC pipe installed beneath the concrete slab of the basement and connected to a pipe that runs up and out of the house. A fan draws the gas through the pipe and exhausts it.

It is much easier to design for radon mitigation before the fact than to go back and install pipes under the slab or basement floor if a problem is detected. It doesn't cost very much to rough in the system as the house is being framed. It can be left inactive and a fan added later if tests show the recommended levels of radon have been exceeded.

Use safer products

Using green products is one of the best ways to improve indoor air quality. Specify building products that contain fewer hazardous materials, and suggest to homeowners that carpet, furnishings, and other household goods be chosen with the same care. For example, builders can use formaldehyde-free products when they are available (medium-density fiberboard, certain door cores, and fiberglass batt

insulation are three such products). Specifying low-VOC paints and water-based rather than solvent-based clear finishes will help. Using less carpeting is yet another avenue, as is installing direct-vent, sealed-combustion furnaces and water heaters.

Filter the air

Furnace filters were designed to protect the fan motor in your furnace, not your health. The original fiberglass filter was designed to filter coal dust out of the air to help the fan last longer. We still use those filters today even though a wide range of better filters are available. Pleated media, electronic, and electrostatic filters are all more effective. Some of them are capable of filtering out dust measured in millionths of a meter.

Kitchen cabinets made with conventional particleboard off-gas formaldehyde long after installation. Specify greener materials, such as wheatboard.

Ventilation

As described more thoroughly in chapter 9, ventilation is vital for human health. Fresh air should be part of our daily lives, yet we spend 90% of our time inside buildings where stale air is cycled and recycled through heating and cooling equipment. We wonder why we feel groggy at work in the afternoons. Bringing fresh air into the home is a requirement for health and safety. And ventilation is the only way to dilute unwanted toxic gasses.

When you suspect a problem

If there's a suspicion of a problem when a house is finished, or occupied, the first step is to test the air. There are experts in mold mitigation, industrial hygienists who specialize in air contaminants, and indoor air-quality experts who have been trained to deal with a range of potential problems. Usually the best way to find

- Use the full range of green-building strategies to eliminate sources of moisture inside the building envelope that contribute to the growth of mold.

- Make sure the house is adequately ventilated and that air is filtered where possible to remove contaminants such as animal dander and pollen.

- Learn to recognize the sources of chemical contaminants and isolate or eliminate those products from inside the building envelope.

- Look for safer alternatives to products that leach or off-gas hazardous materials.

- Install carbon monoxide detectors.

- Seal the wall between an attached garage and the rest of the house.

- Install a radon collection system beneath the concrete slab or basement floor and rough in a means of exhausting the air as the house is framed.

- When air quality problems are suspected, hire an expert to test the home.

one is to start with a list of specialists from a local green-building program. To find one, start by calling your local building office or contacting your state chapter of the U.S. Green Building Council. Local experts are always better because they know what types of mold are prevalent in the area and have learned to recognize typical building failures in that particular climate. If no one can be found, a new national program is being developed by National Jewish Hospital in Denver, Col., and should be in place by 2008. A test kit will be able to identify various types of IAQ contaminants.

Interior Finishes

It's not hard to sell clients on a tight, well-insulated house when they know they'll be comfortable and have lower energy bills and less maintenance to look forward to. That part should be easy. Choosing green interior finishes doesn't offer the same kind of payback. Those decisions have to be based on something not as obvious but equally important—a healthy interior that won't cause illness or allergies, and an opportunity to use materials with a low environmental impact.

Many conventional materials—including particleboard, paint, adhesives, and sealants—give off noxious chemicals that turn a well-sealed, energy-efficient home into anything but a safe haven. Some are obvious. Common sense tells you that a solvent-based floor finish that has a powerful smell days after it was applied can't be doing you any favors. But many others pose more subtle hazards, such as the particleboard interiors of kitchen cabinets or countertop substrates that off-gas formaldehyde. We routinely use these and other building products that pose potential health risks even though a variety of safer alternatives exist.

Choosing Environmentally Friendly Products

As a rule, it's best to select the least-toxic material, which is not always as simple as it

THE GREEN FACTOR

Interior finishes come as one of the last stages of construction. Virtually all the other steps that create a green house have been taken. What remains is wall and floor finishes, paint and caulk, countertops and cabinets, and the many other details that give a house much of its aesthetic character. Decisions about these materials are important for their potential effect on the health of the people who will live in the house, as well as on how much money they'll spend to maintain it. In choosing what materials to use, here are some of the key considerations:

- **Toxicity.** Some common building products emit unpleasant and even dangerous fumes that can persist long after homeowners have moved in.

- **Durability.** Building materials that hold up to the rigors of family life are worth the investment, reducing the frequency of repairs or replacement and making interiors less troublesome to maintain.

- **Resource conservation.** Reusing salvaged materials or choosing products that have been made with recycled material means fewer resources have to be committed to making something new.

- **Sustainability.** As with other building materials, floor and wall coverings come from a variety of sources. The best choices are products that are renewable.

A green interior includes products made from sustainably harvested materials, which have low embodied energy and contribute to indoor air quality. Choices continue to increase dramatically as manufacturers respond to new consumer interest.

In general, let's just say that the risk to occupants from a toxic building product or building assembly—whether synthetic or natural—is lower if the agent is not inhaled or touched. Building products and materials that do not off-gas are preferable to those that do. Less toxic alternatives should be used in place of more toxic materials. But remember, these material choices should be made in context. For example, if an oil-based stain or finish offers a better, more durable result than its water-based counterpart, it's probably a better choice, providing it can be applied offsite and allowed to cure before it's brought into the house. In that case, its VOC content won't be an air-quality issue for homeowners.

Most green products are made to be durable. That's part of what makes them green. But durability, like toxicity, sometimes come with caveats. For example, a finished concrete floor is a very durable option but also comes with tradeoffs for the environment. Dissecting the pros and cons of this material is typical of the mental juggling we can go through with all interior products when trying to build green.

Concrete is generated by mining lime and baking it at 3,500° to produce portland cement. That takes a lot of energy. You can order concrete that contains fly ash, which is good because fly ash is a recycled industrial by-product (for more, see chapter 4, p. 79), but fly-ash concrete takes longer to cure, which can delay construction scheduling. Fly-ash concrete is less likely to crack, but it can be more difficult to work with. If the concrete floor is capped with finished flooring that contains formaldehyde, homeowners can be adversely affected. If concrete itself is the finished floor, that saves valuable natural resources but it may be treated and sealed with chemicals that can be noxious.

appears. Materials should be chosen not in a vacuum but after considering the context in which they will be used. In attempting to build in a truly green fashion, there will be tradeoffs. At times, a more toxic material may be a better performer and less expensive. So we have to ask what risks will the material pose to people living in the house. Will it off-gas before they inhabit the space yet last longer than its environmentally preferable alternative?

Concrete used as the finished floor conserves resources by reducing the amount of material used on the interior. A side benefit is concrete's high thermal mass, an advantage in passive-solar design.

Use recycled and refurbished products

In addition to specific concerns about product choice as it relates to the building and its occupants, we benefit by taking a step back and considering the environment as a whole. Never discount a recycled, refurbished, or remanufactured product that can be used in place of a new one. Also consider the "Cradle-to-Cradle" principle articulated by architect and designer William McDonough, the idea that every product should have more than one life—there's no real "grave" for any material.

Ask whether the material was produced in the least disruptive manner possible. Can it be recycled at the end of its useful life? Will the application be durable? How much energy was used to make the product (its "embodied energy") and how far did the product travel to reach your doorstep?

Recycled glass in a concrete matrix is a very popular green countertop.

WHAT IS "EMBODIED ENERGY"?

It takes a certain amount of energy to produce everything that's used to build a house, an energy price tag called its "embodied energy." This can include the energy required to extract raw materials from the ground or forest, the energy used directly for manufacturing, and the energy it takes to transport the material in the many steps along the way.

Something as simple as a rock taken directly from the site and used to make a fireplace has an energy investment associated with it, even if it's only the few calories we burn lifting it from the ground and carrying it to the hearth.

But that's certainly a lot less than the embodied energy represented in a granite countertop that was quarried halfway across the world. Although they're both stone, one product is more energy intensive than the other.

There are no global standards for measuring embodied energy, nor is embodied energy the only way of comparing the greenness of different building products. But it is a factor and, in general, green builders favor products with a low energy investment over those that someone moved mountains to produce.

CREATING AN INTERIOR AIR BARRIER

Creating an interior air barrier is an important component of energy efficiency and structural durability. Air barriers help to keep conditioned air inside the house where it belongs, reduce the amount of moisture that gets into wall and ceiling cavities, and prevent wind from washing through insulation inside the walls.

The Energy and Environmental Building Association suggests that interior air barriers (or what it calls "airflow retarders") can consist either of polyethylene plastic or the drywall and framing itself. Foam insulation sprayed into wall cavities can serve the same purpose; damp-spray cellulose, the EEBA says, is not as effective.

Some air barriers, such as polyethylene plastic, also work as a vapor retarder and halt the flow of moisture into walls where it can condense on cold surfaces. According to the EEBA, whatever material is used should be impermeable to the flow of air, applied continuously, and durable enough to last the lifetime of the building.

One simple and reliable technique is the Airtight Drywall Approach (ADA). This amounts to sealing potential air leaks in exterior walls with compressible, closed-cell foam or caulk so that the drywall becomes the air barrier. ADA addresses the usual trouble spots—at top and bottom plates, at the rim joist, around windows and doors, and around light switches and receptacles. If the gasket material is not available locally, suppliers who carry it include Resource Conservation Technology in Baltimore, Md., and the Shelter Companies in Burnsville, Minn.

Is ADA effective? Yes. As reported by the U.S. Department of Energy, one ADA house that was tested had 0.67 to 1.80 air changes per hour (ACH) at 50 Pascals pressure, which approximates a 20 mph wind, while an identical home without ADA had 2.23 to 2.59 ACH. More interesting, the department said that an airtight house consumes one-third less energy than an unsealed house.

Nothing is as simple as it seems. Making the best green decision is the act of weighing benefits against risks and making the best choice we can at the time. Few materials pass every test, but making safety, durability, and resource conservation an important part of the mix is a big step in the right direction. Interior finishes start going in when the house has cleared its insulation inspection. But before the drywall goes up we go back to building science basics and decide how to create an effective interior air barrier (see the bottom sidebar on the facing page).

Drywall

Unless you live in a part of the country where plastering is the norm, gypsum drywall is the product of choice for finishing walls and ceilings. It's inexpensive, available just about anywhere, and goes up quickly. Drywall consists of a gypsum core and paper outer layers. But is it green? The paper making up the outer layers of drywall already has a high green quotient because it's made from recycled paper. Instead of standard drywall, look for the type whose core is made with recycled residue from air scrubbers at coal-fired power plants (U.S. Gypsum makes this variety). It's stronger and denser than standard varieties so it's more durable. It's typically used in schools, prisons, factories, and other facilities that get a lot of hard use. Higher density also makes it better at holding heat in an otherwise low-mass house. On the downside, this kind of drywall is more expensive and heavier than standard drywall. Installers gripe when they have to put it on ceilings. You can get the benefits of greater thermal mass and durability by using it on walls alone.

On the near horizon for residential use is a new type of drywall with an unusual ability to absorb and release heat. Micronal® PCM

Gypsum drywall is often the first choice for finished interior walls. A good green option is to look for drywall made with recycled residue from industrial air scrubbers, which is denser and stronger than the standard version.

SmartBoard® incorporates a waxlike substance in the gypsum core. The unique attribute of this "phase change" material is that it melts and solidifies (changes phase) in a narrow range of temperatures close to typical indoor air temperatures. As it does, the material absorbs large amounts of heat (to melt) and then gives off that heat as it solidifies. Phase-change drywall holds great promise for passive solar design, offering the advantages of high-mass materials like stone or concrete without the associated high cost.

"Phase change" drywall has the ability to absorb and release energy, giving it the advantages of a high-mass material in passive solar design. It's expected in U.S. markets shortly.

CLAY PLASTER

No matter what kind of drywall you use it will need priming and painting. An alternative for indoor wall finishes is natural plaster, a popular finish material available in a variety of colors that's applied to primed and sealed gypsum drywall, blue board, or other suitable substrate. Plaster typically consists of a mix of clay, pigments, stone dust, and sometimes plant fiber such as straw. It requires more skill to apply than paint, at least to get professional results. Clay plasters can be applied by trowel to almost any primed wall surface. Other plasters can contain lime and sometimes portland cement, both of which are highly alkaline substances, good for reducing mold but harsh on skin, eye, and lung tissue, so special attention to safety should be taken during installation.

Plasters are thought of as living finishes and may take some extra care to maintain if you experience a crack or chip in the surface. They are very natural, breathable surface covers that are often preferable for clients with chemical sensitivities, as they do not contain any VOCs.

Natural clay plaster is an alternative to paint. Low in toxicity, it can be applied over a variety of substrates.

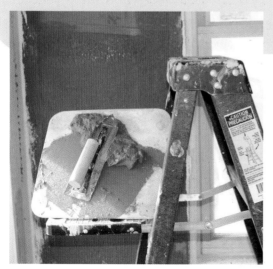

The product is being developed by BASF, which is now introducing it in European markets. The company says Knauf will offer the material under its own label and hopes to have it available in the U.S. in the very near future.

Paints, Finishes, and Adhesives

After pursuing all the green building strategies that have brought a house to this stage, choosing low-VOC or no-VOC paints should be a no-brainer. Volatile organic compounds are substances that easily convert to gas at room temperatures, and they can trigger asthmatic or allergic reactions as well as pollute the atmosphere. The incrementally higher cost of low/no-VOC paints is well worth it, especially when you consider the relatively large areas that are painted—ceilings, walls, and trim add up to a lot of square footage. The EPA requires paint manufacturers to list VOC content. However, only those VOCs that can result in the formation of smog are tested. Many other compounds containing VOCs may also be part of

Latex paint has largely displaced oil-based formulations, but go a step further by choosing low-VOC or no-VOC varieties that are now available from most major paint manufacturers.

Choosing a low-/no-VOC paint is only half the battle. You also have to consider any tints that are added to color the paint. Choose the color you want first, then find out from the manufacturer whether the tints needed to make it add VOCs back into the paint. Pastel colors typically have the fewest VOCs and dark colors have more.

a paint formulation. Your best bet is to select a paint that contains less than 50 grams of VOCs per liter (g/l).

Major manufacturers are jumping on the green bandwagon and the result is a growing number of paints with low or no VOCs. They are sold under a variety of trade names, such as Benjamin Moore's EcoSpec or Sherwin Williams' GreenSure® products. If you like a particular brand of paint, ask the supplier for the low-VOC version. Oil-based paints in general are becoming less common, not only because latex paints are so much better than they used to be but also because oil-based formulations contain more hazardous solvents.

Low-VOC paints should be applied with plenty of ventilation, just like conventional paints. When possible, keep windows and doors open. You can keep fumes downwind by placing a fan in the doorway so it blows air out of the room, or an exhaust fan in a window. Work your way through the room so you're always upwind of fresh paint.

RATING PAINTS

Green Seal, an independent nonprofit organization that offers green product certification (www.greenseal.org), has created criteria for evaluating paint that prohibit some toxic compounds and limit others. Methylene chloride, benzene, vinyl chloride, phthalates, and ketones, for example, are on the list of materials that are completely banned. Standards also require paints to meet performance standards for hiding power (opacity), scrubability (abrasion resistance), and ease of maintenance (stain removal).

Low/no–VOC paint, water-borne wood finishes, and urethane floor finishes work well and are as durable as conventional products.

Water-based wood finishes

Wood finishes, particularly solvent-based floor finishes, can be especially harmful to the health of children. The old generation of "Swedish floor finishes" are one of the most toxic elements brought inside the home. They're sold on the basis of durability, but the chemicals that make for low maintenance off-gas for a month or more. People with asthma and other respiratory problems can have a major problem as these finishes cure. Today, there are a range of water-based products that perform almost as well without the potential hazard. A company called BonaKemi manufactures low-VOC floor finishes with various levels of durability, from casual household to basketball court tough. AFM Safecoat produces a low-VOC water-based finish and a very low-VOC, no formaldehyde Polyureseal BP® that can be applied as an alternative to solvent-based finishes. Water-based wood finishes for trim, handrails, and other exposed wood are now in the finish mainstream. They don't behave or look exactly like their solvent-based equivalents but they are getting better. For one thing, they don't penetrate the wood in the same way that oil does, so they don't impart the same amber

quality to bare wood that's so appealing about an oil finish. Old-timers may miss the rich quality of a penetrating stain and oil-based finish. If oil-based finishes are used, they should be applied offsite whenever possible and brought to the job after they have cured. That's not always possible, of course, but cabinets, interior casework, and some trim certainly can be finished offsite before installation. Using prefinished flooring is an option with the same advantages.

Water-based wood fin-ishes are a healthier choice than their solvent-based counterparts. Performance and ease of application are improving.

Not only does it eliminate floor finish from the jobsite but the flooring doesn't need sanding and can be walked on as soon as it's installed.

Low-VOC adhesives and caulks

As noxious as some kinds of finishes seem to be, you'll find the highest concentration of known carcinogens in solvent-based adhesives. Toluene, xylene, and other petrochemicals typically found in common construction adhesives are known, as warning labels in the State of California tell you, to cause nerve damage, brain damage, kidney damage, and cancer. There is no reason to continue using these products. Virtually all major manufactur-

ers offer urethane-based adhesives that are not only stronger but bond to wet wood, a problem for solvent-based adhesives.

For each specific adhesive application look for the VOC content on the tube or can. It should be less than 150 g/l and lower if possible. If it has a health warning and the ingredients include petrochemicals, ask your supplier for the safe, environmentally friendly alternative. Often it is not as visible on lumberyard or hardware shelves.

Interior Cabinets

Much of the standard cabinetry on the market today contains particleboard made with a urea formaldehyde binder that emits formaldehyde and other harmful chemicals. Worse than new carpeting, most adhesives and binders for wood products contain high levels of formaldehyde that can off-gas for years. But there are a growing number of alternatives, such as panels made from compressed wheat straw and MDI resins that do not emit formaldehyde. Using these agriculturally derived materials diverts waste from landfills or, worse, local incinerators while also giving farmers a secondary source of income. Other alternatives for cabinets include Medite™, a brand of formaldehyde-free medium-density fiberboard, and SkyBlend®, a wood fiber board made without urea formaldehyde. When considering these options, remember that the more recycled fiber used in their production the better. Recycled content saves trees.

For cabinet faces, a variety of green-friendly species is available. In addition to FSC-certified wood in a number of species, there is Lyptus® Eucalyptus, a plantation-grown rapidly renewable wood that looks like mahogany, and a variety of bamboo products, another rapidly renewable resource. To conserve even more resources, use real wood veneers or recycled content veneers with a substrate that does not contain formaldehyde. Using veneers

Kitchen cabinetry made with wheatboard or other formaldehyde-free materials are healthy indoor choices. Wood veneers, which make the most of diminishing natural resources, are an alternative to solid lumber.

Bamboo plywood, *made with a rapidly renewable resource, is an attractive option to conventional cabinet materials.*

from sustainably managed sources stretches the resource a lot further than making solid wood cabinet doors.

Green Seal has also developed specifications for cabinetry that call for low VOCs, no harmful chemical components, and performance standards for durability and mold and mildew resistance—much like its performance standards for paint. As interest in green products grows, manufacturers are responding with cabinet lines designed to satisfy consumer demands for a healthier indoor environment. Taking advantage of what's available starts with knowing what to look for.

Countertops

Homeowners have a tremendous range of choices for countertops, and with a few caveats almost all of them can comfortably be used in a green home. These are by definition food-contact surfaces, so the likelihood that counter materials will shed harmful chemicals is remote. Problems, where they occur, have more to do with the substrate than the countertop itself, or possibly the distance that some materials must be transported before they are put into service.

Linoleum and laminate

Manufactured with linseed oil, pine resin, and wood flour, linoleum is making a resurgence as a flooring material after years of living in the shadow of sheet vinyl. It can also be used as a countertop, showing the same durability and an ability to "heal" itself from minor abrasions and knife marks. Linoleum should be installed over a formaldehyde-free substrate with a low-VOC adhesive to keep it green.

High-pressure plastic laminate is a great bargain for countertops. It consists of resin-soaked layers of kraft paper topped by a decorative top surface. Manufacturing has become increasingly sophisticated so products can now look like wood, stone, and a variety of other materials. Although it won't tolerate high heat and it can be scratched, laminate is otherwise an extremely durable product. Like linoleum, its weakness is the substrate rather than the material itself. But if you choose a formaldehyde-free product, this is a good green choice.

Solid surface

There are many solid surface products on the market, all tracing their histories to DuPont's well-known brand Corian®. Solid surface is an inert, nonporous plastic resin with a mineral filler that, like laminate, can take on the appearance of a variety of materials. These surfaces are durable and minor dings can be sanded and buffed out, but watch out for high heat and sharp knives. Solid-surface countertops are relatively expensive. Once again, pay attention to what substrate the 1/2-in.-thick material is mounted on. Specify exterior-grade plywood, formaldehyde-free MDF, or wheatboard to keep it green.

Solid-surface countertops have great potential for innovation. There are now more materials available that contain recycled content and provide all the benefits of their non-recycled counterparts. They include paper composite countertops such as Richlite®, which uses pulp from sustainably managed forests, and PaperStone™, which incorporates up to 100 percent recycled paper pulp, much of which is post-consumer. Both can be sealed with mineral oil to improve moisture and stain resistance.

Stainless steel

Stainless steel is great for commercial kitchens, although it has slowly migrated into residential kitchens along with the stainless-steel appliances that mimic a commercial look.

IceStone® countertop material is VOC free and made with concrete and 100% recycled glass.

Pros love it because it's nonporous, cleans up quickly, and is virtually indestructible. Because it scratches so easily, that new, shiny look rapidly dulls into a very used look. Stainless steel that has been patterned reduces the visual impact of scratching. Steel is a good electrical conductor, making ground fault circuit interrupters all the more important. Stainless counters are typically bonded to a substrate of medium-density fiberboard, so the usual cautions about formaldehyde off-gassing apply here. Although there are plenty of green attributes with stainless steel, its high cost is not one of them.

Tile

There are many types of tile, from ceramic to porcelain, earthenware to glass, terrazzo and other aggregates, all of which make for a durable and, at times, less expensive countertop surface. Looking for tile with recycled content is your best green option. Tile is hard on

Richlite® is paper combined with phenolic resin and then baked to form a durable alternative to stone and solid surface.

Stainless steel makes an extremely durable, nonporous countertop that's easy to keep clean. If you want to keep it green, install it over a formaldehyde-free substrate.

glassware but extremely durable and the huge selection of sizes, colors, and patterns make it easy to customize. While tile can be pricey, most isn't. Here grout, not the tile itself, is the green issue. Not only should it be nontoxic but grout should also be sealed regularly, every three to six months. Without a sealer, grout can become a matrix that collects bacteria. Keeping it sealed means keeping it safe.

Wood

Just about any kind of wood can be fashioned into a countertop, but the conventional choice is maple butcher block, available as either edge-grain or end-grain slabs. Maple is tough, shock resistant, and close-grained, meaning it doesn't offer a lot of open pores where food and bacteria can collect. Butcher-block counters are often made from recycled material

*Ceramic tile makes a **long-lasting,** nonpolluting countertop but look for nontoxic grout and keep the grout sealed to keep bacteria out.*

gleaned from the furniture and flooring industry —a green advantage. If using another species, look for an FSC label, but it's probably a good idea to stay away from open-grained woods, such as oak, unless they are very carefully sealed (oak turns black when the seal fails and it's exposed to water). The green issues with wood are two-fold: maintenance and finish. Because wood is susceptible to water damage, maintaining a good finish is important. Finishes should be nontoxic.

Another woodlike option is bamboo, an engineered product made by cutting bamboo stalks into strips and gluing them back together. Bamboo is growing in popularity for flooring, and the same attributes make it an attractive green choice for a counter. Manufacturers have developed a variety of exotic looks that you won't find with wood (see www.plyboo.com).

This countertop made from reclaimed wood makes a beautiful and green countertop. Wood must be sealed carefully, especially around the sink, and it should be resealed as the finish wears through.

Stone

All stone is a "natural" product. Its porosity determines its functionality as a countertop, and most stone must be periodically resealed. Some marbles, such as travertine, for example, can be porous and harbor bacteria. Other choices include soapstone, slate, and granite. The green issue is where the stone comes from. Because it's so widely used, granite for U.S. countertops is mined all over the world, meaning that it can have a lot of embodied energy by the time it winds up in a kitchen in Chicago. When choosing stone, look for something quarried from a closer source. The more local it is the better.

Stone composites are a relatively recent addition to the stone category. Silestone® and Zodiaq® are two brand names. They consist mainly of quartz with a small amount of binder. These counters have fewer maintenance issues than natural stone because they are nonporous and don't need sealing. Prices are competitive with natural stone.

Concrete

Concrete is the new darling in the world of countertops. It can be formed into an infinite variety of shapes and enlivened with pigments, inlays, and decorative aggregate. So, from an aesthetic point of view, concrete counters have much to recommend them. Green-wise, concrete makes a very durable, heat-resistant surface. The downside is maintenance. Like stone, concrete must be resealed occasionally to resist stains. Concrete may also show hairline cracks, which can be a sign of character for some homeowners but a detraction for others. Here is where fly-ash concrete is an advantage since it is less likely to crack over time.

It takes a lot of energy to produce cement, the key ingredient of concrete, but no countertop material is immune from this argu-

Heat resistant and durable, natural stone makes a long-wearing and beautiful countertop. Look for locally or regionally quarried stone to reduce transportation costs and lower its embodied energy. Shown here are granite (top) and soapstone (bottom).

Concrete is a green choice for countertops, though it is porous and will stain if it's not sealed or waxed periodically. Sonoma Cast Stone claims that its NuCrete™ counters are impervious to stains.

ment. Moreover, it takes relatively little cement to produce a counter. So, on balance, this a good green choice.

Green Flooring

There is a wide variety of green flooring in the marketplace today. What makes flooring green? Here, many factors come together: durability, non-toxicity, renewable sourcing, and transportation. The challenge is to determine which of these qualities are most important and how they reflect aesthetically. No product has everything so it often amounts to comparing apples to oranges and making what seems like the best choice.

Two general considerations for flooring are its thermal mass and its compatibility with radiant-floor heat, if that's the kind of heating system you have. Some sustainable flooring options, such as ceramic tile or concrete, are also good heat conductors, making them smart choices over radiant floors. Their thermal mass, higher than that of wood, complements passive

solar design. Other products, such as certain kinds of wood, may not be appropriate for radiant-floor systems because of the risk of warping or splitting. Ask your supplier for the manufacturer's recommendation before installing.

Finished concrete floors

When used as the finish floor, concrete containing high fly-ash content serves several green purposes. For one, it saves the expense of installing another flooring material, like wood or carpet. It also makes use of an industrial by-product, a decided green advantage. And concrete, unlike carpet, doesn't harbor allergens, dust, and mold so it contributes to high indoor air quality.

A variety of finishing techniques can also produce dazzling visual results. Pigments applied to concrete as it cures, or acid-based pigments applied to concrete once it has set, can produce beautiful surfaces that look at home even in formal living spaces. Choose the right contractor and you'll get concrete that becomes a two-dimensional sculpture on the floor. The trick is to look for an experienced installer, not necessarily someone who specializes in sidewalks and driveways and is trying to learn something new.

Linoleum and vinyl

Many people refer to sheet vinyl flooring as "linoleum," a natural mistake. After all, linoleum was widely used until vinyl gradually shouldered it aside. But that's changing and linoleum is once again available. It makes a better choice than vinyl because it's manufactured with less toxic materials.

Linoleum is made with fewer noxious chemicals than sheet vinyl. The word "linoleum" is derived from Latin words for linseed and oil.

While preferable to vinyl from a chemical standpoint, linoleum doesn't have the same protective surface and must be polished occasionally to resist stains. Manufacturers recommend it be installed professionally. Be prepared for an odor from the linseed oil that off-gasses an aldehyde, which is not toxic for most people and will dissipate.

Vinyl flooring is very popular, but from a green standpoint it's a product to avoid. Plasticizers called phthalates used to make PVC soft are a health hazard, especially in nurseries and play spaces where children will come in to close contact with the material. Recycled-content vinyl flooring is better than virgin material, but with so many other flooring choices available it doesn't make sense to choose this one.

After years of playing second fiddle to sheet vinyl, linoleum is making a comeback. It's made from less toxic ingredients but needs more maintenance than vinyl.

Bamboo

Bamboo is a rapidly renewable resource and also a durable flooring choice. Bamboo matures in 3 to 5 years versus the 40 to 60 years that oak or cherry need to mature to flooring quality. Bamboo comes in two grain patterns— flat sawn or vertical grain—and typically with either a blond or caramelized finish.

There are a few caveats. Of the thousand or so varieties of bamboo only a few are appropriate for flooring. Of those few, some

Bamboos are from a large family of grasses, not wood. There are 1,000 or so species that grow in a variety of climates and terrains. Some can grow 4 ft. per day and are large enough in only a few years to be turned into a variety of building products.

are better than others in dry climates. When inappropriate species are cut and milled into flooring, the result can be cupping, shrinking, or delaminating. The old adage "you get what you pay for" really applies to bamboo these days. When you see newspaper ads for cheap bamboo flooring, run the other way. Go with a company like Plyboo or Timbergrass, a supplier that has been in the business for over a decade and offers high-quality flooring.

FSC-certified wood flooring

Available in solid wood and as engineered, prefinished varieties, FSC-certified flooring is available across the country. The volume of certified flooring is increasing every year as more landowners get their wood lots certified

and distribution improves. A growing number of exotic species are coming into the market from South America and Asia where certification is catching on as a way to improve market share.

Be aware that some certified engineered flooring contain urea-formaldehyde as the internal adhesive with only the wear layer (4 mils to 6 mils thick) actually made of certified materials. Core materials may come from any number of other species. Other brands, however, are made with formaldehyde-free adhesives and are definitely preferable (EcoTimber is one company selling these flooring products). To find out what you're buying, you'll have to ask the supplier for details. Companies that produce formaldehyde-free versions, however, are likely to make a point of it.

Cork

Cork flooring has become synonymous with green interiors. It is beautiful and has natural anti-bacterial qualities, is soft underfoot, is made from recycled materials, and comes from a renewable source. Cork flooring is typically made from the waste cork left over after bottle stoppers are manufactured. It has become so popular that it is sometimes made from raw cork. Cork comes from the cork oak native to Spain and Portugal. The "corks" are punched out of the sheet and the rest is ground and turned into flooring. The only downside is that cork trees grow only in a limited geographical area in the Mediterranean. All attempts to create cork plantations in other parts of the world, like California, have failed. So it is a limited resource for the future.

The bark of a cork oak is first harvested when the tree is about 25 years old, a cycle that can be repeated every decade or so throughout the tree's 150- to 250-year lifespan without affecting its health. Harvesters remove about 50 percent of the bark in any one harvest and age it for three to six months before turning it into a variety of products, including bottle stoppers.

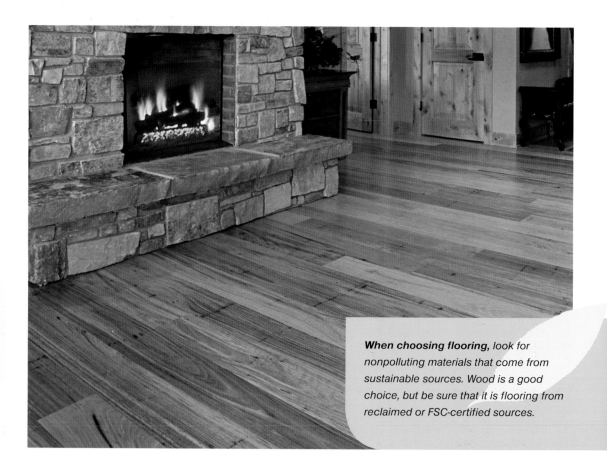

When choosing flooring, look for nonpolluting materials that come from sustainable sources. Wood is a good choice, but be sure that it is flooring from reclaimed or FSC-certified sources.

Cork flooring comes from the bark of the cork oak, a tree that lives for up to 250 years and can be stripped of some of its bark every decade without harming the tree.

Natural carpets

Carpeting for a green home should be made of natural materials, such as wool or sisal with jute backing. Fibers are woven into the backing or bonded with real rubber—avoid carpeting made with styrene-butadiene latex binder, an indoor air pollutant. Although natural wool sounds great from a green standpoint, its desirability depends on where the wool comes from. Domestic wool is fine, but if the wool is imported from Iceland or New Zealand it has probably been fumigated with a USDA-required insecticide that is off the charts in terms of toxicity.

Carpet

Wall-to-wall carpet is an anathema to good indoor air quality. Not only does it off-gas itself (many carpets introduce over 100 chemicals into the home) but it collects dust, dander, and chemicals that are tracked in from outdoors. Its fibers absorb gases from other products. The Carpet and Rug Institute has worked with the EPA for a decade to create the Green Label program. This involves testing random samples off the production line for VOC emissions. They have recently introduced the Green Label Plus program that is stricter about emissions. The

Carpeting made from natural fibers is preferable to carpeting whose binders off-gas indoor air pollutants.

Carpet squares from recycled content are an attractive alternative to conventional carpeting. These are made with a tight weave for long life, and individual squares can be replaced if they become stained or damaged.

RECYCLED CONTENT CARPET

There are several varieties of carpet made with recycled content. Most common is recycled "pop bottle," or PET, carpet. Polyethylene terephthalate is what water bottles and soda bottles are made from. It has been an alternative to nylon for many years and is easily recycled into fabric and carpet fiber. While it is a recycled product, it still uses synthetic latex as a binder so it doesn't enhance indoor air quality. Inexpensive, low-fiber-count carpets have been known to crush in high traffic areas like stairs and doorways.

commercial carpet industry has been more aggressive in conforming to this new certification but always ask before ordering whether the carpet meets the program requirements.

A great alternative to conventional residential carpets it to use commercial carpets from Interface or Collins and Aikman. They have a lower pile and tighter weave and are designed for long-term use. InterfaceFlor™ is a new residential carpet tile product that uses recycled-content fibers and can be lifted and replaced if a square is stained.

Tile

Tiles make durable and attractive flooring that's easy to install and doesn't come with a learning curve like some green products. Most tiles are very durable; a key green consideration is whether they contain recycled content. As with many products, sourcing is an issue. Look for local, then regional, and finally domestic sources.

The best and greenest way to install tile is in conventional thickset mortar. The floor will last longer, will be less likely to crack, and has the lowest toxicity. Thinset mortar is a combination of cement and epoxy. It is the next best option as the epoxy sets up quickly and off-gasses for only a short time. If you plan to use adhesive and grout, look for water-based, nontoxic products.

Glass tile made from old bottles, auto glass, and recycled fluorescent light tubes or ceramics can be found with a quick search of the marketplace. These tiles are highly acclaimed for their rich color and durability.

Natural pebble stones (left) are an alternative to ceramic tile flooring (below).

Recycled rubber flooring

Rubber flooring is attractive for its resilience. Most often found in gyms and health clubs, it's also a good flooring option for commercial kitchens—places that usually have good ventilation. Rubber off-gasses during most of its life. Recycled content reduces some of this effect but the smell is constant. It is a much better product for outdoor play areas than for children's playrooms inside.

Reclaimed flooring

Reclaimed flooring is available locally and through various sources nationally. While old-growth wood is not a green flooring choice, reclaimed old-growth timber flooring can be your way around this problem. Vast quantities of old-growth lumber can be found in old ware-houses, buildings, bridges, and other structures. Reclaimed wood provides the benefits of old-growth timber without the environmental costs. Another source for wood products is local lumberyards that reclaim urban forests when trees die or are cut down to build new homes and businesses.

Pay attention to where the materials in your home come from, how they are made, and what they might emit into indoor air. Reclaimed materials are readily available and cre-

BEST PRACTICES

- Establish an effective interior air barrier.

- If available, choose drywall whose core is made with residue that's taken from air scrubbers at coal-fired power plants.

- Choose low-VOC or no-VOC paints, caulks, and adhesives as well as water-based finishes rather than solvent-based products.

- Avoid wood products that use urea-formaldehyde as a binder.

- Use wood products made with renewable or recycled content.

- Consider the distance that building products must be shipped and choose those produced locally or regionally over those that come from overseas.

- Specify wood that's certified by the Forest Stewardship Council.

- If carpet is used as a floor covering, favor natural materials such as wool or sisal but avoid products that contain styrene butadiene latex binders and wool that must be fumigated when it enters the country.

Reclaimed wood makes excellent flooring. It's not only green because it's recycled, but it also has a character and presence that new flooring just doesn't have.

ate unique creative spaces. The marketplace is filled with nontoxic alternatives to the everyday paints, sealants, and adhesives we're used to buying. Creating a well-designed space that will last throughout a home's various inhabitants is as important as selecting materials with recycled content and low embodied energy.

Landscaping

Builders are not necessarily gardeners or landscapers. Judging from the uniformity of exterior design in many housing developments, the last step of construction is to rake and seed the yard and move all construction equipment off the site. That's the end. In no time, homeowners are happily fussing over expanses of bright green grass—watering, fertilizing, applying herbicides and insecticides, and, of course, pushing or riding a lawnmower around to keep it all under control. It's so perfectly normal. And it doesn't make the least amount of sense.

Give the same building site to a professional landscaper or landscape architect and it becomes an opportunity no less interesting, and promising, than designing a green house. Thoughtful landscaping can accomplish everything that green building is intended to do: conserve natural resources, promote healthy

Collectively, Americans spend $25 billion on lawn care a year, according to the EPA. One acre of lawn costs from $400 to $700 a year to maintain, and the average American will spend the equivalent of a full workweek, 40 hours, cutting the grass.

THE GREEN FACTOR

Good green landscaping doesn't have much to do with hydro-seeding a lawn when construction is complete. In fact, it's more about eliminating acres of grass that soon become a major contributor to water and air pollution, consume thousands of gallons of water a year, and create a maintenance regime for homeowners.

Landscaping for a green home involves a careful assessment of what's on the site, a construction plan that minimizes disruption to natural features and vegetation, and encouraging native plants that work in harmony with the house. Key considerations:

- **Water consumption.** Native plants have learned how to survive without extra watering.

- **Energy efficiency.** The right vegetation cuts energy bills by buffering the house against winter winds, blocking intense sunlight during the summer, and increasing solar gain in winter. Heating and cooling bills can be substantially lower with the right green landscaping.

- **Reduced runoff and cleaner air.** A reduction or elimination of chemical additives to lawns and gardens means fewer pollutants in local waterways. Getting rid of the lawnmower means cleaner air.

- **Resource conservation.** If we can learn to recycle plastic and glass, why not "recycle" organic material into valuable compost for our own gardens. The practice reduces the load on sewage treatment plants and landfills and results in healthier vegetation.

A LAWN YOU DON'T MOW

As a kid my job was to cut the grass, and we had quite a lot of it. We had a ride-behind Gravely® as sturdy as a tank, and I spent many summer afternoons in a wake of dust, exhaust, noise, and grass clippings. Ever since, I've had an aversion to this traditional American pastime.

As an adult I've lived in either suburban or rural houses that all came with lawns attached, and I thought that cutting the grass was just one of those things you had to get used to. By June, the lawn usually needed cutting twice a week—if left unattended it would be knee-high in a few weeks. I managed to avoid fertilizer but occasionally we had moles, which meant grub-killing chemical insecticides.

A few years ago my wife, a landscape gardener, found a solution: grass you never had to cut. It's called sheep fescue, a variety that prospers in Maine where we live without extra watering and without fertilizers. Best of all it doesn't grow more than 5 in. tall. Then it just stops.

Sheep fescue seed isn't cheap, and it isn't available at local hardware stores or garden centers. We buy it over the Internet for about $8 a pound. Nor would a lawn of sheep fescue be featured in a magazine ad for Toro lawnmowers. It's a little scruffy, a little shaggy, and it's not a brilliant green.

But it fits right into my wife's landscaping scheme of native and low-maintenance plantings. Best of all, we gave away the lawnmower.

—SG

living, and lower maintenance requirements for homeowners. Instead of becoming a burden that consumes an alarming amount of water, energy, and time, and pollutes both air and water in the process, landscaping can become a net gain.

Landscapes are more than lawns, and just as no single house design is appropriate for all climates there is no generic landscaping template that can be used everywhere. A successful plan is adaptive to its environment and undertaken with as much forethought as the house itself. In the end, the two work together. Landscaping becomes not so much a disconnected feature but a way of helping the house become even more efficient.

Evaluate Site and Climate

Creating a green landscaping plan begins with understanding what you have to work with, including climate, soil, and plants that are already growing on the site. Ideally, this comes before building starts, not as an afterthought after the lot has been stripped and the house constructed. To encourage plants that will thrive with a minimum of water and other maintenance, planning should include a look at the following:

- solar exposure at different times of the day as well as seasonally

- soil type on the site

- wind patterns, including direction and average strength seasonally

- temperature swings throughout the year

- snow and rainfall patterns

- native plants that are attractive to people and wildlife

According to the American Society of Landscape Architects, there are four climatic zones in the U.S.: cool, temperate, hot-arid, and hot-humid. But within each of them, there are any number of local climatic zones and

Planting native and drought-tolerant species conserves water and lowers the need for chemical pesticides and fertilizers, both keys to green landscaping.

Before construction begins, take a survey of what kind of plants are growing on the site. One goal for green builders is to keep site disruptions to a minimum and encourage the return of those species when the house is finished.

even on the same lot there may be microclimates that are best for certain types of vegetation. It's not enough to visit a local nursery and look only for plants rated Zone 4 hardy, for instance, because you happen to be building in a Zone 4 region. Soil types are no less variable. The same site may have sandy loam, heavy clay, and anything in between. Soil pH as well as type, along with local temperature swings and solar exposure, all help determine what will grow and what won't.

A landscape designer or architect can be as valuable as any other subcontractor in studying these and other conditions that ultimately affect a landscape plan. If you're not planning to hire a professional, there should be a variety of local sources to offer guidance no matter where you're building. In the San Francisco Bay area, for example, a program called "Bay-Friendly Gardening" is available online (see www.stopwaste.org) with a variety of landscape suggestions that are suited specifically

CLIMATIC ZONES

	Temperate	Hot-Arid	Hot-Humid	Cold
OBJECTIVES	Maximize warming effects of sun in winter. Maximize shade in summer. Reduce impact of winter wind but allow air circulation in summer.	Maximize shade late morning and all afternoon. Maximize air movement in summer.	Maximize shade. Minimize wind.	Maximize warming effects of solar radiation. Reduce impact of winter wind. Avoid micro-climatic cold pockets.
ADAPTATIONS				
Position on slope	Middle-upper for radiation	Low for cool airflow	High for wind	Low for wind shelter
Orientation on slope	South to southeast	East to southeast for afternoon shade	South	South to southeast
Relation to water	Close to water; avoid coastal fog	On leeside of water	Near any water	Near large body of water
Preferred winds	Avoid continental cold winds	Exposed to prevailing winds	Sheltered from north	Sheltered from north and west
Clustering	Around a common sunny terrace	Along E–W axis, for shade	Open to wind	Around sun pockets
Building orientation	South to southeast	South	South 5° toward prevailing wind	Southeast
Tree forms	Deciduous trees nearby on west; no evergreens near on south	Trees overhanging roof, if possible	High canopy trees; use deciduous trees near building	Deciduous trees near building; evergreens for windbreaks
Road orientation	Crosswise to winter wind	Narrow; E–W axis	Broad channel, E–W axis	Crosswise to winter wind
Materials coloration	Medium	Light on exposed surfaces, dark to avoid reflection	Light, especially for roof	Medium to dark

Source: Landscape Planning for Energy Conservation, Charles McClenon-Editor, Environmental Design Press 1977, Reston, VA. page 69

to the region's Mediterranean climate. In other parts of the country, county extension offices offer the same kind of locally tailored information. Experts are well-schooled in local growing conditions and native plants. They may even be able to help you test your soil.

Working with What's There

Once equipment moves onto the site, the idea is to cause as little disruption as possible. Topsoil that is moved to accommodate site work should be stockpiled elsewhere so it can be reused when construction is finished. Removing every tree and shrub within 100 ft. of the foundation may make it easier for some of the subcontractors to work, but it doesn't make any sense if plants have to be reestablished later.

Large trees deserve especially careful attention. It's true they are more difficult to remove after the house is built, and large trees right next to the house have the potential for causing problems—roots that grow where you don't want them, leaves and needles that clog gutters and encourage mold on the roof, to say nothing of the damage that a downed tree can inflict. But it's equally difficult to replace a large tree that's been removed unnecessarily. As we discussed in chapter 3 (see p. 42), evergreens on the north side of the house help block cold winter winds. Deciduous trees on south-facing exposures serve a dual purpose, keeping out hot summer sun but increasing solar gain in winter.

According to the U.S. Department of Environmental Protection, plantings can lower air-

Large trees are among the most valuable assets of any building site. Deciduous trees are a valuable ally in passive solar design by tempering summer's heat but permitting the winter sun to warm the house.

conditioning costs by 25 percent and heating bills by between 25 percent and 40 percent, for overall energy savings of 25 percent. Step under a tree and the air temperature can drop 25 percent. Trees can be used to channel wind as well as block it, aiding natural ventilation in the house or helping to shield solar collectors and photovoltaic panels from snow accumulation. Landscaping plans should be developed in conjunction with the early development of the architecture of the house so that the two may fit together in a cohesive design to optimize the beauty while saving energy and water.

Soil management

By planning ahead, soil that's on the site can remain healthy for use after construction is over. Removing the top 6 in. of topsoil in areas that will be disturbed by construction and stockpiling it for later use will help keep soil healthier. That, in turn, will help reduce storm water runoff and erosion while reducing the future need for chemical fertilizers and irrigation systems. Topsoil can be stored in an area that's marked for future paving so it won't be disturbed. It's also a good idea to fence off areas on the site to help keep soil from being compacted. Limit trucks and other equipment to areas that will be paved later. Compaction reduces the ability of soil to hold air and water. The idea is to keep as much of the site as possible in its original condition.

Water conservation

Protecting topsoil also has a bearing on water conservation, a major objective of green gardening. Healthy topsoil retains its ability to hold water, meaning that planted areas will need less supplemental watering later. According to the Bay-Friendly Landscaping Guidelines, 1 cu. ft. of soil holds roughly 1.5 quarts of

water for each 1 percent of organic matter. Keeping as many of the native plants onsite intact during construction helps ensure a landscape fully adapted to that site and climate. Plants will live with little extra care.

Water distribution for the property is most effective when it's considered as part of the overall landscaping plan, not as an after-

The Las Vegas Valley Water District warns residents that watering vegetation during rainy periods gives plants more water than needed, oversaturating the soil and producing wasteful runoff. Turning off on a single rainy day can save 500 gallons of water. A "water smart" home can save as much as 75,000 gallons of water a year.

When they are used, irrigation systems should be designed to minimize waste. Water distributed via in-ground "soaker hoses" gets to the roots where it's needed, and it doesn't evaporate as quickly when mulched properly.

Spraying water indiscriminately into the garden is less effective than in-ground distribution. Timers and rain meters that limit spray operation when soil is already damp are improvements.

thought. Sprinklers are a cheap and foolish way to use water. They place the water on leaves rather than in the soil where roots can absorb the moisture. More that one-third of sprinkled water evaporates before permeating the soil. In-ground irrigation uses less water with better results. It can be placed on a timer or connected with a rain meter that shuts the system down if the soil is already wet.

A rainwater collection system (and pre-plumbing for a gray-water system) can help reduce the amount of potable water used for irrigation. Water catchment can be as simple as a barrel placed at the base of a gutter down-spout or as elaborate as a system that includes filtration as well as oversized storage. To capture the full potential of runoff, start by measuring the square footage of the roof of the house. Then multiply that by the average rainfall in the

Water catchment is a good green strategy. *It can be as simple as placing a rain barrel beneath a gutter downspout.*

RAINWATER CATCHMENT SYSTEM

Capturing rainwater and using it to irrigate a vegetable garden pays dividends on many levels. Even a system that incorporates nothing more than a plastic rain barrel can be an effective means of conserving water.

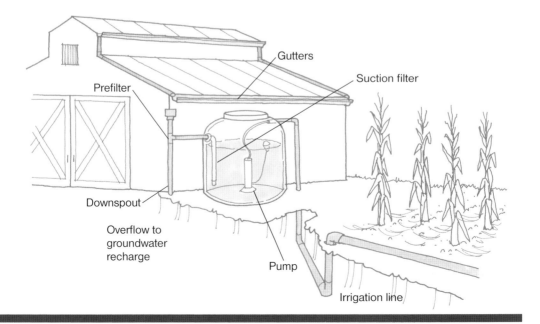

Gutters

Suction filter

Prefilter

Downspout

Overflow to groundwater recharge

Pump

Irrigation line

area to get the number of gallons of water the roof can produce (an online conversion program can help you with the math; www.online conversion.com is one of them).

Decreasing runoff also helps protect the biology of the water in streams and rivers by reducing polluted runoff. Using permeable surfaces for sidewalks and driveways allows rainwater to percolate through subsurface soil, which filters out impurities and pollutants before the water gets into the water table or a nearby stream. Water that's dumped directly into storm sewers takes with it any contaminants it picks up along the way.

Lawnmowers gulp 580 million gallons of gas a year. To keep all of that grass green and pest-free, Americans apply 67 million pounds of pesticides a year to their lawns and in the process poison between 60 million and 70 million birds in the U.S. alone.

Energy conservation

Plants can have a major impact on home energy use and comfort. This is where architecture meets landscaping. Dense conifers to the north and west in most climate zones help reduce the wind speed of winter storms. They can also spread the wind around the house to reduce drafts and air infiltration inside. A combination of low bushes, such as junipers, and evergreens make an effective windbreak. A windbreak placed twice the distance from the house as the trees are tall reduces the wind effect on the house by 75 percent.

WINDBREAK EFFECT

Trees planted a distance from the house can be an effective buffer against winter winds, reducing heating loads and making the house more comfortable.

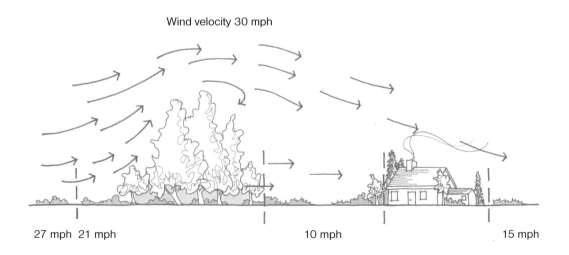

Wind velocity 30 mph

27 mph 21 mph   10 mph   15 mph

Summer cooling is where landscaping can have a major impact. Shading east and west windows with bushes and trees dramatically reduces the heat buildup from low solar angles in morning and afternoon. The hotter your climate in the summer, the more important it is to shade western windows. Depending on the climate zone, deciduous bushes are the most beneficial for blocking light. The root ball should be at least 4 ft. from the house to prevent foundation damage as the plant matures. Bushes around the house also help to keep moisture out of the basement or foundation area. Victor Olgyay, one of the pioneers in designing for specific climates, found that proper shading and windbreaks could reduce home energy use by up to 22 percent.

Overall shading of the house in the summer is especially important in southern climates. A mature stand of trees that shades the house from hot summer sun can reduce the temperature in the surrounding area by 15° and reduce radiant heat gain. By placing plants carefully, the passive solar arc around the southern exposure of the house can be preserved. When trees are too close to the southern exposure, trunks and branches can reduce solar gain in winter by 50 percent, depending on the species.

Deciduous trees help take the wilt out of brutal summer weather and lower cooling costs in the process.

Integrated Pest Management

Pests are not really pests once you have an understanding of their purpose in the grand scheme of things. All living things have some role to play in maintaining a healthy ecological balance even if they are an annoyance. It's hard to wax poetic on the wonders of ecology when you're swatting mosquitoes or pulling Japanese beetles out of the tomato plants.

Encouraging a diversity of native plants will provide a landscape that is adapted to the pests of that area while natural biodiversity will help keep plants healthier. With healthier plants, the need for chemical pesticides is less. And that should keep all of us happier.

Planting native, drought-tolerant species is especially important in arid parts of the country where demands on clean water are high and likely to get worse.

AFTERWORD

Getting to Zero Energy

So what does all this mean when Monday morning rolls around and everything at the office is the same as it was last week?

There is no such thing as the perfect green home. Every house is unique. Each is built in a specific climate where there are varying amounts of sunshine; winds blow from a different direction by season and each site affords different views. Local building products are available or not, there will be small children in the home, or not. And so forth. There is no single green building solution that meets all possible conditions.

The best way to start is to take on some aspect of green building and get really good at it. Don't try to do everything at once. Take on energy conservation and increased R-values in walls and roofs. Get a blower door test done on one of your homes. Try changing the paints and finishes you have always used. Test materials in your garage or on your own home. See what works best for you and your trade contractors. Identify the resistance points in your company or with your trades. Education is the top priority any time you are making changes in your business. Let them know *why* you are making the changes.

At the same time, there are certain inevitabilities that will affect all of us. Climate change will bring about increasingly weird weather. Floods and droughts will be more frequent, occur in strange places, and last longer. Hurricanes will become more intense as the oceans warm. More frequent and unusual tornados will strike unexpected places. The weather is unpredictable even when it is normal. Build to withstand the harshest weather conditions you can imagine for your region.

We will reach "peak oil" during the life span of homes built today. What that means is that all forms of energy will become increasingly expensive and with little forewarning by the powers that be. Natural gas is in greater demand just as it is starting to decline from existing wells in the U.S. How much will heating and cooling our homes cost in 5, 10, or 20 years? All we know is a lot more than it does today.

Fresh water will be one of the things that is most radically affected by climate change. When and where it rains will shift all over the globe. Snow pack in mountain areas that provide the water for agriculture in the summer may be hardest hit. Less snow pack means less irrigation water, which affects food prices. Since globalization is so entrenched, particularly when it comes to food, when climates are impacted in Chile food prices go up in the U.S. Grains are particularly vulnerable to fluctuating water availability. China's grain is irrigated with fossil water that is predicted to go away in as little as two years. Their demand for wheat will affect U.S. wheat prices. The price of corn is already rising as it is diverted away from food to produce ethanol.

We are not growing old trees anymore. The ones that are still standing are the ones that anchor the forest ecologies of the world. At the current rate of deforestation and clear-cutting, our forests are destined for agriculture, even if that means replanting with mono-cultures of Douglas fir or eucalyptus. Our voracious appetite for wood, paper, and other forest products makes for a dire future for the planet's forests (the lungs of the planet—our primary defense against climate change) and all the wildlife that lives within their protective canopies. If we don't reverse this trend soon, many of the plants and animals we take for granted will be seen only in zoos and arboretums.

Time for Change Is Now

This story can go on and on. We are at a critical juncture in the history of humans on earth. With 40% of the world's resources going into buildings, 66% of the electricity generated used for heating, cooling, and lighting buildings, the demand for new coal-burning power plants grows ever stronger. China is planning to build one coal-burning power plant a week for the next 20 years. There are 154 new coal-fired plants on the drawing boards in the U.S. in 42 states. There are currently about 600 coal plants in the U.S. that, according to the Union of Concerned Scientists, burn 1.4 million tons of coal every year.

It's time to start planning, designing, and building homes that reduce the need for new coal-fired plants and help us prepare for the inevitability of more expensive power. Building homes that produce as much energy as they consume and allow their owners to collect and store rainwater are things that we can do now.

Build for the Future

Let's take it step by step with a summary of what builders can do to create the home of the future.

Siting   Face the long axis of the house south. Size the windows for optimal passive solar gain. Size the thermal mass on the floor or illuminated walls relative to the glazed areas for a higher solar contribution. Provide enough south-facing roof area to accommodate current or future solar collectors. Plan early for landscaping that will help with shading the east and west windows in summer to reduce cooling loads.

Foundation   Always consider any foundation material as part of the building system. From slabs to crawl spaces to basements, insulate them as well as possible on the exterior before backfilling. Grade foundation drainage away from the house and backfill with gravel that will allow water to flow to the foundation drainage system to prevent hydrostatic pressure on the foundation wall.

Framing   Always use advanced framing techniques with FSC-certified lumber. In cold climates, frame walls for R-24 or higher insulation. Insulation should reduce or eliminate the cavity effect by preventing air movement between the studs (structural insulated panels are one model of no-cavity effect). Place 1 in. of closed-cell rigid foam on the exterior of the sheathing to keep the dew point of the wall outside of the cavity. Install a drainage plane, and flash all penetrations and intersections perfectly to protect the building from moisture for its entire life span.

Roofing   Use the longest-lasting material you can afford that is designed for your climate. Make sure the entire roof assembly creates an air barrier from the living space below, which means no open areas around plumbing, duct-work, or chimneys. Insulate 50% higher than code requires.

Windows   Install low-e windows at a minimum. Wherever possible, install super glass in fixed-glass locations. Design for solar gain and reduce exposure to western summer sun. Casement windows usually have better air sealing and can be opened to catch breezes. Use windows with a solar heat gain factor of 0.33 or lower for east and west windows, especially in hot climates.

Plumbing   Optimize the design of the plumbing using a trunk and branch system. Reduce the size of supply lines to $3/8$ in. to maximize flow and reduce heat loss. Install a sealed combustion water heater with an EF of 0.62 or higher. Insulate all hot water lines throughout the house. Install an on-demand hot water pump. Reduce flow rates at all fixtures and faucets below code. Conserve as much as possible. Use dual-flush toilets. Pre-plumb for gray water segregation.

HVAC   Install only high-efficiency sealed-combustion furnaces and boilers with efficiencies above 90% and air conditioners with 14 SEER or higher. Better yet, use evaporative cooling in dry climates. Make sure the mechanical equipment is sized properly to meet the dramatically reduced energy load of the house and no more. Provide for fresh air with mechanical ventilation. Keep equipment and all ductwork inside the insulated envelope. Reduce air pressure differentials throughout the house. Seal all ducts with mastic. Have the ducts tested. Consider geothermal heat pumps. In humid climates, a well-sealed and insulated house may require central dehumidification when temperatures are moderate but humidity is high.

Electrical   Design daylighting to provide light to all rooms in daytime use. Design electric lighting carefully for the tasks and uses of each room. Use dimmers and occupancy sensors to minimize lighting requirements. Reduce electrical loads everywhere. Install compact fluorescent bulbs or LED fixtures wherever possible. Provide circuit switches to cut power to "always on" phantom loads. Install the most efficient appliances possible. (Energy Star isn't always the minimum-load appliance.)

Insulation and Air Sealing   More is always better. Insulate today to 50% above local code or DOE recommendations for your area. Make the thermal envelope continuous by eliminating thermal breaks or cold spots. Inspect for perfection of installation. Eliminate any air movement inside the wall cavities and through the building envelope. Create an uninterrupted building envelope with the insulation in contact with the air barrier. Keep the dew point outside the envelope by using exterior rigid foam. Use spray foam insulation between garage and all adjacent living spaces. Use spray foam or spray insulation on all band joists, preferably where any two materials meet. Conduct a blower door test. A well-sealed house, with proper ventilation, will maintain more comfortable humidity levels year round, reducing or eliminating the need for humidifiers in cold months and reducing the need for air-conditioning in warm months.

Siding and Decking   Use siding that is as long lasting as the intended life of the building. Cementious siding or real stucco is fire resistant as well as durable. Don't use wood siding or decking unless it is FSC certified. Install recycled-content composite decking.

Solar   Integrate solar hot water systems with radiant heating systems. Provide ample space for hot water storage to meet the heating load requirements. Install enough PV to meet at least 50% of the electrical load of the house. Install a battery back-up system if you want protection for variable grid availability. Use feedback metering to tell you how much electricity you are using at any given moment. Look for net metering in your area that allows you to sell your "extra" electricity back to the local utility through the grid.

Indoor Air Quality Eliminate as many synthetic materials from inside the envelope as possible. Be aware of the constituent chemicals in all surfaces and finishes. Use zero-VOC paints and finishes. Seal formaldehyde-based products before installation. Eliminate solvent-based products from all adhesives and finishes. Provide adequate ventilation to every room. With forced-air systems, install MERV filters rated 6-12. Make sure that houses using forced-air systems have effective air sealing. Install a heat recovery ventilation unit.

Landscaping Install landscaping that is native to your location. Plant drought-tolerant species. Use landscaping to help reduce cooling loads, especially around east- and west-facing windows. Plant edible landscaping for people as well as birds, butterflies, and wildlife. Install a water catchment system based on your annual rainfall.

Taking Steps Together

The only way to prepare for the future is to bring our focus home, literally and collectively. Cities across the country are leading the charge to become Kyoto compliant. In many cases that means reducing their carbon dioxide production by 25% or more. Some cities, such as Portland, Oregon, have already achieved their goals.

But a city is merely a collection of families. If each family takes responsibility for its consumption patterns, its carbon production, and shops locally, we can make a huge difference. We want to keep our sales tax dollars in our communities. Especially around energy.

When we fill our gas tanks it is taxed once and all the profit leaves the community and typically the state. The profits end up in Saudi Arabia, Houston, or Washington, DC. That doesn't help pay for firemen, policemen, teachers, and the folks who run our communities.

If we keep our dollars local, by not buying fossil fuels, the money saved provides local jobs. It can go toward movies, dinner, clothes, and books from companies that pay local sales tax. Those savings are cycled three to eight times before they leave the community. What that means is the city collects three to eight times as much sales tax when energy is saved than when it leaves the community and is sent to oil and gas companies.

In the past it was common practice to build to code and let the government tell us how and what kind of homes we should have. From this point on it is imperative that we determine what the standards should be for our communities. Through LEED and the NAHB green building guidelines the building industry is leading the transition to a more sustainable future. It takes every one of us to lead in our own communities. Your customers are waiting for you to provide the kind of energy-efficient and environmentally appropriate homes that they want. Take a step forward and see if your market responds. Join a local green building program. Start one if there isn't one. See the Resources for help in learning more about green building guidelines.

All of this may be seem overwhelming but each step is a basis for creating homes that are self-reliant, resilient, and versatile. The scale of environmental changes facing us is enormous and unpredictable. It is only common sense to begin making our homes right for the world we really live in. Future-proofing your home is one of the smartest investments you can make today for your customers and your company.

RESOURCES

Manufacturers and Products

AFM, Safecoat, Polyureseal BP coatings:
www.afmsafecoat.com

Air-krete, insulation:
www.bauerspecialty.com

Atlas Roofing, Nail Base:
www.atlasroofing.com

BASF, Micronal PCM SmartBoard
phase-change wallboard: www.corporate.basf.com

Benjamin Obdyke, Cedar Breather and HomeSlicker
underlayments: www.benjaminobdyke.com

Benjamin Moore, EcoSpec coatings:
www.benjaminmoore.com

Bona, finishes: www.bona.com

Bonded Logic cotton insulation:
www.bondedlogic.com

Cardinal Glass Industries: www.cardinalcorp.com

DuPont: www.dupont.com

EcoTimber: www.ecotimber.com

Enerjoy, radiant heating equipment:
www.enerjoy.com

Grace Construction Products:
www.graceathome.com

Hunter Douglas, Duette window shades:
www.hunterdouglas.com

Interface and InterfaceFlor carpet: www.ifsia.com

Knauf: www.knaufusa.com

Medite, engineered wood panels:
www.sierrapine.com

Metlund Pump: www.gothotwater.com

Milgard Windows and Doors: www.milgard.com

Mohawk Flooring, PET carpet:
www.mohawk-flooring.com

Neil Kelly Cabinets: www.neilkellycabinets.com

PaperStone, paper-based countertops:
www.paperstoneproducts.com

Plyboo: www.plyboo.com

Richlite, paper-based countertops: www.richlite.com

Silestone, stone composite: www.silestoneusa.com

SkyBlend, particleboard: www.skyblend.com

SolaHart, solar panels: www.solahart.com.au

Southwall Technologies: www.southwall.com

Tandus carpet: www.tandus.com

Thermafiber Inc., mineral wool insulation:
www.thermafiber.com

Timbergrass, bamboo flooring: www.teragren.com

Trex: www.trex.com

Typar: www.typar.com

Tyvek: www.tyvek.com

U.S. Gypsum: www.usg.com

Weyerhaeuser Co.: www.weyerhaeuser.com

Zodiaq, stone composite: www.zodiaq.com

Associations and Agencies

American Society of Heating, Refrigerating
and Air-Conditioning Engineers: www.ashrae.org

American Forest and Paper Association's
Sustainable Forest Initiative:
www.afandpa.org; www.sfiprogram.org

American Tree Farm System:
www.treefarmsystem.org

APA-The Engineered Wood Association:
www.apawood.org

Bay-Friendly Gardening: www.stopwaste.org

Build It Green: www.builditgreen.org

Canadian Standards Association: www.csa.ca

Carpet and Rug Institute: www.carpet-rug.org

Energy Star, U.S. Department of Environmental
Protection: www.energystar.gov

European Programme for the Endorsement of
Forest Certification: www.pefc.org

Forest Stewardship Council: www.fscus.org

Green Seal, www.greenseal.org

Leadership in Energy and Environmental Design,
U.S. Green Building Council: www.usgbc.org

MASCO Environments For Living:
www.eflbuilder.com

National Association of Home Builders:
www.nahb.org

National Renewable Energy Laboratory:
www.nrel.gov

Oak Ridge National Laboratory: www.ornl.gov

Rocky Mountain Institute: www.rmi.org

Structural Insulated Panel Association: www.sipa.org

U.S. Department of Energy, Office of Energy
Efficiency and Renewable Energy:
www.eere.energy.gov

PHOTO CREDITS

Introduction p. 2 Robert Vente, p. 4 Marc Richmond

Chapter 1 p. 6 Bryan Bowen, p. 7 Red Pepper Kitchen and Bath, p. 8 VaST Architecture, p. 9 Ecofutures Building, p. 10 Mark Chalom, Architect, p. 12 Allen Associates, p. 13 McCutcheon Construction, p. 15 (top) Allen Associates, (bottom) What's Working, p. 17 George Watt Architecture/ Sun Electric Systems, p. 18 Kelli Pousson, p. 19 Kurt Buss, The ReUse People, p. 20 What's Working, p. 21 Marc Richmond, p. 22 John Shurtz, Green Builders of Marin

Chapter 2 p. 26 What's Working, p. 27 Barrett Studio Architects, p. 29 What's Working, p. 31 (left) Doug Parker, Big Horn Builders, (right) Marc Richmond, p. 32 Carl Seville, Seville Consulting, p. 36 What's Working

Chapter 3 p. 43 Marc Richmond, Hammond Fine Homes, p. 44 Yestermorrow Design/Build School, p. 46 Ecofutures Building, p. 47 National Park Service, Mesa Verde, p. 49 (top) Bryan Bowen, (bottom) Ecofutures Building, p. 50 Gettliffe Architecture, p. 51 What's Working, p. 56 Gettliffe Architecture, p. 57 Marc Richmond, p. 59 Ecofutures Building, p. 61 Bryan Bowen, p. 62 (top) Heida Biddle, (bottom) Marc Richmond, p. 63 Marc Richmond, p. 65 Marc Richmond

Chapter 4 p. 67 W hat's Working, p. 68 Ecofutures Building, p. 69 VaST Architecture, p. 70 Ecofutures Building, p. 72 Ecofutures Building, p. 75 Merten Homes, p. 76 Durisol Building Systems, p. 78 What's Working, p. 79 American Coal Ash Association, p. 80 Ecofutures Building, p. 81 (top left, top right) Marc Richmond, (bottom) Scott Gibson, courtesy *Fine Homebuilding*, © The Taunton Press, Inc.

Chapter 5 p. 83 Ecofutures Building, p. 84 What's Working, p. 88 What's Working, p. 89 What's Working, p. 90 (left) Nick Sommer, (right) What's Working, p. 91 (top) Nick Sommer, (bottom) What's Working, pp. 92–93 James Cameron and Kathleen Jardine, Sun Garden Houses, p. 94 What's Working, p. 95 (top) © 1996 Forest Stewardship Council A.C., (bottom) Ecofutures Building, p. 96 Kelli Pousson, p. 97 What's Working, p. 98 What's Working, p. 99 What's Working, p. 100 Ecofutures Building, p. 101 What's Working , pp. 102–103 What's Working, p. 104 Merten Homes, p. 105 (top) Merten Homes, (bottom) Ecofutures Building, p. 106 Kurt Sommer, p. 107 Nick Sommer

Chapter 6 p. 110 Namaste Solar, p. 111 Alan Greenberg, Catherine Greener, p. 113 (top) Marc Richmond, (bottom) Louisiana Pacific, p. 114 Carl Seville, Seville Consulting, p. 115 (top) Atlas Roofing, (bottom) Merten Homes, p. 118 (top) What's Working, (bottom) Benjamin Obdyke, p. 119 What's Working, p. 121 Daniel S. Morrison, courtesy *Fine Homebuilding*, © The Taunton Press, Inc., p. 123 Daniel S. Morrison, courtesy *Fine Homebuilding*, © The Taunton Press, Inc., p. 124 Allen

Associates, p. 125 (top) Marc Richmond, (bottom) What's Working, p. 126 John Mahan, courtesy *Fine Homebuilding*, © The Taunton Press, Inc., p. 127 Robert Vente, p. 128 Edward Caldwell, courtesy *Fine Homebuilding*, © The Taunton Press, Inc.

Chapter 7 p. 130 Robert Vente, p. 133 Robert Vente, p. 134 VaST Architecture, p. 136 (top) Nate Burger, Eco-Handyman, (bottom) VaST Architecture, p. 137 What's Working, p. 141 Alpen Glass, p. 142 What's Working, p. 144 (top) Marc Richmond, (bottom) DAP Inc., p. 146 (top) Marc Richmond, (bottom) Kelli Pousson, p. 147 Daniel S. Morrison, courtesy *Fine Homebuilding*, © The Taunton Press, Inc., p. 148 What's Working, p. 149 Brian Pontolilo, courtesy *Fine Homebuilding*, © The Taunton Press, Inc., p. 150 Robert Vente, p. 151 (top) Scott Gibson, courtesy *Fine Homebuilding*, © The Taunton Press, Inc., (bottom) Andersen Windows, p. 153 SureSill, p. 154 Kelli Pousson

Chapter 8 p. 155 Hammond Fine Homes, p. 156 Nick Sommer, p. 157 What's Working, p. 158 (top) What's Working, (bottom) Marc Richmond, p. 159 Marc Richmond, p. 161 (top) Carl Seville, Seville Consulting, (bottom) Scott Gibson, p. 162 ACT, Inc. Metlund Systems, p. 164 Marc Richmond, p. 167 (left) Robert Vente, (right) Kohler Co., p. 168 (top) Marc Richmond, bottom, BioLet, p. 170 Bill Lucas, Merten Homes, p. 171 Ecofutures Building

Chapter 9 p. 173 What's Working, p. 174 Ecofutures Building, p. 176 Marc Richmond, p. 177 Carl Seville, Seville Consulting, p. 179 (top) What's Working, (middle, bottom) Marc Richmond, p. 180 What's Working, p. 181 (top) Carl Seville, Seville Consulting, (middle, bottom) Marc Richmond, p. 182 Apple Construction, p. 183 What's Working, p. 184 Marc Richmond, p. 185 Marc Richmond, p. 186 (left) Marc Richmond, (right) Vermont Castings, p. 187 Scott Gibson, courtesy *Fine Homebuilding*, © The Taunton Press, Inc., p. 190 Marc Richmond, p. 191 (top) Marc Richmond, (bottom) Robert Vente, p. 193 (top) What's Working, (bottom) Carl Seville, Seville Consulting, p. 194 Marc Richmond

Chapter 10 p. 198 Alan Greenberg, Catherine Greener, p. 199 (left) Robert Vente, (right) Kelli Pousson, p. 200 Progress Lighting, p. 201 What's Working, p. 202 (top) Robert Vente, (bottom) Kelli Pousson, p. 203 (left) Gettliffe Architecture, (right) Marc Richmond, p. 204 Richlite, p. 205 What's Working

Chapter 11 p. 207 US GreenFiber, p. 208 Ecofutures Building, p. 212 Ecofutures Building, p. 214 What's Working, p. 215 Marc Richmond, p. 217 (top) Nate Burger, Eco-Handyman, (bottom) Kelli Pousson, p. 218 David Pierce, Sheep Wool Insulation Ltd., p. 219 (top left, bottom left) US GreenFiber, (right) What's Working, p. 220 Marc Richmond, p. 221 Kelli Pousson, p. 222 What's Working, pp. 224–225 What's Working, p. 226 Marc Richmond

Chapter 12 p. 227 VaST Architecture, p. 228 Merten Homes, p. 229 Carl Seville,

Seville Consulting, p. 230 (top) Benjamin Obdyke, (bottom) What's Working, p. 231 Mark Averill Snyder, courtesy *Fine Homebuilding*, © The Taunton Press, Inc., p. 234 Andrew Wormer, courtesy *Fine Homebuilding,* © The Taunton Press, Inc., p. 235 Ecofutures Building, p. 236 What's Working, p. 237 (left) Kelli Pousson, (right) Ecofutures Building, p. 238 Steve Culpepper, courtesy *Fine Homebuilding*, © The Taunton Press, Inc., p. 240 What's Working, p. 241 (top) VaST Architecture, (bottom) What's Working, p. 242 Tom O'Brien and David Ericson, courtesy *Fine Homebuilding,* © The Taunton Press, Inc., p. 245 courtesy *Fine Homebuilding,* © The Taunton Press, Inc., p. 246 (top) courtesy *Fine Homebuilding,* © The Taunton Press, Inc., (bottom) Allen Associates. p. 247 courtesy *Fine Homebuilding,* © The Taunton Press, Inc., p. 249 Barrett Studio Architects, p. 250 courtesy *Fine Homebuilding*, © The Taunton Press, Inc.

Chapter 13 p. 251 Namaste Solar, p. 252 Bryan Bowen, p. 254 Jeff Mahoney, p. 255 Jeff Mahoney, pp. 256–257 Ecofutures Building , p. 258 Marc Richmond, p. 259 (top) Marc Richmond, (bottom) Ecofutures Building, p. 260 What's Working, p. 261 Ecofutures Building, p. 262 What's Working, p. 263 Namaste Solar, p. 264 Ecofutures Building, p. 265 Namaste Solar, p. 266 (top) Namaste Solar, (bottom) SunSlates/Atlantis Energy Systems, p. 267 (top) Namaste Solar, (bottom) SunSlates/Atlantis Energy Systems, p. 270 (top) Ecofutures Building, (bottom) Kim Master, p. 271 SunSlates/ Atlantis Energy Systems

Chapter 14 p. 273 Carl Seville, Seville Consulting, p. 274 VaST Architecture, p. 275 Odin's Hammer, p. 276 Odin's Hammer, p. 278 Odin's Hammer, p. 279 Hammond Fine Homes, p. 282 Marc Richmond, p. 283 Hammond Fine Homes, p. 284 Marc Richmond, p. 285 Allen Associates

Chapter 15 p. 288 Robert Vente, p. 289 (top) Hammond Fine Homes, (bottom) Marc Richmond, p. 291 Roe Osborn, *Fine Homebuilding,* © The Taunton Press, Inc., p. 292 (top) BASF, (bottom) Kelli Pousson, p. 293 Ecofutures Building, p. 294 Robert Vente, p. 295 Red Pepper Kitchen and Bath, p. 296 American Loft Cabinetry, p. 297 Robert Vente, p. 298 Marc Richmond, p. 299 (top) Richlite, (bottom) Marc Richmond, p. 300 Roe Osborn, *Fine Homebuilding,* © The Taunton Press, Inc., p. 301 Leger Wanaselja Architecture, p. 302 (top) Robert Vente, (bottom) TDS Custom Construction, p. 303 Marc Richmond, p. 304 Robert Vente, p. 305 Marc Richmond, p. 306 Eco Timber, p. 307 (top) Robert Vente, (bottom) Marc Richmond, p. 308 Marc Richmond, p. 309 Marc Richmond, p. 310 Hammond Fine Homes

Chapter 16 p. 313 (top) Robert Vente, (bottom) Marc Richmond , p. 315 Hammond Fine Homes, p. 316 Marc Richmond, p. 317 Denver Water (Xeriscape Colorado), p. 318 Marc Richmond, p. 320 Ecofutures Building, p. 321 photo Tamara Shulman, reprinted with permission of StopWaste.org

INDEX